D1563406

THE PETITE BOURGEOISIE

EDINBURGH STUDIES IN SOCIOLOGY

General Editors: Tom Burns, Tom McGlew, Gianfranco Poggi

The *Edinburgh Studies in Sociology* series publishes sociological works from the Department of Sociology at the University of Edinburgh. The majority of the books in the series will be founded on original research or on research and scholarship pursued over a period of time. There will also be collections of research papers on particular topics of social interest and textbooks deriving from courses taught in the Department.

Many of the books will appeal to a non-specialist audience as well as to the academic reader.

Titles already published

Tom Burns: THE BBC: Public Institution and Private World
John Orr: TRAGIC REALISM AND MODERN SOCIETY: Studies in the Sociology of the Modern Novel
Anthony P. M. Coxon and Charles L. Jones: THE IMAGES OF OCCUPATIONAL PRESTIGE: A Study in Social Cognition
Anthony P. M. Coxon and Charles L. Jones: CLASS AND HIERARCHY: The Social Meaning of Occupations
Anthony P. M. Coxon and Charles L. Jones: MEASUREMENT AND MEANINGS: Techniques and methods of Studying Occupational Cognition

Forthcoming titles

Frank Bechhofer and Brian Elliott: THE SMALL SHOPKEEPER IN THE CLASS STRUCTURE
John Orr: TRAGIC DRAMA AND MODERN SOCIETY: Studies in the Social Theory of Drama from 1870 to the Present
Brian Elliott and David McCrone: PROPERTY AND POWER IN A CITY
Kathryn Backett: THE NEGOTIATION OF PARENTHOOD
Harvie Ferguson: CONFINEMENT AND CHILDHOOD: Two Essays in Experimental Psychology

THE PETITE BOURGEOISIE

Comparative Studies of the Uneasy Stratum

Edited by
Frank Bechhofer and Brian Elliott

First published 1981 by
THE MACMILLAN PRESS LTD
London and Basingstoke
Companies and representatives
throughout the world

ISBN 0 333 23737 4

Printed in Hong Kong

Contents

Notes on the Contributors

Frank Bechhofer was Junior Research Officer in the Department of Applied Economics, Cambridge, from 1962 to 1965. He then became Lecturer in Sociology at Edinburgh University until 1971 when he became Reader in Sociology. He has written several articles on research methods, industrial sociology and stratification. He is co-author of *The Affluent Worker* and editor of *Population Growth and the Brain Drain* and is preparing *The Small Shopkeeper in the Class Structure* (with Brian Elliott).

Colin Bell is Professor of Sociology at Aston University. In addition to the works with Howard Newby he is author of *Middle Class Families*; co-author with Margaret Stacey, Anne Murcott, and Eric Batstone of *Power, Persistence and Change*, and co-author with Sol Encel of *Inside the Whale*.

Suzanne Berger is Professor of Political Science at Massachusetts Institute of Sociology. She is the author of *Peasants against Politics*, *The French Political System*, and *Dualism and Discontinuity in Industrial Societies* (with Michael Piore). She is also editor of *Organizing Interests in West Europe*.

Daniel Bertaux is Chargé de recherche au Centre National de la Recherche Scientifique. He works at the Centre d'Etudes des Mouvements Sociaux in Paris and is the author of *Destins personnels et structure de classe* and numerous papers. He is also editor of *Biography and Society*.

Isabelle Bertaux-Wiame is Attachée de recherche au Centre National de la Recherche Scientifique and works in the Groupe de Sociologie au Travail, Université de Paris VII. Trained as an historian she is now using an oral history approach to the dynamics of socio-historical change and has published articles in this area.

Chris Birkbeck graduated in Geography from Oxford University and is now Research Fellow at the Centre for Development Studies. He is author of various articles on crime and employment in Colombia.

J. F. Conway is Associate Professor of Sociology and Head of the Department of Sociology and Social Studies at the University of Regina,

Saskatchewan. Originally trained as a psychologist he obtained his Ph.D. in Political Science and Sociology at Simon Fraser University. He is the author of a number of articles on Populism.

Brian Elliott was Lecturer in Sociology at the University of Glasgow from 1963 to 1965. He then moved to Edinburgh University where he was Lecturer in Sociology until 1979 when he became Senior Lecturer. He was also Visiting Professor of Anthropology and Sociology at the University of British Columbia, 1973–74. He has written several articles on urban sociology and social stratification and is currently writing *Property and Power in a City* and *The Modern City* (with D. McCrone) and *The Small Shopkeeper in the Class Structure* (with Frank Bechhofer).

Chris Gerry is Lecturer in Development Studies at the Centre for Development Studies, University of Swansea. An economist, he has written on petty production and capitalism and is editor (with Ray Bromley) of *Casual Work and Poverty in Third World Cities*.

Bronislaw Misztal is Associate Professor at the Institute of Philosophy and Sociology, Polish Academy of Sciences, Warsaw. He is the author of four books in Polish 'Peer groups in Urban Culture'; 'Problems of Social Participation and Co-operation'; 'Urban Sociology'; and 'Changes in Small Town Communities under Urbanization and Industrialization'.

Howard Newby is Reader in Sociology at the University of Essex. He is the author of *The Deferential Worker* and *Green and Pleasant Land?*; editor of *International Perspectives in Rural Sociology*; co-author with Colin Bell of *Community Studies*; co-editor with Colin Bell of *The Sociology of Community* and *Doing Sociological Research*; and co-author with Colin Bell, David Rose, and Peter Saunders of *Property, Paternalism and Power*.

Franz Urban Pappi is Professor of Sociology at the Institut für Soziologie der Christian-Albrechts-Universität at Kiel. He is co-author with Edward O. Laumann of *Networks of Collective Action*; editor of *Sozialstruktur-analysen mit Umfragedaten*; and author of numerous articles on social stratification, voting behaviour, methodology and survey research.

David Rose is Lecturer in Sociology at the University of Essex and co-author of *Property, Paternalism and Power*.

Peter Saunders is Lecturer in Sociology at the University of Essex. He is author of *Urban Politics: A Sociological Interpretation* and co-author of *Property, Paternalism and Power*.

Preface

This book has been a long time in the making. Not so much in the business of commissioning the papers, reworking some of the translations and generally editing – though that has taken long enough. But in a sense this book dates back to 1968 when we published a paper on small shopkeepers (Bechhofer and Elliott, 1968). At that time we were planning an empirical study – which we subsequently carried out – in which we construed them as 'marginal' members of the middle class. The rather sparse literature on retail trade and indeed on small business in general available at that time led us to identify a difficult market situation, unpleasant work situation redeemed only by independence, and a status situation which located shopkeepers shakily in the middle class. As we subsequently wrote 'the shopkeepers' claim to be middle class rested upon peculiar features of their market and work situations. In particular, the ownership of modest amounts of capital and the element of autonomy at work seemed to provide the major reasons for distinguishing them from manual workers and placing them with the traditional bourgeois elements of our society. At the same time, it was obvious that the self-same factors marked them off from most of the other groups conventionally labelled "lower middle class"' (Bechhofer *et al.*, 1974). A decade ago at the time of the publishing of the *Affluent Worker* studies and before the Marxist revival changed the face of British sociology, it seemed a reasonable strategy to further the study of the British class structure by examining a group which lay close to the 'margin' of the middle class in the same sort of way as affluent workers were said to lie close to the 'top' of the working class. Even today this notion does not seem entirely silly, as the debate on the labour aristocracy in nineteenth-century Britain shows.

In the course of that decade, both everything and nothing has changed. We have come to see our problem somewhat differently, no longer in terms of marginality but as the location, composition and political significance of the petite bourgeoisie in capitalist and state socialist society. By 1974, when we wrote the paper from which the previous quotation was taken, we had already moved most of the way towards such a conceptualisation. The small shopkeeper was now interesting not because of his marginality but because shopkeepers represented a significant group within the petit-bourgeois stratum and one which seemed to encapsulate many of the most traditional features of that stratum. Those interested in that process of reconceptualisation should compare our paper of 1968 with a subsequent paper on the petite bourgeoisie in the same journal some eight years later (Bechhofer and Elliott, 1976). In the Spring of 1977 when we first started making plans for this book, the petite bourgeoisie was beginning to appear once more on the sociological agenda. Of course, there had been the rather specific interest in the part they played in National Socialism, Poujadism and McCarthyism evident in the political and sociological literature, but now for the first time since the 1930s there was emerging a much more general curiosity about the part they were playing in contemporary societies. In particular, Marxist writers such as Poulantzas (1975) were making a great deal of the importance of this stratum in capitalist orders. Thus, for a long period it had seemed rather eccentric to be interested in such a small and insignificant group which was supposedly disappearing by the hour and, in any event, doomed to extinction. Apart from a very small number of people, notably the members of the SSRC Stratification Seminar, our sociological colleagues seemed less than enthusiastic about the petite bourgeoisie as an object of study. Suddenly, or so it seemed to us, things changed, and from being virtually alone in this rather specialised sub-field, we found ourselves part of a minor fashion.

Yet in another sense very little has changed in the past decade. The petite bourgeoisie may have been put back on the theoretical agenda, but the dearth of empirical material is still evident. It is as if theoretical fashion is almost unaffected by the extent of empirical knowledge. It was this strange disjunction between a reviving theoretical interest and the lack of ethnographic detail which prompted the compiling of this book. At the time of writing, there are some signs that things may be changing. Small business has shown a new political vigour, the new Tory Government is pledged to re-establish the spirit of entrepreneurship and to re-create what to a jaundiced observer seems like the worst aspects of mid-nineteenth-century Britain. There is a corresponding stirring among sociologists which seems likely to produce empirical research. In 1977 it seemed to us that a book which tried to pull together some empirical work would attract some interest; now it looks positively topical. We were personally aware of a good many of the existing studies and ongoing studies, and with the help of friends we were able to trace some more. We eventually decided on a strategy of soliciting pieces from different countries, not because this would permit serious comparative study (the essays are far too disparate for that) but because we hoped to show that the petite bourgeoisie still plays a role in many very different societies, and because such a strategy might be helpful in posing problems which further research could attack. These essays then are not representative of this field of study, nor are they in any sense meant to be definitive accounts of the place of the petite bourgeoisie in these various societies. We provided our authors with a rough outline of some of the problems which we thought interesting and encouraged them to address at least a few of them, but each chapter has been shaped by the specific interests and research commitments of its author and we make no claim that there is one single common theme. We do believe however that it is possible to draw a number of important ideas from them, and in the concluding chapter we have attempted not to summarise those themes but to write an essay ourselves which takes them as its starting point.

We should make a number of apologies and acknowledgements. First must come the authors. All the articles in this book were specially commissioned and written. We must thank especially those authors who produced their chapters promptly, and apologise to them for the long delays in the completion of this book. The fault does not lie entirely with dilatory authors, or indeed dilatory editors. The chapters from Germany, Poland and France were either written in English by their authors or translated. We undertook the more or less extensive revision of these chapters in order to make them stylistically more satisfactory while retaining the flavour of the original and it proved a lengthy task involving considerable correspondence. We thank them all for their scholarship, help, and not least endurance. John Winckler of Macmillan proved a most tolerant editor; if he suspected that the typescript would never materialise he never made his doubts too clear. Our greatest debt is to Terri Ainslie who typed and retyped countless versions of all the chapters with cheerful efficiency, coping alike with our handwriting, four foreign languages and the publisher's house style.

Edinburgh 1979   Frank Bechhofer
                                                        Brian Elliott

References

F. Bechhofer and B. Elliott, 'An Approach to a Study of Small Shopkeepers and the Class Structure', *European Journal of Sociology*, ix (1968) 180–202.

F. Bechhofer, B. Elliott, M. Rushforth and R. Bland, 'The Petits Bourgeois in the Class Structure: the Case of the Small Shopkeepers', in F. Parkin (ed.), *Social Analysis of Class Structure* (London: Tavistock, 1974).

F. Bechhofer, B. Elliott, M. Rushforth and R. Bland, 'The Petits Bourgeois in Industrial Society', *European Journal of Sociology*, xvii (1976) 74–99.

N. Poulantzas, *Classes in Contemporary Capitalism* (London: New Left Books, 1975).

List of Abbreviations

APSA	American Political Science Association
CCAHC	Central Council for Agricultural and Horticultural Cooperation
CCF	Co-operative Commonwealth Federation
CDU	Christlich-Demokratische Union
CESPE	Centro Studi di Politica Economica
CGIL	Confederazione Generale Italiana del Lavoro
CISL	Confederazione Italiana Sindicati Lavoratori
CNEL	Consiglio Nazionale deu'Economia e del Lavoro
CPR	Canadian Pacific Railway
DC	Democrazia Christiana
DGB	Deutscher Gewerkschaftsbund
EEC	European Economic Community
FILTA	Federazione Italiana Lavoratori Tessili e del Abbigliamento
FILTEA	Federazione Italiana Lavoratori Tessili e del Abbigliamento
FIM	Federazione Italiana Metalmeccanici
FLM	Federazione Lavoratori Metalmeccanici
GNP	Gross National Product
ILO	International Labour Office
INSEE	Institut National de la Statisique et des Etudes Economiques
ISTAT	Istituto Centrale di Statistica
ISVET	Istituto per gli Studi sullo Sviluppo Economico e il Progresso Tecnico
MAFF	Ministry of Agriculture, Fisheries and Food
MLA	Members of the Legislature of Alberta
MP	Member of Parliament
NFU	National Farmers Union
PCI	Partito Communista Italiano
PCP	Petty Commodity Production
PSIUP	Partito Socialista di'Unita Proletaria
SGGA	Saskatchewan Grain Growers Association
smd	standard man day
SSRC	Social Sciences Research Council
UFA	United Farmers of Alberta
UFM	United Farmers of Manitoba
UFO	United Farmers of Ontario
UIL	Unione Italiana del Lavoro
UILTA	Unione Italiane Lavoratori Tessili e del Abbigliamento

1 Agrarian Petit-Bourgeois Responses to Capitalist Industrialisation: The Case of Canada

J. F. CONWAY

Political and Economic Background

The agrarian petite bourgeoisie dominated the political debates in Canada during the first few decades of the twentieth century. Their domination was ephemeral and extended only to setting the agenda for the debates since, although they won some concessions, they proved unable to change the course of the development of Canadian capitalism in ways congenial to them. They failed to maintain the momentum of their own class and their efforts to forge successful alliances with the working class and the urban petite bourgeoisie were wrecked on the rocks of their own self-interested view of what the world ought to be like.

The agrarian upsurge awaited the successful settlement of the Prairie provinces – Manitoba, Saskatchewan and Alberta – during the so-called 'wheat boom', a period between 1896 and 1913 when the export of wheat dominated Canadian economic life. It was during this time that the design of the Confederation of the British North American colonies, effected in 1867 and redesigned in 1878, finally 'clicked' and the pieces of the plan fell rewardingly into place. The Confederation strategy depended upon the West. The design – usually called the National Policy – included the following elements: the construction of an all-Canada transcontinental railway; the erection of a tariff wall to encourage domestic industry; the settlement of the Prairie West with farmers who would produce grains, mainly wheat, for export and who would serve as a protected market for Canadian manufactures; and the establishment of a new investment frontier for foreign and domestic

1

finance capital in the new agrarian region. The strategy had been despairingly husbanded during the world Depression of 1873–93 and many had come to believe that it was a foolish dream.

In 1896 prosperity began to dawn, the 'wheat boom' of 1896–1913 began. In terms of the fate of the Prairie West the key to the boom lay in declining transportation costs and rising prices for wheat which 'suddenly brought the virgin resources of the Prairies within the scope of the international market and within the range of profitable exploitation'.[1] Among the other factors involved in the boom was the availability of free and cheap land – land sold for $3.36/acre in 1901 which only became $11.30/acre by the 1930s. Add to these salubrious conditions the fact that the booming American frontier was for all practical purposes settled, and the conditions for both a massive jump in population and a consequent unprecedented leap in occupied and improved lands in the region were established.

The speed of settlement and agricultural development was unprecedented in Canadian history. In the period from 1896 to 1913, 1 million people moved into the three Prairie Provinces, occupied lands increased from 10 to 70 million acres, and wheat produced jumped from 20 million bushels to 209 million bushels (Royal Commission, 1940, pp. 67–8). For the first time the Confederation design was functioning as it ought to have from the beginning; for example, 'the value of the exports of wheat and flour alone in 1913 was greater than the value of all exports in 1896' (Royal Commission, 1940, p. 63). The Prairies were filling up as population moved in and followed the railway to every corner and wheat was being produced in undreamed-of quantities. In the period 1896–1913 it would not be an overstatement to say that 'the settlement of the Prairies dominated the Canadian economic scene' (Royal Commission, 1940, p. 74).

But the production and the export of wheat and the resulting east-west railway traffic was only one cornerstone of the original design. Out of the boom one element of the original capitalist designers of Confederation would gain much – the investors in transportation, the speculators in land, the middle-men who dealt in the international grain market, the banks and trust companies, and the commercial wholesalers and retailers who dealt in consumer commodities all benefited. However that was only one segment of the eager group that watched the final fruition of the long-postponed dream. The other major segment was made up of those industrial-capitalists who had finally abandoned illusions of reciprocity with the US and had moved to a strategy of industrialisation through protective tariffs. The role the West was to play here, too, was crucial.

The population which had been begged, cajoled, lured, and even deceived into coming to settle on the Prairies and to raise the wheat served many purposes. They were, behind the impenetrable walls of the protective tariff, the captive market for the manufactures of Central Canadian capitalists. In a sense, the agricultural population, and the essential, if small in number, wage-earners, that had settled and rendered productive the Prairies, were a capitalist's dream come true – they were forced to buy dear and to sell cheap. The protected manufactures they needed for production – implements, machinery, nails, hardware and so on – for consumption – boots, shoes, clothing, furniture, etc. – and even for amusement – tobacco, liquors, musical instruments, and the like – cost them up to 50 per cent above what they would have paid had there been free trade. At the same time, the commodities they produced for a cash income – grains, especially wheat, and some livestock and livestock products – had to be forwarded through middlemen, each of whom took a share of the final price ultimately gained on the world market, as well as transported vast distances. From the prairie agrarians' point of view, in terms of their share of the final price, they were forced to sell cheap indeed. Add to this the cost of credit needed to buy land, to purchase machinery, and to build buildings, and even the ability and right to produce was subject to a tariff in the form of interest.

Sir Wilfred Laurier's 'prosperous and contented people' of the Prairie Provinces – by 1913 numbering in excess of 200,000 farmers,[2] with a total capital investment of $1,788,693,000 – did not remain so for long. The capital invested in agriculture alone had leapt almost eight times since 1901 (Urquhart and Buckley, 1965, p. 354). They had settled the west and created the agricultural dream. Yet the vast majority were neither prosperous nor contented.

For the most part[3] the settlers were small capitalists who embraced the basic tenets of the system of private enterprise and extolled individualism and entrepreneurial ability. But they had been brought into being by big capitalists for purposes beyond their control. Almost immediately there was a clash of interests. In the first instance, some of the best lands of the vast region had been alienated to the Hudson's Bay Company (one-twentieth), to the Canadian Pacific Railway (CPR) (25 million acres, and more as work progressed, of choice lands bordering the main line and the branches – the best land for a settler), as well as to the colonisation land companies and many other friends in the government. Hence they found that in order to expand and develop their holdings, they must purchase lands already owned. Second, they found themselves at the dubiously tender mercies of a legislated railway monopoly which, until the Crows Nest Pass Agreement of 1897 gave some relief for export grain shipments as well as the inward movement of settlers' effects, charged freight rates, coming and going, of an excessive nature. Third, as mentioned above, they found themselves forced to buy all their manufactured necessaries and conveniences at prices inflated mercilessly by a protective tariff. More generally speaking, they found themselves involved in a highly sophisticated capitalist agriculture concerned with the extensive industrial cultivation of highly specialised cash grain crops for a distant market. In short, they found themselves immersed, inextricably, in an economic situation which, for them, had all the vices of a 'free market' – insecurity, price fluctuations, high production costs, speculation – and none of the virtues – windfall profits, high reward for the entrepreneurial function, good return on investment – at least none so far as the overwhelming majority of grain producers was concerned.

It was in this economic context that the agrarian petite bourgeoisie in Canada began to organise a Populist challenge to the course of Canadian development.

Theoretical Considerations

The concept of 'Populism', defined best by V. I. Lenin (1963, vol. 1, pp. 340–1) as '. . . a protest against . . . bourgeoisdom (i.e., capitalism) *from the peasant's, the small producer's point of view . . .'* has been rarely applied in analyses of the agrarian agitation in Canada. Indeed, despite the enormous attention devoted by scholars to all facets of the agitation, and most particularly to its final political stages in Alberta (the Social Credit League) and in Saskatchewan (the Co-operative Commonwealth Federation), no widely accepted theoretical approach has emerged.[4]

S. M. Lipset's *Agrarian Socialism*, C. B. Macpherson's *Democracy in Alberta*, and W. L. Morton's *The Progressive Party in Canada*, the most influential treatments of the agitation, all share, despite their many disagreements, one central assumption. They all emphasise the *regional* rather than the *class* nature of the agrarian agitation. With the singular and only occasional exception of Morton, the works generally refuse to locate the particular character of the phenomenon, especially in Alberta and Saskatchewan, in the general character of the national agitation of the agrarian petite bourgeoisie against the form and content of capitalist modernisation under the terms of the National Policy of Canada. Consequently, scholarship in Canada considering the agitation has tended to over-emphasise the regional focus of the agrarian agitation and to de-emphasise its class focus, a focus which, for a time, united the leading sectors of the English Canadian agrarian petite bourgeoisie nationally from the Maritimes to British Columbia. As a result, theoretical clarity on this most crucial political class struggle in the early stages of Canada's developing political economy has suffered.

There is no doubt that a great deal of theoretical confusion surrounding the agrarian agitation has much to do with the complexity of the phenomenon. Agrarian agitations have had so many political and economic faces – from the revolutionary left to the counter-revolutionary right – and have occurred in so many strikingly different milieux – from Louisiana to Alberta to the steppes of Russia – that one despairs of finding an encompassing theoretical organising principle for grappling with the phenomenon in general. This problem is dealt with satisfactorily by the concept of Populism as developed by Lenin.[5]

In Lenin's schema, Populism is viewed as the characteristic response of the agrarian petite bourgeoisie, and other small, independent commodity producers, to the threat posed by capitalist industrial modernisation. Such modernisation is a threat because of the unavoidable consequences of unfettered capitalist development for all small producers: either they enlarge themselves at the expense of others or they go out of business and join the ranks of wage-labour. This dynamic applies as much to agriculture as it so obviously does to handicraft production. Inevitably industrial techniques come to be applied to the production of agricultural commodities, particularly in the area of the modernisation of machinery, to the point where the individual producer must apply the modern techniques and expand his land-holding in order to produce more as the new competition lowers the prices received on the market. As the Draconian logic of capitalist development begins negatively to affect the agrarian petite bourgeoisie, that class, more or less politically united, begins to attack aspects of capitalism while retaining a commitment to its essence for the petite bourgeoisie – private property and small commodity production.

As a result, the agrarian petite bourgeoisie is simultaneously hostile to and supportive of elements of the capitalist economy which ensnares it. Its interests are neither completely those of labour nor completely those of capital. Consequently, the agrarian petite bourgeoisie's politics vacillate, now expressing progressive views, now expressing reactionary views, now expressing progressive and reactionary views simultaneously. The instability of its place in the capitalist economy, exaggerated during times of crisis and rapid modernisation, is reflected in unstable politics. To quote Lenin, (1963, vol. 1, p. 503):

> . . . the Narodnik (Populist) in matters of theory, is just as much a Janus, looking with one face to the past and the other to the future, as in real life the small producer is, who looks with one face to the past, wishing to strengthen his small farm without knowing or wishing to know anything about the general economic system and about the need to reckon with the class that controls it – and with the other face to the future, adopting a hostile attitude to the capitalism that is ruining him.

Consequently the petite bourgeoisie in general, and the agrarian sector in particular, tends to idealise and glorify small commodity production for its own sake (i.e. 'a way of life') while criticising commodity production on a large scale. Thus the Populist critique of capitalism reveals '. . . an extremely superficial understanding, that it is the artificial and incorrect singling out of one form of commodity economy (large-scale industrial capital) and condemnation of it, while utopianly idealising *another form of the same* commodity economy (small production)' (Lenin, 1963, vol. 2, p. 220). Ignoring, or never fully understanding, their real location in the larger economy, it is not surprising that Populists fail to see themselves as representing a class from the past which stands between the proletariat and the bourgeoisie and whose interests lie with neither, yet whose historical fate it is to join one or the other as the logic of capitalist competition threatens its members' ability to exist.

In this way Lenin's theoretical approach provides the most complete framework for an analysis of the Populist phenomenon in all its complexity, contradiction, and generality. Such a perspective refrains from over-stating Populism's critique of capitalism as well as from overlooking Populism's reactionary features. Lenin's perspective locates the movement in the concrete class structure of developing capitalism and focuses on the consequence of an uncontrolled development of modern capitalism for the petite bourgeoisie. On the one hand, we see Populism's general assault on capitalist modernisation which transforms the small property of the many into the big property of the few as well as imposing, as industrialisation must, heavy costs on the agricultural sector to provide the capital, labour, and cheaper food so essential to modernisation. On the other hand, we note Populism's profound reluctance to reject the fundamental principles of capitalist production – private property, commodity production, competitive self-enrichment – which often forces it to adopt programmes which tend to oppose development and modernisation. In this way one recognises that Populism is the political expression of the petite bourgeoisie in the class struggle and hence one can begin to understand clearly both the progressive and reactionary faces of the doctrine.

It is this theoretical perspective which informs the following characterisation of the Populist response to capitalist industrialisation in Canada.

The Populist Agitation in Canada, 1900–30

Prior to the wheat boom, agrarian organisations had flourished in the more settled regions of Central Canada and the Maritimes (Wood, 1924). And in the days of early settlement in the Prairie West a number of organisations had been essayed in an effort to redress agrarian grievances.[6] However, the successful settlement of the Prairie West made the agrarian petite bourgeoisie a power in the land not only because of their increased share of the population, not only because of the new economic importance of wheat, but also because the Prairie agrarian petite bourgeoisie began to pioneer new forms of organisation and to act with a new militancy. Too often the Prairie agrarians are seen in isolation from their counterparts in Ontario, Quebec and the Maritimes. Indeed, part of the popular mythology of the history of the Prairie West holds that much of the agitation that occurred can be attributed to the harsh environment which the settlers confronted and conquered. Yet a close examination of the record shows that, from the beginning, such agitations had more to do with Senators than seasons, with railway charges than locusts, with land policies than frost, with tariffs than poor yields, and with the hundredfold man-made calamities of a corrupt and unresponsive political system than with the inevitable natural calamities that befell grain growers. As well, it is clear that the basic critique of capitalism and the options posed for a redress of agrarian petit-bourgeois grievance had been long expressed by agrarian organisations such as the Dominion Grange of the Patrons of Husbandry and the Grand Association of the Patrons of Industry, both active in Canada in the later part of the nineteenth century. Like the roots of the organised farm movement itself, the roots of the developing agrarian petit-bourgeois ideological perspective[7] can be traced, during the later part of the nineteenth century, to these organisations.[8] As can be expected, the farmer and his vocation was elevated to the primary moral and historical status in the hierarchy of man's sundry occupations.

The intensity of the positive view of their own vocation in agrarian petit-bourgeois ideology was matched by the intensity of the disdain they held for non-productive occupations: they assailed the businessman, the professional, the entrepreneur, and most odious, those in the trusts and monopolies. They contrasted the manipulative shrewdness of such groups with the productive primacy of their own vocation; their own innocent but crucial knowledge to the sneaky methods of business enterprise and city ways. Urban classes, with the exception of an aloof respect granted to the industrial working class and to the crafts, were seen as little more than parasites. As for the entrepreneur, the banker, and the speculator:

> . . . the only sounds that will ever charm his ears will be the clink of gold and the only perfume that will refresh his organs of smell will be the dusty, musty parchments, silent witnesses of his ill-gotten hoard, his nature will become sordid and his position will ever be a painful vacancy of soul.[9]

The early agrarian petit-bourgeois organisations saved their most severe contempt and strongest attacks for the corporations, the trusts, the banks, and the railways – especially the railways. In 1881, one Grange leader sounded this warning:

> The growing power of the railway monopoly is a matter that in the near future will require not only the combined efforts of farmers, but of all other industrial organisations to hold them in reasonable check. Experience has shown that the corporate powers that give them existence and enable them to manage these necessary, artificial highways is rapacious, it is marked by encroachment and usurpations, it assumes rights which belong to the people . . . and with surprising effrontery it warns the people against attempts to recover the rights that they have so innocently yielded.[10]

The farmer's voice, the *Toronto Sun*, in an editorial in 1892, saved its strongest words for the monopoly, or the combine:

> The combine is strong and sinewy in its limbs as a gorilla, its head contains the brain of a shrewd despot, the eye of the far-seeing tiger, the wrath of the all-consuming hyena. It sees everything, it cogitates upon everything, it devours everything, and in its capacious belly it converts the pawned wedding ring of the pallid mother, the pawned shoes of the shivering babe, the pennies of the half-starved newsboy, the pledged tools of the workman into the dollars that make its members fat and strong.[11]

As for politicians, there was nothing but cynicism. As a Grange leader, quoted in the 22 November 1892 edition of the *Toronto Sun*, declared:

> Our parliaments are composed largely of the hirelings of railway companies and the laws are made to suit the purpose of their employers . . . [Political parties had become] . . . essentially a union for political plunder.[12]

The party system was viewed as a fraud since it was ' . . . the anvil on which our chains are forged, partisan politics is the anaesthetic given while it is being done'.[13]

However, there was one urban class brought into being by industrial capitalism for which the early Grange had a qualified respect: the industrial working class. The one qualification was that the urban working class did not share in the exhilarating benefits of rural life. Yet the Grange saw in the industrial working class the farmers' natural ally in the struggle for economic and social justice. They began to grope toward a general labour theory of value, though they retained the belief that agriculture always would precede industrial activity in its wealth-producing importance.

For our purposes, it is sufficient to note that the early efforts at farmer-labour unity failed effectively to materialise. However, the active and militant sections of the organised agrarian petite bourgeoisie did begin to develop a complete ideology which reflected their real place in the system of production and which, more or less, reflected the interests of the agrarian petite bourgeoisie as a class. Hann, in his excellent pamphlet on the ideological perspectives of the agrarian petite bourgeoisie in this early period (on which the preceding characterisation depends heavily), sums up the overview of this advanced and organised section of the agrarian petite bourgeoisie:

> The society that the farmers looked forward to was one in which all parts worked together to produce wealth. If wealth continued to be distributed unevenly, then the future seemed to portend dark things. They looked not to the state to correct this maldistribution but to the integrity of every group engaged in the real production of wealth. Farmers and labourers would have to define their interests and demand their just share of the national wealth. Farmers would have to overcome the natural isolation of their occupations and band together into organisations like the Grange and Patrons in order to protect their rights to a just return for the efforts they expended. The ultimate goal was a community in which the economy served the needs of its inhabitants rather than the profit needs of urban capitalists. Social harmony would be possible only if groups like the Grange and Patrons could band together to control the arrogance of those in power. (Hann, 1973, p. 10)

Many of these early ideological themes recurred as the organised agrarian petit-bourgeois movement matured and gained experience.

With the turn of the century the earlier experiments in agrarian organising bore more permanent fruit in the Prairie West. The new efforts 'had wider aims than the granges in the older provinces' (Porritt and Annie, 1913, p. 434) which dated back to the 1870s:

> They [the new Prairie agrarian organisations] were organised (1) to free grain growers from the exactions of elevator owners at shipping points . . . (2) to relieve grain growers from the exactions of a combine which existed among grain buyers at Winnipeg, and (3) to work for lower railway rates from interior shipping points to the railway terminals on Lake Superior . . . (Porritt and Annie, 1913, pp. 434–5)

The organising went extremely well.[14]

The story of the Prairie agrarian struggle to gain the co-operative control of the annual harvest has been told many times.[15] It was their greatest collective success and, as such, led to a developing self-confidence and class strength which set the stage for their political efforts to transform the structure of Canadian capitalism. This political offensive is the more interesting story.

The protective tariff had always been an abiding grievance among the Prairie agrarian petite bourgeoisie. And, of course, the roots of the protective tariff grievance reached far back into the origins of the Canadian farm movement in general (Wood, 1924, pp. 92–8). It was the patent injustice of the protective tariff that crystallised the near united opinion of farmers across Canada during this period. The arguments against the tariff were commonplace enough among free traders the world over. But among those who were farmers and free traders the arguments reached a pitch of anger, disgust and disillusionment that could only finally result in organised and independent political action. As one farmer put it in 1904:

> . . . when governments compel by protective tariffs the consumers of Canada to pay from twenty-five to fifty per cent upon the necessaries of life than their natural value in the world's market . . . a few that are loud at clamouring may eke out an unnatural existence or become millionaires at the people's expense . . .[16]

The protective tariff meant that the farmers' costs of production were inflated on every item essential to grain production: from wire nails to tractors and combines. Yet the farmer was forced to accept an unprotected and highly competitive world market situation when he sold his produce. Thus the cash return to the individual farmer was threatened at both ends of the complex process that led from seeding to the sale of grains. Consequently, each year the farmer faced an uncertain inflow of cash and a certain set of fixed costs of production. The inevitable boom and bust cycle in such a situation came to dominate the farmer's economic life. As a result, the issue of the protective tariff became a focus of uninterrupted political agitation whose intensity ebbed and flowed with the international price of grains, especially wheat.

Another spectre haunted the agrarian petite bourgeoisie: that of rural depopulation and the ultimate and irreversible triumph of urban industrial capitalism. They saw this process as largely a consequence of protection. The concern had long persisted, especially in Central Canada where rural depopulation was a serious demographic trend during the 1870s, 1880s, 1890s and early 1900s.

In the period from 1901 to 1930, therefore, one can witness a last great national agitational effort to slow, to stop, or to reverse the trend to the decimation of rural Canada. In a sense, it was the last hurrah for the passing, pre-industrial, agrarian mode of life that had persisted prior to industrial capitalism, which, once in motion, proceeded to work its inevitable logic on the demographic landscape. The spectre of rural decimation and depopulation contributed in no small measure to the incredible assault launched by the more conscious sectors of Canada's agrarian petite bourgeoisie. Never before and never since were Canada's farmers so united and strong.

In developing their critique, the organised agrarians increasingly insisted that 'you of the Big Cities' (Moorhouse, 1918, p. 11) must come to recognise that 'this business of backbone farming is the backbone of Business in General' (Moorhouse, 1918, p. 14). As a contemporary observer, Moorhouse argued that agriculture was the sole source of new wealth:

> Day by day the great mass of the toilers in the cities go to work without attempting to understand the fluctuations of supply and demand. They are but cogs on the rim, dependent for their little revolutions upon the power which drives the machinery. That power being Money Value, any wastage must be replaced by the creation of new wealth. So men turn to the soil for salvation – to the greatest manufacturing concern in the world, Nature Unlimited. This is the plant of which the Farmer is General Manager. (Moorhouse, 1918, p. 14)

This kind of realisation was slow in dawning on the farmer. However, the 'upward struggle with market conditions' (Moorhouse, 1912, p. 15) had fostered this insight along with a sense of abiding grievance with 'the currents of organised commercialism' (Moorhouse, 1918, p. 32).

By 1909 the organised farmers had established themselves nationally with the founding of the Canadian Council of Agriculture. The new national organisation moved quickly. By December 1910, the Council was able to bring 811 delegates to a 'Siege on Ottawa' (Sharp, 1948, p. 48). There, on 16 December 1910 they presented a series of resolutions which came to be known as the 'Farmers' Platform of 1910' (Morton, 1967, pp. 297–301). The platform represented the clearest distillation of the agrarian petite bourgeoisie's thinking up to that point. Of course, the delegates led off their presentation on the question of the tariff demanding reciprocal free trade between Canada and the United States 'in all horticultural, agricultural and animal products, spraying materials, fertilisers, illuminating, fuel and lubricating oils, cement, fish and lumber'. They also demanded 'reciprocal free trade . . . in all agricultural implements, machinery, vehicles and parts of each of these'. However, a qualification was introduced by a resolution supporting the Imperial preferential system, although they wanted this phased out in order to establish 'complete free trade between Canada and the Motherland within ten years'. Furthermore, the delegation declared a willingness to face direct taxation in order to make up the revenue lost to the government by such a gradual move to a free trade policy. The resolution on the tariff also reiterated the deep concern of the agrarian petite bourgeoisie regarding rural depopulation and the rapid increase in urban, industrial population.

The 1910 platform also called for various government interventions: a government-owned and operated Hudson's Bay Railway, government ownership of terminal elevators, a government chilled-meat industry, federal legislation to aid in the incorporation of co-operatives, and amendments to the Bank Act and the Railway Act. The document is mute on issues directly of concern to the industrial working class or on general reforms in areas that did not directly relate to the specific interests of the agrarian petite bourgeoisie. Such an effort, though unsuccessful in general terms, was to be attempted later.

Earlier that year, in June 1910, Prime Minister Laurier had become the first incumbent Prime Minister to tour the west. His reception was mixed:

> Everywhere he went he was welcomed enthusiastically. But everywhere he went he also found that after the ceremonies of welcome came the farmers' petitions. (Brown and Cook, 1974, p. 159)

His reception impressed Laurier and had not a little to do with his marginal support of a degree of free trade with the United States the next year. However, in general terms, he emphatically rejected the Farmers' Platform. Laurier is quoted as saying, 'The requests of our farming friends are too radical to stand the test of discussion and have no chance to be adopted in the east.'[17] Indeed, Laurier knew well the attitude of the manufacturers of the day and found himself trying to strike what he believed to be a reasonably judicious balance between contradictory claims. Indeed, it was in this context that limited reciprocity was adopted as a policy by the Laurier administration. The overall impact was nowhere near what the farmers wanted, but it caused a political furore which led to the Liberal defeat that year.[18]

The farmers saw the agreement as a small first step, but an important breakthrough toward their ultimate goal of free trade. Opposition to the agreement from Canadian capitalists was instantaneous and near complete. As the *Weekly Sun* put it, 'They [the business community] see that the promised success of the agitation by the farmers for opening of the American market to farm products may be a prelude to an assault on the whole citadel of Special Privilege'.[19]

Many prominent Liberals, including Clifford Sifton, the former champion of free trade, broke with Laurier and went over to the opposition. But the spearhead of opposition came from powerful capitalist interests:

Much of the opposition came from the business, financial and manufacturing community in Toronto and Montreal. In the vanguard of the suddenly mounting wave of resistance to reciprocity was a group of eighteen Toronto Liberals led by Zebulon Lash, a leading Toronto lawyer, and Sir Edmund Walker, President of the Canadian Bank of Commerce. On February 20 they issued a manifesto opposing the agreement and calling upon the country to block its approval. Reciprocity, they claimed, would destroy the Canadian economy which had developed on an east-west axis and would lead eventually to Canada's absorption into the United States. (Stevens, 1970, p. 2)

Combined with these sentiments, the powerful Canadian Manufacturers' Association 'regarded the agreement as the thin edge of the wedge, to be followed by more extreme measures of free trade' (Masters, 1961, p. 18). Some manufacturers were directly affected negatively – especially millers, packers, canners, and brewers – since 'free trade in natural products meant that the prices of their raw materials would rise to American levels' (Masters, 1961, p. 18). The arguments that Canadian industry needed protection from foreigners and that Canadian resources should be conserved for Canadians were also mounted. The debate became near hysterical: advocates of the reciprocity measures were accused of being disloyal, even treasonous, annexationists. American politicians, like the Speaker of the House of Representatives, Champ Clark, didn't help with their tendency to hyperbole. Clark, at one point, said 'I am for it, because I hope to see the day when the American flag will float over every square foot of the British North American possessions clear to the North Pole.'[20] Such gaffes were grist for the mills of super-patriots who accused Laurier of the next thing to deliberate treason.

  The results of the 1911 Reciprocity election were not only a defeat for Laurier's Liberals but a staggering blow to free-traders. Although the total vote cast for each party was close – 665,594 Tory to 625,103 Liberal – an analysis of the seats won told a much different story (Stevens, 1970, p. 183). The Tories swept Ontario 73 seats to 13. The Liberals narrowly won Quebec 38 seats to 27. The parties split Nova Scotia, 9 seats each. New Brunswick went Liberal 8 seats to 5. The Tories won all 7 of British Columbia's seats. The parties split Prince Edward Island, 2 seats each. The agrarians rewarded Laurier's small efforts: the Liberals taking 8 of Saskatchewan's 10 seats and 6 of Alberta's 7 seats. Surprisingly the Tories won Manitoba 8 seats to 2. Of 221 seats in the House, the Tories took 134 to the Liberals' 87. Once again Canada had voted for the National Policy. The free-traders, even the modest free trade policy of Laurier, had failed to convince the industrialists or the working class.

The 1911 results did not discourage the organised agrarian petite bourgeoisie, on the contrary they declared that 'if a Liberal tariff was unsatisfactory, a Conservative tariff will be doubly so' (Sharp, 1918, p. 50). Support for independent political action therefore grew. Rather than retreating from the 1911 defeat, the organised agrarian petite bourgeoisie went on a new political offensive.

1911 was an important year for the agrarians for a reason other than the Laurier defeat. 1911 was a Census year and the Census figures portended an ominous future for the agrarian petite bourgeoisie. They revealed that rural population had declined from 62.4 per cent in 1901 to 54.4 per cent in 1911. Urban population had increased from 37.6 per cent in 1901 to 45.6 per cent in 1911 (MacDougall, 1913, p. 24). More significantly, as Table 1.1 reveals, more and more people were involved in non-agricultural occupations by 1911 and the trend worsened in each census year. Moreover, although the absolute number of occupied farms in Canada was not to begin its decline until 1951, rural decline had already begun to occur in Central Canada and the Maritimes between 1901 and 1911.

TABLE 1.1   Percentage of labour force in agricultural and non-agricultural occupations in Canada, 1901–31

	Agricultural	Non-agricultural
1901	40.21	59.79
1911	34.28	65.72
1921	32.72	67.28
1931	28.75	71.25

Source: Urquhart and Buckley, 1965, Series C1-7, p. 59

The reaction of the organised agrarian petite bourgeoisie to these trends was, naturally enough, strongest in Central Canada, especially Ontario. The resentment often spilled over to colour the agrarians' attitude to the industrial workers, rendering co-operation difficult:

In Ontario, where industry exerted its greatest pull, rural de-population was most pronounced and most resented. The provincial platform of the UFO placed it first among the reasons for the farmers' entering politics . . .

The loss of rural population was attributed by the farmers to the tariff, which favoured industry at the expense of agriculture. The short working day and high wages of the city, which protected industry and extravagant governments sanctioned, enhanced the attractiveness of the city over the country. These conditions were maintained by legislatures in which farmers had ceased . . . to be represented in proportion to their numbers. The remedy for protective tariffs and rural depopulation was therefore to elect farmers to the legislatures . . . (Morton, 1967, pp. 72–3)

The period from 1911 to 1919 was therefore characterised by a new agrarian petit-bourgeois political offensive, though an offensive somewhat muted by the patriotic demands of the Great War. This period was characterised by the Canadian organised agrarian petite bourgeoisie's move to class political action at both federal and provincial levels. The events – involving, as they do, the end of the wheat boom in 1913, the short-circuiting of Depression by the Great War of 1914, and the post-war crisis – are complex. Limitations of space make a complete and satisfactory analysis impossible. Suffice it to say that the debates regarding independent political action among the leading sectors of the agrarian petite bourgeoisie continued. However, post-war developments made the decision inexorable: industrialism and urbanisation accelerated; agriculture experienced an inadequate and uncertain prosperity; depression followed peace quickly and post-war politics were racked with serious class conflict.

In response, the Canadian Council of Agriculture issued a further edition of the Farmers' Platform in 1918 which was submitted to member organisations in 1919, and revised for the purposes of the 1921 election. The document came to be known as the 'New National Policy' and was much more far-reaching and complete in its proposals than earlier documents had been. The tariff issue still occupied centre stage and a series of complex steps were advocated for its gradual removal. The document also advocated a more progressive taxation system, a series of democratic political reforms, and more positive government intervention to support agriculture. The biggest disappointment was for those who were advocating a stronger basis for farmer-labour political unity. The documents' labour programme was weak and vague, stating merely:

We recognise the very serious problem confronting labour in urban industry resulting from the cessation of war, and we urge that every means, economically feasible and practicable, should be used by federal, provincial and municipal authorities in relieving unemployment in the cities and towns; and, further recommend the adoption of the principle of co-operation as the guiding spirit in the future relations between employer and employees – between capital and labour. (Morton, 1967, pp. 302–5)

Armed with this 'New National Policy' the organised agrarian petite bourgeoisie marched into political action. For the first time they had a 'comprehensive programme, which, put into effect, would have re-shaped the development of the Canadian economy' (Morton, 1967, p. 62).

A large part of their arsenal was the post-war Depression. With the cessation of the activity of the Canadian Wheat Board, which had been established to regulate war time wheat sales and prices, free trading was accompanied by a sharp decline in wheat prices (MacGibbon, 1932, pp. 64 ff.). In August 1920, No. 1 Northern wheat sold for 2.69\frac{1}{2}$ to $2.74 per bushel. By September it had risen to $2.85 per bushel. By December it was $2.00. In 1923 it fell to 93$\frac{1}{4}$ cents per bushel. Between October 1920 and December 1923 the price for wheat declined 67 per cent (MacGibbon, 1932, p. 64).

Very quickly the organised agrarian petite bourgeoisie won some notable political victories. In the 1919 election, the United Farmers of Ontario won the largest bloc of seats. They had not expected to win and were ill-prepared to govern (Morton, 1967, p. 85). In the 1923 election they went down to inglorious defeat (Morton, 1967, p. 210). The UFO Government was broken asunder by the debates between those who wished to keep the movement an agrarian movement and those who wished to 'broaden out' in order to attract a larger base of support. In 1921, the United Farmers of Alberta (UFA) entered politics and swept the province to govern there until 1935 (Patton, 1928, p. 389). In 1922, the United Farmers of Manitoba formed the government there as well (Morton, 1957, chap. 16). Gradually, the new Manitoba government edged back into the Liberal fold since the majority of Manitoban Progressives had always regarded themselves as 'advanced Liberals' (Morton, 1957, p. 397). With the exception of the UFA, none of the Farmer Governments survived the first few years in power intact. Nor were they successful in carrying out the programmes upon which they had secured election. Had the UFO succeeded in 'broadening out' and surviving as a political alternative, had the UFM not been riddled with loyalist 'Liberals in a hurry', had the UFA acted more boldly, the political topography of Canada would have perhaps been fundamen-tally transformed. Such 'might have beens' are the idlest of speculations, since the very nature of the movement made such outcomes unlikely from the beginning. The divisions within the movement, the vagueness of their programmes, the insipid attitude to labour, the ultimately unrealisable goal of returning agriculture to its former position of pre-eminence in a developing industrial capitalism fore-doomed the orga-nised farmer governments. They simply could not agree on an adequate and effective policy towards labour. They simply could not agree on the role of the state in the economy. On each basic issue, the movement was split irremediably. Inevitably these weaknesses found their expression in the sorry fate of the Progressive party at the federal level.

In the federal general election of 1921 the Progressive party won 65 seats, the second largest group of seats in the House (Morton, 1967, Chap. 4). They declined to become the official Opposition, and, according to most scholars,[21] this was the beginning of their demise. However, that was only a symptom of the deeper divisions and contradictions within the movement we have already noted. The Progressive party's biggest single bloc of seats came from Ontario, a fact often overlooked by those who insist on the sectional nature of the movement. With the exception of Quebec, there was no part of the nation in which the Progressives had not made a presentable showing, certainly enough to form the electoral base for a new agrarian petit bourgeois political party with the evident capacity to govern in terms of national support. The fact that the Progressive party was unable to do so had less to do with its sectional nature and its coyness about Parliament and the party system than with the political and ideological ambiguities and contradictions that made up the organised agrarian movement. There was simply no agreement on the items which would be essential for the organised agrarian petite bourgeoisie to win the confidence of other classes in the society, especially the industrial working class and the urban petite bourgeoisie, in order to govern effectively. Yet it was the organised agrarian petite bourgeoisie's finest hour in national politics: they had run in 149 seats and won 65 of them (Scarrow, 1926, p. 36). They appeared to have reached the threshold of similar successes in political action to compare with their successes in business co-operation.

The almost overnight disintegration of the Progressive movement is well described in Morton's *The Progressive Party in Canada* and there is no need to re-hash the details here. Probably it is correct to say that the Progressive's refusal to become the official Opposition and thereby to adopt the party system and cabinet government ensured its gradual extinction as an organised political party. Yet no one should be astounded at that principled decision given the previous twenty years of agitation. It would have been unthinkable for the Progressive party to have embraced the party system after having denounced it for years as a source of evil and corruption in national political life.

In the 1925 federal election the Progressives contested only 72 of the 245 seats. They won only 24. In Ontario they held 2 seats with 2.4 per cent of the popular vote: a drop of 25.3 per cent. Now in truth they could be called sectional. Their years of confusion, disorganisation, and indecision in Parliament had lost them much credibility even among their loyal base in the Prairie West and rural Ontario. More galling, perhaps, and ominous for the next election, was the fact that the strongly protectionist Conservatives gained 23 of the Progressive seats to the 18 the Liberals gained (Scarrow, 1962, p. 50). In the 1926 federal election the Progressives only contested 37 seats, retaining 20 (Scarrow, 1962, p. 64). They persisted on into the 1930 federal election to hold 12 seats with

3.2 per cent of the popular vote, with 9 of the seats and about half their vote in Alberta (Scarrow, 1962, p. 77). By 1935, 15 of Alberta's 17 seats went Social Credit and only three candidates in Manitoba maintained the lonely vigil, running as Liberal-Progressives (Scarrow, 1962, p. 91).

The Progressives had been truly a meteoric political phenomenon, entering and exiting from the effective political stage in the short space of five years. Yet they had had a significant impact: they had wrung some important concessions from the Liberal government and Canadian politics were never the certainty they had been prior to the phenomenon. Most importantly, and not surprising, the Progressives had won significant concessions for their agrarian base, which perhaps goes part way in explaining their demise.[22] In 1922 they won the restoration of the Crow's Nest Pass statutory freight rates (which were suspended in 1919) on grain and flour in transit by rail to the lakehead, and on a variety of westward-bound commodities, including agricultural implements. They also won some tariff relief on agricultural implements and motor vehicles. The Progressives are also credited with winning significant federally sponsored agricultural credit legislation. And for a time, they appeared to have won the re-establishment of the Wheat Board which had been suspended in 1920, much to the chagrin of most farmers who attributed much of the big drop in grain prices in the post-1920 period to that suspension, just as many of them had attributed the high prices gained during the War to the Board. As it turned out, the Wheat Board victory was short-lived as the Manitoba legislature refused to pass the necessary enabling legislation (Morton, 1967, pp. 157–8).

The crisis in the Progressive party merely revealed the crisis at its base: the farmers' organisations confronted serious problems and a massive decline in their membership in the early 1920s. It is ironic, if understandable, that in what appeared to be their greatest political hour, the organised agrarian petite bourgeoisie appeared to be disintegrating:

> Moreover, after 1921, which was the year of highest membership in the farmers' organisations, there was a great falling-off in the number of paid-up members. High cash incomes down to 1920, growing discontent, and the stimulus of political action, had increased the membership to record heights. Thereafter the decline in membership was rapid, from sixty thousand members and sixteen hundred clubs in the UFO, for example, to half that number of members and a quarter that number of clubs in 1922. . . . Nor did the membership of the associations increase in succeeding years, as prosperity grew. The organisation of the Wheat Pools, the waning of political interest, and the rise of the new Farmers' Union, weakened the farmers' organisations and diminished their political strength in all the provinces except Alberta, where organisation made good the loss of members. (Morton, 1967, pp. 211–12)

In such a situation there is no wonder that the organised farmers very quickly left overt political action.

By 1923, in fact, the UFO officially declared itself out of politics and devoted itself to educational and co-operative work (Morton, 1967, p. 216). The SGGA had never gone into provincial politics and only half-heartedly into the federal fray behind the Progressives (Morton, 1967, p. 231). The UFM went through a more gradual metamorphosis which brought it back into the Liberal fold (Morton, 1967, pp. 226–31). The UFA lived long enough as government in Alberta to be completely decimated by the Social Credit party in 1935. In March, 1923, the Canadian Council of Agriculture withdrew its support of national political action, leaving political questions to the various provincial organisations (Morton, 1967, pp. 173–5). This decision also had the effect of removing the national organising locus for the Progressives.

The decision of the Canadian Council of Agriculture effectively ended the brief intrusion of the organised agrarian petite bourgeoisie into national politics: indeed, it meant the end of organised agrarian activity in provincial politics, as events were to prove. In future, the actual organisations of the agrarian petite bourgeoisie concerned themselves with economic action, business co-operation, and pressure group and educational activity. The business of politics was to be left to specifically political organisations. The difficulties encountered in attempting to govern Ontario and Manitoba, as well as the spectacle of Progressive dissension in Parliament, re-kindled the argument that political action would breed division and destroy the farmers' organisations. Events had seemed to confirm this contention.

In the meantime, the organised agrarian petite bourgeoisie was busy building those edifices to business co-operation: the Wheat Pools. In 1923 the Manitoba legislature had refused to pass the enabling legislation for the re-establishment of the Wheat Board, which had earlier (1922) been approved by the House of Commons and the Saskatchewan and Alberta legislatures. As a result, the efforts to re-establish the Wheat Board were abandoned, as was the voluntary pool project under the leadership of the Canadian Council of Agriculture (Patton, 1928, pp. 203–11). Attention therefore was focused on winning voluntary Pools at the provincial level. By 1930 the Pools had 242,614 members with 15,646,522 acres under contract, representing 55.5 per cent of Prairie farms. Also by 1930 the Pools had 1655 country elevators, with a 58 million bushel capacity in all the Prairies (MacGibbon, 1932, pp. 343–4).

Yet, as we have seen, many of the most important of the grievances of the agrarian petite bourgeoisie could only be addressed and redressed through political action. The tariff, despite the modifications, remained essentially intact. The near-complete reliance on grain production, especially wheat, remained to plague Prairie prosperity. Rural depopulation continued and capitalist industrialisation and urbanisation accelerated unchecked. Vulnerability to the ups and downs of the international market remained. What security had been won, had been won by the self-organisation of the agrarian petite bourgeoisie into Wheat Pools and other commodity co-operatives. Control over the costs of production continued to elude the farmer. Railways continued to impose their freight rates with impunity, save for the small measure of relief provided by the Crow Rates. The political clout of agrarian Canada, and of the Prairie West, continued to be virtually ignored but for this or that gesture of conciliation flung by Liberal or Tory federal governments. And such prosperity as had been won in the 1920s, as it turned out, depended on uncertain markets in an increasingly competitive world market (Royal Commission, 1940, p. 115). Therefore, although the organised agrarians' initial ventures into politics had failed significantly the need for political action remained.

The arrival of the Great Depression in 1930 precipitated the agrarian petite bourgeoisie into Canadian politics once more and with considerably different results. Their biggest mark was made in Alberta and Saskatchewan, the only remaining provinces in which they continued to be the most numerous class[23] and, coincidentally, the two provinces which were the most completely shattered by the impact and consequences of the Depression of the 1930s. The forms, even some of the demands, of the renewed agrarian agitation changed, but much of the content remained strikingly the same. As Sharp (1948, p. 188) notes:

> When it [the agrarian revolt] re-appeared under the stimulus of depression and agricultural distress, it came garbed in a new dress and waving new banners, but most of the slogans were the same. They were similar because the fundamental demands were similar . . .

This time, however, they came not dressed in farmers' garb but in a more general wardrobe, as the new political organisations strove to represent and to win a broader than narrowly agrarian base of support.

Old Wine, New Bottles: The Social Credit League in Alberta and the Co-operative Commonwealth Federation (CCF) in Saskatchewan

The immediate impact of the Great Depression on Alberta and Saskatchewan was severe[24] and ultimately devastating. It was a calamity of national and international proportions: but, in Canada, it was more calamitous for the regions principally economically dependent on the production of primary products and most calamitous for those regions mainly engaged in the production of primary food products.

The Canadian staple-based economy experienced the brunt of the Depression since one-third of Canada's national income was derived directly from abroad and two-thirds of Canada's exports were raw materials. Canada's economic success, such as it had been, had largely derived from the extraction and export of raw and semi-raw materials (foodstuffs, newsprint, lumber, minerals) to foreign markets. Crucial to this capacity was an expensive transportation system and basic infrastructure which had been built mainly with borrowed foreign capital. The result of this was:

> The application of this vast capital and of advanced techniques to virgin resources became the principal basis of our economic life. It involved a narrow specialisation in the production of a few export staples, heavy fixed charges, and a precarious dependence upon the commercial policies of other countries. (Royal Commission, 1940, pp. 193–4)

These factors were worsened by the fact that Canada's two leading exports – wheat and newsprint – faced a problem of world over-production and severe downward price pressures as well as a seriously over-extended internal credit system (Royal Commission, 1940, p. 144). All these factors combined to produce a rapid and steep fall in export prices with particularly disastrous consequences for Canada (see Tables 1.2 and 1.3).

Clearly, in Canada, 'those furthest out on the long arm of this lever were the farmers, the fishermen, the lumbermen and the miners, in whose rigid costs (freight rates, taxes, mortgage interest and cost of equipment) the fixed interest charges were expressed' (Royal Commission, 1940, p. 146). The problem of indebtedness was so severe that by 1932–3 servicing the debt took fully one-third of the total receipts derived from Canada's exports.[25]

The incidence of the Depression, due to the regionally based structure of the Canadian economy, fell heaviest on the farmers and other primary producers, especially in the Prairie West, in particular, as well as, obviously, the unemployed across the country and the investors in common stock (Royal Commission, 1940, p. 148). Furthermore, those industries which were protected by tariffs actually did relatively better in the Depression since their prices declined considerably less than the decline either in the cost of living or in wholesale prices. By 1933, the cost of living had declined 22 per cent, prices of tariff-protected manufactures by only 14 per cent, all wholesale prices by 30 per cent, export prices by 40 per cent, and farm prices by 49 per cent.[26] Canada's farmers' share of the national income fell from 15 per cent in 1929 to 7 per cent in 1933, whereas the share of the national income won by wage and salary earners in the tariff-protected industries improved marginally

TABLE 1.2 The decline in export prices and economic activity, Canada, 1929–33

	The prices of 17 major exports	Export prices of farm products	All wholesale prices	Index of employment	Index of industrial production
1929 June	100	100	100	100	100
1930 June	82	70	90	93	80
1930 December	66	42	80	87	74
1931 June	62	42	74	83	64
1931 December	61	41	72	80	61
1932 June	54	37	68	72	59
1932 December	47	30	66	67	52

Source: Royal Commission, 1940, Book 1, p. 144

TABLE 1.3 Canadian export prices, 1929–1933

	All exports (ex. gold)	Wheat	Cattle	Lumber	Newsprint	Copper	Dried cod fish
1929	100	100	100	100	100	100	100
1930	84	70	87	87	100	75	82
1931	66	44	59	75	91	50	56
1932	60	41	46	67	79	38	44
1933	60	45	37	68	62	44	42

Source: Royal Commission, 1940, Book I, p. 146

(1929–14 per cent; 1933–15 per cent). As well, salaries and wages in the naturally sheltered industries and occupations (transportation and communication, merchandising, government and education, banking, insurance and the professions) improved their relative positions – earning 29 per cent of the national income in 1929 and 35 per cent by 1933. Table 1.4 reflects the disparity in the incidence of the Depression in terms of occupation and region as expressed in declines in net money income. The table reveals that Prairie farmers were the hardest hit in

TABLE 1.4 Depression decreases in net money income

	Percentage change in 1932–3 average income from 1928–9 average income
Agriculture – prairies	−94
Fisheries	−72
Salaries and wages in construction	−68
Agriculture – Eastern Canada and British Columbia	−64
Salaries and wages in exporting industries	−50
Total national income	−41
Dividends received by stockholders	−40
Salaries and wages in the protected manufacturing industries	−37
Income of small business and the professions	−36
Salaries and wages in the sheltered occupations	−30
Miscellaneous income	−18
Bond interest, property income from life insurance and interest on farm mortgages received by individuals	+13

Source: Royal Commission, 1940, Book I, p. 150

terms of net money income declines, their 1932–3 income representing a
94 per cent decline over their 1928–9 income: more than double the
decline in national income. Other producers of primary products and
workers in export industries and construction experienced declines in
excess of 50 per cent. On the other hand, those involved in the so-called
sheltered industries and economic activities experienced declines of
money income considerably below that reflected in total national
income. A notable exception to the general pattern, and one to keep in
mind, is the fact that those involved in the private credit business
actually experienced a 13 per cent *increase* in money income during the
period under consideration. These decreases in net money income by
occupation, region, and economic activity category found a regional
reflection in the *per capita* income decline experienced by each of the
provinces.

In the case of Alberta, *per capita* income fell from third place, second
only to British Columbia and Ontario and well above the national
average in 1928–9, to fifth place, well below the national average in
1933: reflecting a decline of 61 per cent (Royal Commission, 1940, p.
150). The only province which experienced the Depression more
seriously, in terms of income declines, was Saskatchewan.

The political consequences of the Depression were to renew the
vigorous expression of the traditional agrarian petit-bourgeois grievances regarding their place in the Canadian political economy:
grievances about the tariff, the grain pricing system, the credit system,
corporate monopolies, though far from new, took on a new urgency in
the context of the Great Depression. Such agitations were joined
increasingly by those mounted by the unemployed and the organised
working class on similar issues, but with a different focus.

In Alberta the United Farmers of Alberta government, the only
surviving organised agrarian petit-bourgeois government, crumbled
under the impact of the Depression. Serious estrangement grew between
the UFA government and the UFA membership. In response to the
Depression the government became more orthodox, parsimonious and
rigid, refusing to respond courageously to the crisis. In response, in
contrast, the UFA membership and its mass base among the Albertan
agrarian petite bourgeoisie, began to toy with two sets of depression
remedies – the co-operative commonwealth and social credit. The
Saskatchewan agrarian petite bourgeoisie also began to consider the
two remedies.

In fact the 1932 UFA Convention manifesto was, by today's standards at least, 'a strange mixture of co-operative commonwealth
and social credit' (Betke, 1971, pp. 135–6). As it turned out, the UFA
Government was unwilling to adopt either set of ideas aggressively,
losing for itself any hope of retaining the major portion of its mass base.
While the UFA government was taking hesitant and moderate steps to

deal with the crisis, the rank-and-file was pushing for the simple and drastic solution of a debt and tax moratorium as an interim programme to the wider reforms implicit in the ideas of social credit and the co-operative commonwealth (Betke, 1971, p. 118).

In the Autumn of that year, 1932, the Social Credit movement in Alberta was launched by school teacher and part-time radio evangelist William Aberhart, who began to introduce social credit ideas into his religious radio broadcasts (Irving, 1959, Chapter 3). The story of Aberhart's Social Credit League's campaign has been told in detail in many published works and a number of dissertations,[27] therefore there is no need to reiterate the full story here. The significant point is that ideas of monetary and credit reform, Douglas Social Credit most prominent among them, which had had a significant following for many years in Alberta thanks largely to the agitations of the organised agrarian petite bourgeoisie, were rapidly becoming a popularly perceived panacea to the particular character of the Depression crisis in the Prairies, especially Alberta. Public and private debt, particularly the interest charges on that debt, were central to the Prairie crisis in the Depression years. In 1932, for example, debt interest charges were taking fully 29 per cent of the Alberta government's total expenditures, in 1933 it rose to 32 per cent, falling marginally to 28 per cent in 1934. In 1932 such payments almost equalled total combined Provincial Government expenditures in education, public health, and public welfare. Besides the provincial debts, for which the provincial governments were directly responsible, one must add the considerable municipal and school board debts throughout the provinces. Private farm mortgage debt in Alberta by 1932 was estimated at $162 million – and much higher if all forms of private debt were taken into account. In Saskatchewan, private farm mortgage debt was estimated in 1931 at minimally $117 million. Hundreds of farmers were forced to appeal to the Debt Adjustment programme in their province for some compromise arrangement in order to avoid foreclosure. Many experienced foreclosure. Yet ironi-cally, even when agricultural production remained at good levels, as it did in most of Alberta, prices were impossibly low. The result was that the fruits of the farmers' production were siphoned off to finance and re-finance debts acquired from expansion during earlier, more prosperous times. This 'poverty in the midst of abundance', a Douglas Social Credit notion that Aberhart in Alberta and T. C. Douglas[28] in Saskatchewan were to use to good effect, was increasingly seen to be unnecessary and unjust, especially in the context of the national calamity of the magnitude of the Depression and more especially when it was seen that financial institutions were doing very well even during the Depression.

Aberhart was able to use a particular and crude re-interpretation of Social Credit doctrine, one which Major Douglas himself was to repudiate, which capitalised on the very real crisis of debt and depression as well as on Alberta's political legacy of popular support for monetary and credit reform, to march irresistibly to provincial office. Almost overnight, Aberhart was able successfully to challenge the UFA for the undisputed political leadership of Alberta's agrarian petite bourgeoisie. Interestingly Aberhart, uncommitted as he was to notions of group government and strictly class organisation, was able also to win the political leadership of Alberta's small working class from the Labour party. The Social Credit League emerged, phoenix-like, from the ashes of the UFA.

In January 1933, a split between the UFA government and the UFA organisation, when the UFA voted to affiliate with the Co-operative Commonwealth Federation, became nearly irreconcilable (Betke, 1971, p. 148). The UFA, out of the January 1933 Convention, issued a 'Declaration of Ultimate Objectives of the United Farmers of Alberta' (The UFA, 1 February 1933). The document re-affirmed a 1932 Convention commitment to the idea of 'a Co-operative Commonwealth and declare it to be our ultimate objective . . . '. The document went on to call for the 'nationalisation of currency and credit', a planned economy, and the 'public ownership or socialisation of all natural resources, industrial and distributive equipment essential to the welfare of society'. The UFA Board of Directors modified and expanded this last public ownership position by adding:

Therefore, as initial steps with this end in view, it will be necessary to:

  (i) obtain political power;
 (ii) nationalise or socialise the monetary system, which is the key factor in the means of distribution;
(iii) pass legislation guaranteeing security of tenure by instituting a perpetual use lease on homes and lands, instead of titles.

We recognise the necessity of the right of title and possession of all natural resources being vested in the state. In the progressive steps towards this end, socialisation of certain natural resources and utilities would be imperative such as:

1. Health, educational and recreational facilities;
2. Receiving facilities, including sites for elevators, stockyards, creameries, packing plants, warehouses, etc.;
3. Transportation facilities;
4. Power plants, factories, workshops, coal mines, oil fields, etc.;
5. Telephone, telegraph, radio broadcasting . . .

(*The UFA*, 1 February 1933)

For all practical purposes, the UFA government ignored both the document and the fact of affiliation with the CCF. During the 1933

Session only Labour MLA's introduced aspects of the Co-operative Commonwealth programme as resolutions in the House (Alberta Legislature, 1933, p. 219). On the other hand, calls for currency and credit reform abounded throughout the Session. On 7 March 1933, the House passed a resolution calling for a managed monetary system under national control (Alberta Legislature, 1933, p. 90). While the merits of Social Credit and the Co-operative Commonwealth programmes for coping with the Depression were being batted back and forth in the House, Aberhart's campaign for Social Credit became more and more intense (Irving, 1959, p. 51 ff.).

The pressure on the Government from the UFA rank and file was enormous. The agitation for Depression remedies – whether Social Credit or the Co-operative Commonwealth – had served dramatically to increase the UFA's membership by 1934.[29] The 1934 Convention was heated – calls for monetary reform of various kinds were commonplace. At the same time there were heated and often confused debates around the idea of the co-operative commonwealth, most particularly on the issue of the nationalisation of the land and the use-lease proposal.[30] It is fair to say that many among the UFA membership shared the conviction that ideas of the Co-operative Commonwealth and of Social Credit could—indeed, should—be reconciled. Increasingly, the fact that the Provincial government seemed to be avoiding both sets of ideas, angered many UFA'ers, particularly when they were confronted, by Government loyalists, with dire predictions of defeat if the Government went too far, too fast down either road.[31]

The debate reflected a popular demand, emanating from the agrarian petite bourgeoisie, for a shift in the perspective guiding agrarian petit-bourgeois politics. The traditional position, reflected by the UFA government, had not been able to cope with the Depression.

The UFA's diagnosis of the root problems in the political and economic order has been typical of the national organised agrarian petite bourgeoisie's analysis. The party system was at fault. Through the party system the economic order itself had been corrupted by special, well-organised, deeply entrenched interests which, due to their wealth and power, were able to dominate politics by corrupting and dominating the parties and, in turn, dominating and corrupting the economic order and, ultimately, all of civil life. The tariff system, the most unnatural of all economic systems, had been politically established by parties in order to reward the special interests which in turn used their enhanced wealth and economic power further to deepen their control of the parties. This control, mutually reinforcing, made it increasingly impossible to use either of the major parties as vehicles for serious reform. Furthermore, the unnatural economy, dominated by special interests, protected by tariffs, increasingly became more unnatural – monopolies and trusts emerged, squeezing out the small industrial producer, and exacting excessive tribute from farmer and consumer in the form of higher prices, mercilessly inflated behind an impenetrable wall of legislated protection. As a result, concentration accelerated, unjust prices were imposed on necessary commodities with impunity, and the high industrial wages, made possible by the high prices and unnaturally excessive profits, attracted the people from the countryside to towns and cities. Thus rural depopulation and urban concentration accelerated.

On the other hand, farmers and other small producers, with no organised power, found themselves unable either to compete with the large concerns or to gain a decent price on an unprotected market for their commodities. Furthermore, such small producers and farmers, especially farmers, were vulnerable to a number of other unjust exactions from merchants, mortgage companies, grain traders, and transportation concerns. In this context, the interest rates they were forced to pay on the necessary credits they were forced to seek from private financial institutions reflected merely one of many injustices imposed by the special interests who dominated the parties and therefore Parliament and were able, as a result, to impose their will and to seek their own advantage unconcerned with the general good.

The solution to this sorry state of affairs was not a Bolshevik revolution, nor the massive public ownership of the economy, nor, finally, after many bitter experiences with the Liberal party, reforms through the existing party system. The solution, first of all, was to organise along class lines in order to become powerful in the land, just as the special interests, who were highly organised, had done. Thus the organised agrarian petite bourgeoisie proceeded to organise themselves and urged other classes to do likewise. Related to this solution was the necessity for economic co-operation – the carrying-over of the principles of social and political self-organisation into selected economic areas. Such co-operative economic organisation, again a practice engaged in by the special interests when they formed monopolies and trusts, fixed prices and interest rates, and shared out the market, was not to be done at the expense of individual enterprise but to enhance individual enterprise and to ensure a fair return to the agricultural entrepreneur. Thus the organised agrarian petite bourgeoisie went into the co-operative buying and some co-operative production of agricultural inputs and consumer necessities as well as, more massively, into the co-operative marketing of their produce, particularly grains, in order to ensure the maximum return of the final price received to the individual producer.

The proper role of government in these efforts was certainly not to use its legal power to impede, but to facilitate, encourage, and when necessary, concretely to support such co-operative enterprises. For a time, too, there was a strong sentiment that the state should enter directly into managing some of the grain-handling infrastructure by owning and operating the railways, the elevators, the terminals, and the ports as utilities and at cost. But opinion among the agrarian petite bourgeoisie remained divided on this matter, and of course, governments, including those controlled directly by the organised agrarian petite bourgeoisie and those heavily influenced by it, proved reluctant to pursue such policies. Further, there was a strong current of opinion, reflected in the long-lived agitation for monetary and credit reform, which argued that the state should own the banks and other financial institutions and that capital ought to be mobilised for the use of actual producers at low or cost-related interest rates. There was a strong sense of injustice at the prevailing practice which saw that the passive owners of capital could make fabulous returns by lending out their capital to others, the real producers of new wealth, who then proceeded to do the work and to take the risks for marginal and insecure profits. This, and all other forms of economic parasitism, were constantly attacked and denounced. Even later, as the Great Depression deepened, the organised agrarian petite bourgeoisie, like the UFA, when circumstance moved them to advocate the public ownership of all resources, including land, the policy was heavily qualified by the perpetual use-lease policy which would ensure individual entrepreneurial ownership in fact if not in law. The role of the state, then, was significant but always subordinated, even among its staunchest advocates, to the enterprise and initiative, if not of the legalistic owners of capital, then certainly of the actual producers of real wealth, especially the farm producer.

Obviously the traditional parties were not going to carry out a programme motivated by such a critique which would, if the diagnosis were correct, lead to the gradual but inevitable extinction of many of the special interests, certainly of those whose existence depended upon their influence on and control of the party system. Gradually, after much debate, the organised agrarian petite bourgeoisie moved to the position that the principle of self-organisation ought to be carried into the electoral political realm as well as the economic realm. The organised agrarian petite bourgeoisie decided to go directly into electoral politics. But their view was not to win power at provincial or federal levels in order to become another special interest which corrupted public life for its own benefit. Rather, their view was that they, the farmers, would go into politics as a class just as other classes – workers and industrialists and so on – would. The elected representatives – bound to their respective classes and controlled through the initiative, the referendum, and the recall – of all classes would meet in Parliament and Legislatures unfettered by the game of party politics, and proceed rationally to select the most competent members as a Cabinet which would then act upon the will of the House. The process was seen to be one of rational discussion and reasonable compromise leading to class harmony and good, fair government.

Advocates of Co-operative Commonwealth and Social Credit remedies clearly maintained that this traditional posture of the organised petite bourgeoisie was not enough, particularly in the context of the Great Depression. Co-operation would not bring a living price for agricultural products when that price was nowhere to be had in the market-place. Calls to the House of Commons for monetary and credit reform would not prevent the foreclosure and seizure of the farms of defaulting farmers whose work and productivity remained high, nor would they stop the lion's share of provincial, municipal, and school taxes which many had to sacrifice to pay, going as interest and service charges on loans made to settle and build the Prairies. Fair government would not lower the price of production inputs or the cost of living, nor would it put food on the table nor clothes on the back, nor provide jobs for the asking. The new agitations appealed directly to the agrarian petite bourgeoisie, around its organised sector, and argued that indeed the provincial governments could be doing more, indeed they could implement Social Credit or the Co-operative Commonwealth and solve all problems of the Depression. Admittedly, the new agitations, unlike the political agitation of the organised agrarian petite bourgeoisie appealed to the working class, the urban and small town petite bourgeoisie, the professions, etc., but they had to win the agrarian petite bourgeoisie to win the provinces and the agitations reveal that key awareness repeatedly. In other words, the new agitations argued that the provincial state could be used directly and aggressively in the interests of the small producer and his allies against the forces of big capital and its allies.

In Alberta, the Social Credit advocates won the debate and gained leadership of the agrarian petite bourgeoisie in the 1935 election. Led by a group unencumbered by any responsibility for the UFA regime's perceived incompetence and a leader of outstanding organisational and propaganda capabilities, the newly formed Social Credit League swept the province in a whirlwind election campaign. The greater attractiveness of Social Credit doctrine to the agrarian petite bourgeoisie was understandable. It proposed no massive programme of public ownership, no serious encroachment on individual entrepreneurship. Rather it advocated a concerted attack on the financial system and the issuance of dividends charged against the province's credit as the route back to prosperity. The establishment of free, or at least cheap, credit, combined with the emergency provision of relief, would salvage the true free enterprise system of small production and, by bringing finance capital to heel, replace the dominance of the banks with the dominance of the productive individual of small property.

The Alberta Social Credit government embarked, between 1935 and 1945, on a series of legislative confrontations with finance capital and the federal government which involved the disallowance of eleven provincial statutes by the federal cabinet and the reservation of three proposed statutes by the Lieutenant-Governor. Had the legislation been allowed to stand the province's financial institutions would have been transformed into instruments of cheap credit for the benefit of small producers. The laws in question would have unilaterally cut interest rates, declared a moratorium on debt collection, prevented foreclosure for debt, and transformed banks into community-controlled credit clearing houses.

The CCF in Alberta remained the major opposition force to the Social Credit government until the 1944 election. However, in Saskatchewan the story of agrarian petit-bourgeois politics was different.[32] The CCF movement there emerged on a political stage uncluttered by a farmers' government. It was able to battle Social Credit ideas successfully among the agrarian petite bourgeoisie, particularly after the disallowance of Alberta legislation made it clear that the federal power, in co-operation with finance capital, was simply not going to allow the establishment of anything remotely close to Social Credit. The version of the Co-operative Commonwealth which emerged in Saskatchewan was an interesting reconciliation of selected aspects of Social Credit grievance if not doctrine, of the principle of co-operation as a major form of social ownership, and of the public ownership of selected sectors of the economy. More importantly, from the outset, the CCF in Saskatchewan proclaimed that it would carry out its programme with due regard to the limitations imposed by the constitution. Like the Social Credit in Alberta, the CCF in Saskatchewan denounced the banks and mortgage companies. However, the Saskatchewan CCF also developed a more general criticism of the capitalist system. Like the Social Credit in Alberta, the CCF in Saskatchewan promised and provided provincial government intervention in establishing programmes of debt readjustment in order to weather the Depression emergency. Unlike the Social Credit, the CCF promised the public ownership of utilities and of selected natural resources in order to expand the public revenues and to foster some industrial activities related to agriculture. The story of the Saskatchewan CCF's struggle for the power they finally won in 1944 is complex and fascinating. Suffice it to say that, upon their victory in 1944, the CCF government in Saskatchewan embarked on their promised programme though by 1948 they began to shy away from too much public enterprise in areas other than utilities.

Conclusion

It must be noted that the Social Credit in Alberta and the CCF in Saskatchewan each claimed that their movement was the legitimate and linear descendant of the agrarian protest movement. It was not just that much of Social Credit doctrine and CCF doctrine had been picked up and popularised by the earlier agrarian movement, but that in itself was significant. But, clearly, the two movements' activists in Alberta and Saskatchewan had absorbed all the essential grievances that had wide currency among the agrarian petite bourgeoisie and that had been so well, though finally inadequately, articulated by the organised agrarian petite bourgeoisie.

The CCF and Social Credit movements represented rearguard actions of the national agrarian petite bourgeoisie's efforts to reconstruct Canadian capitalism in ways congenial to the small producer. The failure of the national effort laid the basis for the successes of the provincial efforts. When Depression struck again the agrarian petite bourgeoisie spawned new movements in the provinces in which they were still the most numerous class and embarked on new efforts at reconstruction. Their further failure to win an opportunity to apply their Depression remedies nationally ensured that they would have to retreat to purely provincial strategies. As it turned out, thwarted in their desire to reconstruct capitalism, both movements, in different ways, sought concessions from it that would (and largely did) cushion their constituencies from the negative consequences of an unregulated capitalism.

NOTES

1. Royal Commission, 1940, p. 67; see also Mackintosh, 1935, p. 10, Easterbrook and Aitken, 1967, pp. 400–1.
2. The figure of in excess of 200,000 farmers is calculated from the fact that according to the 1911 census there were 199,203 occupied farms on the Prairies (of which 178,182 were owner-occupied) and this figure grew to 255,657 (200,000 owner-occupants) by the 1921 census. See Urquhart and Buckley, 1965, p. 351. These facts, combined with a chart provided in Haythorne, 1965, p. 9, suggest that if the estimate errs, it errs on the conservative side.
3. It should be noted that in this work we are focusing on the agrarian petite bourgeoisie engaging in the production of agricultural commodities for a cash market. The full story of the Prairie working class has yet to be told. Yet in 1913, and for some years to come, it would be fair to say that the prosperity of the overwhelming majority of the working class in the Prairies rose and fell with that of the farmer. Much of their wage-labour – construction, transportation, service – was related directly or indirectly to settlement and agricultural production and forwarding. The same held probably even more true for those involved, at least as salaried functionaries or small entrepreneurs, in servicing the farming population, in trade, finance, commercial, and professional occupations.
4. For a more complete discussion of the theoretical issues see Conway, 1978.
5. See Ionescu and Gellner, 1969 for an example of the diverse usage of the term. See Walicki, 1969 for a detailed account of an analysis of Russian

Populism from Lenin's perspective and a vindication of that perspective.
6. The Manitoba and Northwest Farmers' Protective Union, the Settlers' Union in Saskatchewan, the Society of Equity and the Patrons of Industry all made their appearance on the Prairies. See A. S. Morton, 1938, pp. 93–5; Stanley, 1936; Black, 1913; and W. L. Morton, 1957.
7. It should be noted that it is not being suggested that the ideological perspectives about to be characterised were universally held by the agrarian petite bourgeoisie. Indeed, as the collapse of the UFO, UFM, and, later, of the UFA provincial governments, as well as the disarray of the Progressive party, were to prove, when it came to the crunch, the movement found itself unable to impose ideological hegemony over the whole of the agrarian petite bourgeoisie. Yet, as we will see later, the very indecisiveness and internal contradictions which were to wreak such havoc on the movement were themselves features of the newly matured agrarian petit-bourgeois ideology. It is fair to say, though, that until the 1920s, there was a fairly universally shared ideology among the agrarian petite bourgeoisie, especially those in the agrarian activist organisations. The fact that the ideology, and the movement, collapsed when faced with concrete tasks says as much about the nature of the class which espoused it as it does about the ideology itself.
8. An excellent overview of this ideological orientation is provided by Hann, 1973.
9. Mrs C. Moffatt, 1886, cited in Hann, 1973, p. 9.
10. *Proceedings of the Dominion Grange*, vii, p. 5, cited in Hann, 1973, p. 12.
11. *Toronto Sun*, 7 June 1892, cited in Hann, 1973, pp. 12–13.
12. *Toronto Sun*, 22 November 1892, cited in Hann, 1973, p. 14.
13. *Toronto Sun*, 6 June 1893, cited in Hann, 1973, p. 14.
14. See MacGibbon, 1932, Chapter iii; Porritt and Annie, 1913, Chapter xvi; Moorhouse, 1918, Chapters ii, iii and iv; Wood, 1924, Part iii (Chapters xiv to xviii); Fowke, 1957, Part Two; Patton, 1928, Chapter iii; Sharp, 1948, Chapter iii.
15. The following are fairly definitive: Patton, 1928; Moorhouse, 1918; MacGibbon, 1932; Colquette, 1957; and, of course, Fowke, 1957.
16. 'From a Farmer's Standpoint', correspondence between R. J. Vair and C. A. Mallory (one page, no place of publication, 1904), cited in Hann, 1973, p. 13.
17. Sir Wilfred Laurier, quoted in Brown and Cook, 1974, p. 161.
18. For the complete story see Callahan, 1937; Ellis, 1939; Glazebrook, 1942; and Masters, 1961.
19. *Weekly Sun*, 15 March 1911, cited in Brown and Cook, 1974, p. 161.
20. Quoted in Masters, 1961, p. 19.
21. See Morton, 1967 and W. Young, 1969 for this argument.
22. See Patton, 1928, pp. 389–90 for the concessions won.
23. In 1930, 35 per cent of Manitoba's population was 'gainfully occupied' in agriculture. The figures for Saskatchewan and Alberta were 60 per cent and 51 per cent respectively. (Royal Commission, 1940, p. 121).
24. See Safarian, 1970 for the full account of the Depression's consequences for the economies of Canada and her regions.
25. 'In 1930 about 40 per cent of all the capital invested in Canadian business

(excluding farms) and government securities was owned abroad.' (Royal Commission, 1940, p. 146).

26. Royal Commission, 1940, p. 149. The figures that follow are to be found in tables on the same page.

27. Irving, 1959 remains the most detailed description of the process by which Aberhart led his movement to power; Macpherson 1953 remains the most cogent theoretical discussion of the political theory of Social Credit and its application under Aberhart; Mallory, 1954 is the best, and only detailed, description and analysis of the confrontations between Social Credit legislation and the federal power of disallowance; Barr, 1974 is a good capsule history of the movement in Alberta.

    Unpublished MA theses and PhD dissertations on the Social Credit interlude abound. Among the most useful are: Schultz, 1959; Sinclair, 1972; Anderson, 1972; Pashak, 1971.

    More popular and partisan, and quite useful if read carefully and critically, are the following: Hooke, 1971 (Mr Hooke was a Social Credit Cabinet Minister for 26 years); Johnson and MacNutt, 1970; and, of course, Douglas, 1937 is particularly useful, especially as it contains the correspondence between Aberhart and Douglas upon Aberhart's ascension to the Premier's Office.

28. T. C. Douglas became Saskatchewan's CCF Premier in 1944. He should not be confused with Major Douglas, originator of the Social Credit doctrine.

29. The 16 January 1934 *Calgary Albertan* reported a 1934 membership of 13,000 compared to a 1933 membership of 8000.

30. *Calgary Albertan*, 19 January 1934.

31. One delegate at the 1934 convention said, 'It is better that we should go down to defeat than resort to political expediency.' *Calgary Albertan*, 19 January 1934.

32. The major published works on the CCF and its successor, the New Democratic Party (NDP) are: Lipset, 1971; McHenry, 1950; D. Morton, 1977; W. D. Young, 1969; and Zakuta, 1964. The number of published articles on the CCF are too numerous to mention. As well, theses and dissertations abound on all aspects of the phenomenon. The most useful, from the author's perspective, are: Johnson, 1961; McLeod, 1959; Silverstein, 1968; and Sinclair, 1972.

REFERENCES

Alberta Legislature, Journals, vol. xxx.

O. A. Anderson, *The Alberta Social Credit Party: an Empirical Analysis of Membership, Characteristics; Participation and Opinions* (unpublished Ph.D. dissertation, University of Alberta, 1972).

J. J. Barr, *The Dynasty: The Rise and Fall of Social Credit in Alberta* (Toronto: McClelland & Stewart, 1974).

C. F. Betke, *The United Farmers of Alberta, 1921–35: The Relationship Between the Agricultural Organisation and the Government of Alberta* (unpublished MA thesis, University of Alberta, 1971).

N. F. Black, *History of Saskatchewan and the Old North West* (Regina: North West Historical Co., 1913).

R. C. Brown and R. Cook, *Canada, 1896–1921: a Nation Transformed* (Toronto: McClelland and Stewart, 1974).

J. M. Callahan, *American Foreign Policy in Canadian Relations* (New York: Macmillan, 1937).

R. D. Colquette, *The First Fifty Years: A History of the United Grain Growers Limited* (Winnipeg: The Public Press, 1957).

J. F. Conway, 'Populism in the United States, Russia and Canada: Explaining the Roots of Canada's Third Parties', *Canadian Journal of Political Science*, XI (1978).

J. F. Conway, *To Seek a Goodly Heritage: The Prairie Populist Resistance to the National Policy in Canada* (unpublished PhD dissertation, Simon Fraser University, 1978).

C. H. Douglas, *The Alberta Experiment* (London: Eyre & Spottiswode, 1937).

W. T. Easterbrook and H. Aitken, *Canadian Economic History* (Toronto: Macmillan, 1967).

L. E. Ellis, *Reciprocity*, 1911 (New Haven: Yale University, 1939).

V. C. Fowke, *The National Policy and the Wheat Economy* (Toronto: University of Toronto, 1957).

G. P. Glazebrook, *Canadian External Relations: An Historical Study to 1914* (Toronto: Oxford University Press, 1942).

R. Hann, *Some Historical Perspectives on Canadian Agrarian Political Movements: the Ontario Origins of Agrarian Criticism of Canadian Industrial Society* (Toronto: New Hogtown Press pamphlet, 1973).

G. V. Haythorne, *Labour in Canadian Agriculture* (Cambridge, Mass.: Harvard University, 1965).

A. Hooke, *30 + 5: I Know, I was there* (Edmonton: Co-op Press of Alberta, 1971).

G. Ionescu and E. Gellner (eds.), *Populism: its Meanings and National Characteristics* (London: Weidenfeld & Nicolson, 1969).

J. A. Irving, *The Social Credit Movement in Alberta* (Toronto: University of Toronto Press, 1959).

A. W. Johnson, *Biography of Government: Policy Formation in Saskatchewan 1944–61* (unpublished PhD dissertation, Harvard University, 1961).

L. P. V. Johnson and O. J. MacNutt, *Aberhart of Alberta* (Edmonton: Co-op Press of Alberta, 1970).

V. I. Lenin, *Collected Works* (London: Lawrence & Wishart, 1963).

S. M. Lipset, *Agrarian Socialism: The Co-operative Commonwealth Federation in Saskatchewan* (Berkeley: University of California Press, 1950, reprinted 1971).

J. MacDougall, *Rural life in Canada: its Trends and Tasks* (Toronto: University of Toronto, 1913).

D. A. MacGibbon, *The Canadian Grain Trade* (Toronto: Macmillan, 1932).

D. McHenry, *The Third Force in Canada: The Co-operative Commonwealth Federation, 1932–48* (Toronto: Oxford University Press, 1950).

W. A. Mackintosh, *Economic Problems of the Prairie Provinces* (Toronto: Macmillan, 1935).

T. H. M. McLeod, *Public Enterprise in Saskatchewan: The Development of*

Public Policy and Administrative Controls (Harvard: unpublished PhD dissertation, Harvard University, 1959).

C. B. Macpherson, *Democracy in Alberta: Social Credit and the Party System* (Toronto: University of Toronto Press, 1953).

J. R. Mallory, *Social Credit and the Federal Power in Canada* (Toronto: University of Toronto Press, 1954).

D. C. Masters, *Reciprocity, 1846–1911* (Toronto: Canadian Historical Association, 1961).

H. Moorhouse, *Deep Furrows* (Toronto: McLeod, 1918).

A. S. Morton, *History of Prairie Settlement* (Toronto: Macmillan, 1938).

D. Morton, *Social Democracy in Canada: NDP* (Toronto: Hakkert and Co., 1977).

W. L. Morton, *Manitoba, A History* (Toronto: University of Toronto, 1938 reprinted 1957).

W. L. Morton, *The Progressive Party in Canada* (Toronto: University of Toronto Press, 1950, reprinted 1967).

L. B. Pashak, *The Populist Characteristics of the Early Social Credit Movement in Alberta* (unpublished MA thesis, University of Calgary, 1971).

H. S. Patton, *Grain Growers' Co-operation in Western Canada* (Cambridge, Mass.: Harvard University, 1928).

E. Porritt and G. Annie, *Sixty Years of Protection in Canada 1846–1912: Where Industry Leans on the Politician* (Winnipeg: Grain Growers Guide, 1913).

Royal Commission on Dominion-Provincial Relations, *Report* (Ottawa: King's Printer, 1940).

A. E. Safarian, *The Canadian Economy in the Great Depression* (Toronto: McLelland & Stewart, 1970).

H. A. Scarrow, *Canada Votes: a handbook of Federal and Provincial Election Data* (New Orleans: Hauser Press, 1962).

H. J. Schultz, *William Aberhart and the Social Credit Party: a Political Biography* (unpublished PhD dissertation, Duke University, 1959).

P. F. Sharp, *The Agrarian Revolt in Western Canada: a Survey Showing American Parallels* (Minneapolis: University of Minnesota, 1948).

S. Silverstein, *The Rise, Ascendancy and Decline of the Co-operative Commonwealth Federation Party of Saskatchewan, Canada* (unpublished PhD dissertation, Washington University, 1968).

P. R. Sinclair, *Populism in Alberta and Saskatchewan: a comparative analysis of Social Credit and the Co-operative Commonwealth Federation* (unpublished PhD dissertation, University of Edinburgh, 1972).

G. F. C. Stanley, *The Birth of Western Canada: a history of the Riel Rebellions* (Toronto: University of Toronto, 1936).

P. Stevens (ed.), *The 1911 General Election: A Study in Canadian Politics* (Toronto: Copp Clark, 1970).

M. C. Urquhart and K. A. H. Buckley (eds.), *Historical Statistics of Canada* (Toronto: Macmillan, 1965).

W. D. Young, *The Anatomy of a Party: The National C.C.F., 1932–61* (Toronto: University of Toronto, 1969).

W. Young, *Democracy and Discontent: Progressivism, Socialism and Social Credit in the Canadian West* (Toronto: McGraw-Hill, 1969).

A. Walicki, *The Controversy over Capitalism: Studies in the Social Philosophy of the Russian Populists* (Oxford: Clarendon Press, 1969).

L. A. Wood, *A History of Farmers' Movements in Canada* (Toronto: Ryerson, 1924).

L. Zakuta, *A Protest Movement Becalmed: A Study of Change in the C.C.F.* (Toronto: University of Toronto, 1964).

2 Farming for Survival: The Small Farmer in the Contemporary Rural Class Structure

HOWARD NEWBY, DAVID ROSE, PETER SAUNDERS AND COLIN BELL

The major problem faced by the small farmer is not dissimilar to that faced by other petit-bourgeois groups in contemporary society: how to ensure survival under conditions which threaten increasing economic marginality and eventual extinction. The tenacity of the small farmer in the face of such a threat has, of course, entered the folklore of English[1] historical experience. The yeoman virtues of sturdy independence and solitary self-help have long been prized and celebrated as a source of strength in the English national character and, although we shall not be discussing the metaphysical niceties of this viewpoint here, it is worth pointing out that this perspective continues to infect much of the thinking and writing on what has come to be known as the 'small farm problem'. In this context the small farmer[2] has been a 'problem' since the state decisively intervened in the organisation and support of British agriculture during and immediately following the Second World War. For a less charitable interpretation of tenacity is obstinacy, and from the perspective of agricultural policy-makers the small farmer represents an obstacle to the rationalisation of British farming along more efficient and cost-effective lines.[3] Indeed, since the entry of the United Kingdom into the European Economic Community the small farmer has found himself at the centre of political controversy over the financing of the Common Agricultural Policy, so that the 'problem' of small farmers is now not only one which concerns agricultural policy-makers but consumers, too.

The basic theme of this paper is to demonstrate how the small farmer is coping with a situation in which he is, if not quite 'non-existent, historically speaking', then at least under increasing pressure to preserve his existence as an independent entrepreneur. The trend towards fewer, larger productive units in agriculture is a long-standing but accelerating one. Farming is becoming less and less a dignified and Arcadian 'way of life', in which the small farmer could find a reasonably secure, if frugal, niche, but a rationally organised business with principles little different from those of much urban-based manufacture. How the small farmer has reacted and adapted to the changes implicit in this process will be our major concern in this paper.

This is a concern which also underlies much of the sociological literature on small farmers in the British Isles, although it has been somewhat differently expressed in terms of the encroachment of *gesellschaft* upon *gemeinschaft* or urban upon rural values. Beginning with Arensberg and Kimball's pioneering study of County Clare (Arensberg and Kimball, 1968) a series of anthropological studies carried out mostly in the 1950s and early 1960s emphasised the importance to the small farmer of 'keeping the name on the land' and of the risk of downward social mobility were he forced to give up farming and seek employment elsewhere (see, for example, Rees, 1950; Williams, 1956; Nalson, 1968). A general theme to emerge from these studies was therefore the notion that the 'rationality' of the small farmer could not be understood in purely utilitarian terms, but was a set of values and beliefs moulded by the (local) social structure in which he was located. What to an agricultural economist might therefore appear to be irrational or erroneous could be explained in sociological terms. Guided as they were by the theoretical and methodological prescriptions of structural-functional anthropology, two institutions received particular attention: the kinship system and the system of local social status (see Arensberg and Kimball, 1968; Rees, 1950; Williams, 1956, 1964; Nalson, 1968; Jenkins, 1971). Studies of rural Wales also emphasised the Welsh cultural tradition, particularly its embodiment in non-conformist religion (see Day and Fitton, 1975 for a summary and a critique). Later studies (for example, Williams, 1964; Nalson, 1968) were also concerned with the mechanisms whereby a 'degree of fit' could be ensured between the kinship and landholding structures, both intra- and inter-generationally.

Taken collectively these studies represent a point of departure, sociologically and historically, for this paper. However, they deal with theoretical questions, a historical period and geographical locations which are very different, on the whole, from ours. For example, most of these studies (with the exception of Littlejohn, 1963) emphasise the *gemeinschaftlich* qualities of the local social structures which they analyse. However, as we have already indicated, we shall be concerned with the consequences to the small farmer of the dictates of the market for agricultural produce and the nature of the constraints which they place upon his entrepreneurial behaviour. The economic conditions under which the small farmer operates have changed markedly since these studies were written, to say nothing of the technological changes which have accompanied them. Moreover, this paper is based upon data gathered in a very different location – geographically, agriculturally and socially – from those which predominate in the existing literature. Hitherto the studies of small farmers have been carried out in pastoral, mainly upland, farming areas. This is, of course, as it should be: such areas contain a preponderance of small farmers and small farmers are disproportionately located there. Nevertheless in our study of farmers in East Anglia (Newby *et al.*, 1978) we obtained data from a sample of small farmers, despite their being somewhat atypical of agriculture in the region as a whole. This enabled us to discuss the overall class structure of the area, as well as to highlight the differences between this group and the larger farmers and landowners in whom, because of our theoretical concerns, we were more interested. Our initial task must therefore be to describe this sample, to locate it within the context of East Anglian agriculture and to place it in the more general context of modern agriculture in England.

Farming for Survival in Suffolk

The data presented in this paper are based upon interviews carried out in 1974/5 with a one-in-three stratified random sample of all full-time farmers in an area of 44 parishes in East Suffolk.[4] This area, which is approximately within a ten-mile radius of the market town of Framlingham, shows a high incidence of owner-occupation among its farming population, but in other respects – most notably the distribution of the farms according to size – it is reasonably representative of Suffolk, and East Anglia, as a whole – though not of England and Wales, owing to the generally larger size of East Anglian farms. Comparative statistics are presented in Table 2.1. However, the location was chosen not so much for this reason as to provide comparative material collected by Newby in his earlier study of farm workers (Newby, 1977), although we were also concerned to use this sample as a control with which to compare data collected from interviews with very large-scale farmers across the East Anglian region as a whole (see Newby *et al.*, 1978). As Table 1.1 indicates, these 44 parishes do contain some farms which would be considered large by any standards, including those which apply in East Anglia. We have therefore excluded from our analysis in this paper those interviews conducted with farmers occupying over 300 acres[5] crops and grass, a figure which represents, as we shall indicate, an important dividing line in British agriculture.

TABLE 2.1   Size distribution of holdings in England and Wales, Eastern Region, Suffolk and 44 parishes, 1972

Acreage size group	England and Wales No.	%	Eastern Region No.	%	44 Parishes No.	%
$\frac{1}{4}$ 49$\frac{3}{4}$	102,547	47.4	15,707	54.6	190	42.7
50 – 99$\frac{3}{4}$	43,005	19.9	4034	14.0	73	16.4
100 – 299$\frac{3}{4}$	53,282	24.6	5303	18.4	111	24.9
300 – 699$\frac{3}{4}$	14,141	6.5	2759	9.6	56	12.6
700 – 999$\frac{3}{4}$	1922	0.9	537	1.9	10	2.2
1000 +	1422	0.7	424	1.5	5	1.1
Total	216,319	100	28,764	100	445	100

Topographically the 44 parishes form part of an elevated plateau intersected by shallow river valleys. For the most part conditions are good for arable agriculture, except at the bottom of the river valleys where dairying predominates. The main crops grown in the area are cereals, mainly wheat and barley, with 'break' crops such as sugar beet, broad beans, potatoes and rape. In addition, there are extensive acreages of vegetables grown under contract for food-processing companies, the most significant of which is Birds Eye. Stock are rarely seen outdoors, although most farms in the area have a pig unit which utilises home-grown grain. In general it is an area typical of what Frankenberg (1965, p. 253) describes as the 'capitalist organised, business farming areas' of lowland England. There is virtually no marginal land, hired labour is used quite extensively, but investment in buildings and machinery is also very high. Unlike other areas of Britain, East Suffolk has no tradition of small peasant holdings, farmed by owner or tenant: the predominant relationship on the land has always been that of employer and employee since Saxon times. Even the tenanted farms were of a sufficient size to require a large amount of hired labour, while landlords were never solely landlords, or even absentees, preferring instead to farm some of their land 'in hand'. There is, therefore, no history of landlord-tenant conflict in the area (except against the Church, significantly both an absentee and a non-farmer) and today the cross-cutting ties between landowners and farmers are considerable; nor is their relationship necessarily a hierarchical one. Tenurial status, as we shall see, is a significant aspect of entrepreneurial activity, but the complexities are often so baroque that it does not form a meaningful category for political mobilisation or informal social ranking.

Whatever the vagaries introduced by the weather, by disease or by agricultural politics, farming in the 44 parishes, in common with East Anglia as a whole, is an extremely prosperous activity. The type of agricultural production which dominates the area –cereal growing – is one which has been well served by the scientist and the technologist, by the system of state support for British agriculture since the Second World War and by the conditions of Britain's entry into the EEC. It is an area which has, therefore, been in the vanguard of Britain's 'second agricultural revolution' – the transformation in technology and husbandry management which has enabled British agriculture to double its output during the last thirty years. Indeed, the stability granted to agriculture by continuing state intervention, together with the comparative ease with which cereals production can be mechanised, has promoted a remarkable degree of regional specialisation: sheep have been virtually banished and 90 per cent of East Anglia is now under the plough. Although arable farming therefore predominates irrespective of the size of enterprise, the concentration on crop production is the main factor accounting for the larger overall size of holdings and farm business than exists nationally. The amount of capital which must be employed on modern arable farms renders their optimum size much larger than the norm for British farms generally. Moreover, the problems of capital accumulation are promoting a clear trend towards fewer, larger holdings, with a concentration of production on the larger farms. As Table 2.2 shows, in the last thirty years there has been a large reduction in the overall number of holdings, both nationally and in Suffolk, and this reduction has been concentrated among holdings of less than 300 acres. Thus, while the smaller holdings may predominate *numerically*, in terms of their significance for employment and production, it is the larger holdings that count. In 1974 the top 10 per cent of holdings accounted for 53 per cent of agricultural production in England and Wales.

This trend towards fewer, larger holdings is a long-standing one, but since the Second World War this movement 'from agriculture to agribusiness' has been promoted by successive governments by the ways in which they have intervened in the economic organisation of the agriculture industry. The phrase 'political economy' then has a rather more literal meaning in agriculture than in other sections of British industry. (For detailed descriptions of British agricultural policy since the war see Self and Storing, 1962; Beresford, 1975; Wilson, 1977.) British agriculture is so highly politicised, not only because food is the most essential of life's necessities, but because the economic problems which would beset farming if it were left to a free market would be little short of catastrophic. As agricultural economists long ago pointed out, agricultural commodities are subject to extreme fluctuations in supply and (given virtually inelastic demand) price, because changes resulting from extraneous factors like the weather become magnified by the activities of farmers themselves. Violent fluctuations in price of the kind associated with 'scissor cycles' and 'cobweb cycles' can be extremely

TABLE 2.2   Percentage distribution of holdings by crops and grass acreage size groups, Suffolk and England and Wales, 1945–1974

Size groups	1945 (%)	1955 (%)	1965 (%)	1974[1] (%)	Percentage change 1945–74 in number of holdings
Suffolk					
$\frac{1}{4}$– 49$\frac{3}{4}$	52	57	55	41	−58
50 – 99$\frac{3}{4}$	17	15	14	16	−49
100 –299$\frac{3}{4}$	22	22	21	26	−40
300 +	6	7	10	17	+43
Total	100	100	100	100	−46
England and Wales					
$\frac{1}{4}$– 49$\frac{3}{4}$	62	63	60	46	−57
50 – 99$\frac{3}{4}$	17	16	17	20	−31
100 –299$\frac{3}{4}$	18	17	19	25	−20
300 +	3	4	5	8	+43
Total	100	100	100	100	−42.5

[1] In June 1968, 47,000 insignificant holdings were excluded from the census.
Source: MAFF Annual Agricultural Statistics.

damaging if the periodic slumps in prices are so severe as to render farmers bankrupt, and in commodities involving high capital investment and/or long production cycles this can be a real possibility (see Metcalf, 1969; Capstick, 1970). Such violent fluctuations also inhibit investment and technological innovation, so reducing the efficiency of those farmers who survive. One major aim of state intervention has therefore been to promote the stability and hence the efficiency of agriculture.

This policy objective has, however, tended to conflict with the second major aim of state intervention: support of the low-income problems of farmers. Within a market economy there is a persistent and long-standing tendency for returns to agriculture to decline as a proportion of returns to the economy as a whole as the standard of living of the population increases. Although this could be rectified if sufficient numbers of farmers left the industry to allow equitable incomes for those who remained, this would have to occur on such a historically massive scale as to be unrealistic. An objective of state intervention has therefore been to maintain the income levels of farmers at a level which would allow a 'reasonable' standard of living for the 'efficient producer'. This may be carried out on purely social welfare grounds, as in the subsidies paid to hill farmers, or for strategic reasons in order to maintain indigenous food supplies, or to improve the nation's balance of payments. Insofar as this entails keeping marginal farmers in production, it conflicts with the first objective of state intervention – the promotion of efficiency. Moreover any system of subsidies to farmers will ensure (and has ensured) that the bulk of the payments will go to the largest producers who arguably need least support. This has been, and is, the classic dilemma of state support, which applied to the 'deficiency payments' system which operated until Britain's entry into the EEC and which continues to apply to the Common Agricultural Policy.

It is against this kind of background that the 'problem' of the small farmer must be set. Clearly his economic prospects will depend very much on the level of state support for whatever commodities he happens to be producing. By varying the levels of price guarantees and tinkering with the precise details of their implementation the government has a far-reaching effect on the prosperity of the industry as a whole – and a crucial one on those small producers who are economically marginal. In addition, since the Agriculture Act of 1947 the government of the day has had a variety of other measures at its disposal in order to structure the kind of agriculture which it would like to see, ranging from the imposition of selective import quotas and tariffs to the payment, selectively if need be, of direct grants and subsidies for such items as buildings, machinery and fertilisers. Payments like these have been used selectively as a 'carrot' to encourage rationalisation and concentration in the agriculture industry. In turn, intervention in pricing has enabled farmers to expand their output and productivity without suffering a commensurate loss of income from what would otherwise have been depressed prices. Hence the stimulus has been provided for the wholesale substitution of capital for labour which has become characteristic of British agriculture. However, agricultural support has been so structured that farmers have never *quite* been fully reimbursed for increases in their costs, giving the state a useful 'stick' for goading them into even greater efficiency to make up the difference. Thus the size and scale of the 'marginal' farmer has been allowed to slowly, but inexorably, advance. 'Small' farmers of a decade ago may find themselves uneconomic and out of business, while former medium-sized farmers become increasingly marginalised, as they struggle to accumulate sufficient capital to provide the investment necessary to keep up with the low-cost efficiency promoted by the Ministry of Agriculture.

The problem of 'farm adjustment' is therefore a perennial one (see Ashton and Rogers, 1971), for each generation sees the creation of a new stratum of 'small farmers'. The problem is not, however, a purely economic one. Such is the politicisation of modern agriculture that few small farmers fatalistically resign themselves to the 'hidden hand' of the market. Farmers in general have demonstrated a remarkable ability to mobilise themselves organisationally through the National Farmers Union (NFU), which has taken on the role of negotiating the level of guarantees and other support measures in Whitehall and in Brussels. However, insofar as the NFU has been a party to policies which have threatened the long-term existence of small farmers, it is not perhaps surprising that the formation of breakaway organisations which have challenged the legitimacy of the NFU have tended to occur among small farmers in Wales and the West Country (see Wilson, 1977). Small farmers have also been in the forefront of militant activity outside the formal negotiating procedures, such as the blockading of cattle ships at Ardrossan and Holyhead in 1973. The NFU, careful not to be politically outflanked, has therefore consistently supported measures which at least alleviate the worst problems confronting small farmers (such as the provision of generous payments to encourage small farmers to leave the industry), while politicians, mindful of the number of rural constituencies in which the votes of small farmers are believed to be significant, have not been averse to a modicum of state aid. Moreover, there is no doubt that the social fabric of some rural areas would suffer considerably if small farmers were allowed to be driven to bankruptcy.

Until Britain joined the EEC in 1973, the cornerstone of government aid to small farmers was the Small Farmers' Scheme, introduced in 1958. It was designed to give special assistance to small farms which were potentially economically viable, but which were struggling to overcome under-capitalisation. The assistance took the form of a series of grants for capital and husbandry improvements, made only in accordance with a plan approved by the Ministry of Agriculture's advisory service; later in 1965, a further condition of keeping and using proper farm records was added. (For details of the scheme see Donaldson and Donaldson, 1972, Chapter 12.) The results of the scheme – before it was wound up in 1973 to be replaced by a parallel one operated by the EEC – were somewhat disappointing. Only a little over half of those for whom it was intended received payments under the scheme – and often the results were somewhat unpredictable. A study of the scheme in a part of Devon in 1963 concluded that:

> The composition of the group of farmers with schemes is in many respects untypical of the area as a whole. They tend to be young immigrants to the area, the majority being owner-occupiers. (Bradley, 1963, pp. 6–8)

Rather than providing a prop for the preservation of yeoman virtues, it was allowing 'up-country johnnies' with little farming experience to dabble in uneconomic farming. (There is an interesting echo here of the changes in the area which Williams (1964) found in his study of 'Ashworthy'.) Donaldson and Donaldson argue that, economically, such schemes only give the small farmer 'the doubtful security of a condemned man on a deferred sentence' (1972, p. 159). In other words, despite these ameliorative measures the old contradiction between the efficiency and welfare aspects of modern agricultural policy continue to reassert themselves, and, while the latter may slow the effect of the former, the drive towards increasing efficiency has steadily continued.

Small farmers therefore find themselves swimming increasingly against the economic tide. Yet their tenacity in the face of these unfavourable conditions is remarkable. Although there are problems in interpreting the official statistics, the total number of 'farmers and graziers' showed little change between 1851 and 1951 and there has been only a small downturn (a little over 10 per cent) since that date (see Gasson, 1974). Farmers are therefore an exceptionally stable element of the agricultural labour force. Of course, compared with agricultural workers, farmers have much more to lose by moving out, for it usually involves a downward move in terms of both class and status (Nalson, 1968). Many small farmers will ruefully admit that their activities make economic nonsense – but they prefer to stay put. The economic rationality of the small farmers cannot therefore be taken as a 'given'. From our interviews with small farmers in Suffolk we shall explore their apparently 'irrational' entrepreneurial behaviour so that their tenacity can be accounted for. In East Anglia the small farmer is in a doubly anomalous situation for not only does he suffer from the disadvantages already referred to but being located in an area where large-scale arable agriculture predominates there is an added piquancy to his relative deprivation. We shall therefore not only investigate the mainsprings of his economic activity but explore his political and ideological reactions to his increasing marginalisation.

The Small Farmer as Entrepreneur

Not surprisingly, small farmers share certain common features with other petit-bourgeois groups discussed in the literature. Nor would it be controversial to suggest that such similarities derive most basically from the fact of property ownership, for the traditional petite bourgeoisie was originally defined by both Marx and Weber precisely in terms of this factor. For example, Marx, both in *The Communist Manifesto* and the *Eighteenth Brumaire*, makes it clear that the only factor preventing the petite bourgeoisie from sinking into the proletariat is their property, and this has become a central concern of much of the subsequent discussion. Similarly Weber argues that the life-chances of the petite bourgeoisie depend more upon their market situation as owners than upon any skills they might possess. While this brings his analysis superficially close to that of Marx, Weber nevertheless seeks to explain the very different market situations which separate the petite bourgeoisie, not only from the working class but also from the non-propertied professionals and technocrats and the commercial and propertied class (Weber, 1968, pp. 302 ff. and 926 ff.). In this section we shall follow Weber's analysis in examining the market situation of small farmers in East Anglia. We shall see that there are certain similar features to those described for other petit-bourgeois groups (for example Bechhofer *et al.*, 1971, 1974a, 1974b, 1976, 1978; Roberts *et al.*, 1977). However in some ways small farmers, at least in eastern England, are distinctive, and we wish to examine the nature and importance of their unique qualities.[6]

In a recent essay discussing the findings of a large-scale survey of farms and farm businesses, it was noted that 'families ran farms, and though not true to the same degree, farms were run for families' (Harrison, 1975, p. 21). While it could rightly be claimed that the family is extremely important in any discussion of small business, in agriculture it would appear to have an even greater role to play in the individual farmer's market situation. Take, for example, the problem of how people initially establish themselves as independent farmers. Agriculture, in common with other sectors of the economy where small businesses flourish, is noted for particular values and ideologies among its practitioners. One of the most common (discussed below) is that which stresses the rewards to be gained from hard work and the value of independence. Bechhofer *et al.*, have expressed the general point well with regard to shopkeepers:

. . . the petit-bourgeois stratum is the repository of many of the traditional values upon which a capitalist social order was built. The shopkeeper's passionate individualism and the moral evaluation of work emerge clear enough . . . Moreover, their belief that by hard work and wit you can succeed is crucial to the conception of ours as an open society. Thus the symbolic significance of the stratum resides in the fact that to many their lives appear to demonstrate the possibility of individual mobility. (1974b, p. 124; see also Bechhofer and Elliott, 1978)

However, the shopkeepers studied by Bechhofer and his colleagues had, in the main, established their businesses *by their own efforts*. Most had provided the capital to become independent from their own savings and, insofar as they had made a success of their shops, felt able to congratulate themselves. In farming the situation is rather different, for while there exist certain beliefs about a 'farming ladder' (that is, starting small and, by hard work, thrift and business acumen, becoming bigger) the amount of capital necessary to become a farmer is relatively large, especially for the aspiring owner-occupier. Hence even to start small in farming means thinking in terms of big money, especially in a prosperous farming area like East Anglia with land costing up to £2000 per acre, and tenancies increasingly difficult to obtain.

It is for this reason that the family takes on such great importance and why entry to the farming occupation is so circumscribed (and becoming more so). Recruitment to the ranks of shopkeepers, it appears, takes in a relatively wide section of the social spectrum, the amount of initial capital necessary being comparatively small (Bechhofer *et al.*, 1974b, p. 109). In agriculture the situation is deceptive. While it is unlike almost any other sector of the economy in that it is an industry in which most businesses are small, to be a farmer is in fact, at any rate for owner-occupiers, to be in possession of a small fortune. For example, Harrison has pointed out that while only 1.7 per cent of the population have personal fortunes in excess of £20,000, this is true for 16 per cent of farmers (1975, p. 65).

Small though these sums may be in comparison with business capital arrays in other parts of the economy they are large in terms of personal fortunes and . . . it is very largely personal fortunes that they are. (*Ibid.*, p. 9)

Consequently few farmers can establish themselves by savings and hard work alone, whatever they may believe or claim. Thus among our sample of small farmers in Suffolk 74 per cent were farmers' sons, and almost 80 per cent had inherited from their family either land or the money to buy land. A minority of our sample had by virtue of thrift, bank loans and hard work succeeded in establishing themselves, but most agreed that in the current land market this would generally be a much more difficult proposition, if not downright impossible. For this reason the family will take on an even greater importance, and farming as an occupation will depend to an even greater extent on being born on a farm.

The importance of family background is not unnaturally associated with several other features of the social situation of small farmers. To begin with, much of the sociological literature on the middle class lays great stress on mobility, both geographical and social (for instance Watson, 1964; Bell, 1968). However, sociological accounts of local social systems (for example Stacey, 1969) indicate the key role played in the local organisations by the stable, immobile middle class with its roots firmly in the local community (for example Stacey, 1960; Stacey *et al.*, 1975). Moreover, nothing so enhances immobility and attachment to an area so markedly as property ownership, be it of a small business or of a farm. It was very obviously the case in our study (and our findings confirm those of Harrison, *op. cit.*) that farmers were geographically and socially immobile, and had in the main no other occupational experience. Not only were so many of them the sons of farmers, but only 12 per cent had been employed in more than half of their total jobs outside farming.[7] Consequently, when we take into account the extreme likelihood of farmers having (a) a father who was a farmer; (b) inherited the family farm; and (c) little or no non-farming experience, we would expect geographical mobility to be low. This proved to be the case, 33 per cent of farmers having been born on their present farm and a further 35 per cent coming from within 10 miles of their present farm. Very few farmers were born in urban areas. It is interesting that, just as in certain situations the modified extended family aids the middle-class nuclear family in its upward, spiralist progress (Bell, 1968) so among farmers it is the family which, through inheritance, maintains stability and relative immobility.

To be born into a family which owns a business also makes it less likely that one will have to enter the labour market as a *seller* of labour. This is, perhaps, more true in farming than in other small businesses (Bechhofer *et al.*, 1974b) and it may be for this reason that the educational qualifications of farmers have generally been found to be lower than those of people in occupations of similar status (see Economic Development Committee for the Agriculture Industry, 1972; Roberts *et al.*, 1977, p. 113, make a similar point). While a reasonable level of educational qualifications is extremely important for the aspiring middle-class employee, it may well be less so for self-employed petit-bourgeois groups like farmers. Moreover since most farmers are born into farming, they tend to receive most of their occupational training on the family farm (Economic Development Committee for the

Agricultural Industry, 1972). This particularly applies to small farmers, although small farms can generally provide employment for only one son, and some cannot even manage that (see below). In our Suffolk sample 44 per cent had acquired only a basic elementary or secondary modern education, the remainder having attended grammar or (generally local) fee-paying schools. Furthermore, 86 per cent had received no further education, and the same proportion had no formal agricultural qualifications of any kind.[8] On smaller farms, it appears, sons who are to inherit are expected to leave school relatively early. Not only is their labour needed on the farm but, since they are to inherit the farm anyway, they can learn all they need to know by gaining experience. The consequences of all this for the social mobility of farmers should be obvious (Gasson, 1966; Nalson, 1968).

It is hardly surprising, therefore, that the vast majority of the small farmers in our sample had at least one family member directly involved in work on the farm. Perhaps typically for such family businesses, it was generally the case that other family members were also involved to varying degrees in the running of the farm. For example, 90 per cent of farmers claimed that their wives took an active role. Admittedly the level of involvement here tended to be restricted to answering the telephone, taking messages and running errands, although 14 per cent of farmers said their wives did most of the office work. However, 14 per cent of wives were said to work on the land, make farm policies and issue orders to employees. It was clear that for the most part the definition of 'woman's work' in agriculture was confined to ancillary and non-manual tasks, rather than work on the land itself.[9] An even more stark illustration of the conception of 'woman's work' is the fact that 95 per cent of daughters were reported to have no involvement in the farm whatsoever, and we came across only one daughter who had inherited and was running her father's farm. Our respondents' sons were slightly more involved in day-to-day farming operations but even here 86 per cent of them had no involvement and only 5 per cent were attending to all aspects of the farm as a business. This may seem paradoxical given the emphasis we have placed on farms as family businesses. However, many small farms cannot provide an adequate income or sufficient work for two men, and so sons have to seek some form of alternative employment, either permanently or whilst awaiting their inheritance (cf. Williams, 1964).[10]

Small farmers are generally regarded as a somewhat clannish group, bound together by residential stability and a high degree of intermarriage between their families. Our data on small farmers in Suffolk tend to confirm this stereotype. We have already noted how most small farmers are themselves farmers' sons. Some of them (21 per cent) also married farmers' daughters, and a further 33 per cent were married to the daughters of employers, own-account workers or self-employed professionals. Moreover, 80 per cent of their wives had, before marriage, been employed in non-manual occupations, mostly of a routine kind. Only 10 per cent of wives came from the ranks of the manual working class. These tendencies become even more pronounced when we examine the occupations of the siblings and brothers-in-law of those in the sample. For example, 56 per cent of brothers, and 23 per cent of brothers-in-law were also farmers; a further 19 per cent of brothers were employers or self-employed, as were 14 per cent of brothers-in-law. Consequently, not only is the stereotype of the farmer belonging to the rather enclosed and self-contained world of the farming fraternity largely borne out by our data but even where the close kin of small farmers are not engaged in agriculture they are located in other petit-bourgeois groups. So families and farming are inseparable, just as families and any other form of small business appear to be insepar-able.[11] Indeed 'small firms' and 'little businesses' tend to be defined in the literature in part by reference to the family. A recent investigation into small businesses in Britain, whilst recognising the inherent difficul-ties associated with the definition of the term, commented that 'the all important characteristic which is shared . . . by all small firms . . . is that they are managed by the people who own them' (Bolton Report, 1971, p. xv). Similarly the more extensive American literature on small businesses stresses the importance of the family, the lack of non-family labour and the involvement of the owner in the physical work as well as the management of the business (see, for example, Phillips, 1958 and Hollander *et al.*, 1967). However, on these criteria we would be able to make little distinction between the farmers from the 44 parishes, with whom we are currently concerned, and the other, larger farming enterprises in East Anglia which we also investigated. Agriculture stands in great contrast to most other sectors of the economy in that nearly all farm businesses are relatively small. Consequently most of what we have said about the importance of the family applies with equal, if not greater, force to large farmers, too. If we are to understand what is unique about small farmers (at any rate in East Anglia) we must be more precise.

We can begin with the most salient point about the market situation of small farmers – their position as property owners.[12] Here our research confirms the national survey by Harrison (1975) in terms of such factors as business forms and land tenure. In terms of land ownership it is an often-quoted statement that whereas 90 per cent of land farmed in 1914 was rented, today only about 45 per cent is rented.[13] Land, especially in the inflated land market of the 1970s, represents the owner-occupiers' single most crucial asset. Landlord's capital (the ownership of land and buildings) outweighs tenant's capital ('the money involved in the running of the farm, providing for livestock, machinery, movable plant and equipment, growing and harvesting produce', Clery, 1975, p. 59) by a ratio of 4 : 1 in United Kingdom agriculture. In general,

the smaller the farm in acreage terms, the greater the proportion of land
that is owned (but see Rose *et al.*, 1977, for certain caveats concerning
this). This also proved to be the case for our sample. As Table 2.3 shows
63 per cent owned all the land they were farming and only 14 per cent
were tenants. Some farmers, of course, had mortgages but only 20 per
cent owned land that was wholly or mainly mortgaged. Indeed a general
feature of most small farmers, which they appear to share with other
members of the petite bourgeoisie, is a low indebtedness (Harrison, 1975;
Bechhofer, *et al.*, 1974b). Given these fairly straightforward tenurial
arrangements, and given the relatively small size of business, business
structures tended to be fairly simple. Sole or family proprietorships
accounted for 95 per cent of cases. However, similar though farmers
may be to most small businessmen in terms of ownership, indebtedness
and business structure, there is one major difference which arises in the
case of the farmer and which complicates his life.

TABLE 2.3   Land owned by respondents as
a proportion of land farmed

Percentage owned	Percentage farmers (N = 43)
0	14.0
Less than 25	7.0
25– 49	4.7
50– 74	2.3
75– 99	9.3
100	62.8

We have already noted that there is a greater capital requirement in
agriculture, and that this has arisen in large part because of recent
changes in the land market. This, among other things, has meant an
embarrassingly large capital gain to any farmer who bought all or most
of his land prior to the huge inflation in prices during the 1970s. The
gains have been much larger than anything that most small businessmen
could possibly expect when compared to their original capital investment. And it is not an unmixed blessing when capital taxation has to be
paid. What should have been, and in some ways was, a strengthening of
the farmer's market situation had potentially unpleasant side-effects. On
the one hand if the value of the land which is already owned increases,
then the farmer gains greater borrowing power. Even though purchasing land is made more expensive, it can be offset against land which was
bought much more cheaply. Hence, there opens up a possibility of
expansion. However, to set against this is the threat to owner-

occupation which high land prices could bring through eligibility to high rates of capital taxation. Of the two possibilities, most farmers appeared more worried by the latter than pleased by the former, since 90 per cent of them believed recent land price inflation harmful. This is a new problem for small farmers. Ten years ago, it could never have occurred to most of those in our sample that their businesses could be threatened because of what they represented in terms of personal wealth. This may have the effect of smaller farmers turning to the more complex business structures generally found on larger farms for tax avoidance purposes. It is, to say the least, ironic that *increased* wealth can lead to a threat to the small farmer – and it is especially resented when it might prevent him from handing on a viable business to the next generation.

However, what this situation did reveal was something about the small farmers' attitudes to big business. We asked farmers to comment on the statement that 'big business in this country is too powerful'. We were mindful of the fact that farmers are extremely reliant nowadays on the products of large multi-national concerns such as ICI and Shell for fertilisers and fuel, Ford for tractors and in the sphere of agricultural wholesale companies like Dalgety who are taking over the small family concerns which used to predominate. Consequently, farmers, as small businessmen, might well have views on such developments and the role of big business in general. Almost two-thirds of the sample of small farmers agreed that big business was too powerful, complaining that the large agricultural merchants were not interested in, say, purchasing wheat in the small amounts they had to offer; and that in general it had become impossible to obtain decent terms whether buying or selling. However, the general attitude tended to be fatalistic rather than condemnatory. There appeared to be little resentment towards big business except in the case of land purchases by City institutions – insurance companies, pension funds and so on – and here their anger knew no bounds. Many farmers blamed rising prices of land on the activities of City institutions who began buying land in the depressed conditions of the stock market in the early 1970s. Whether or not high land prices *were* the fault of such activity is not relevant here: many farmers clearly did associate the two. Consequently the attitudes of smaller farmers were especially bitter towards the City investors. Only one farmer in the sample thought City investment was beneficial, while 81 per cent saw it as inimical to agricultural interests. Small farmers often appeared to be genuinely shocked at the thought of impersonal institutions, bureaucratically controlled, being allowed to purchase land for which they had no real love or feeling.

Of course, we would not suggest that farmers are not equally concerned about the economic consequences – especially the threat to succession which is posed. However, the importance of a farmer's personal relationship to the land cannot be overestimated.

Independence is as important to the small farmer as to any other small businessmen, and not for purely economic reasons. Much of the literature on small business emphasises the point that small businessmen do not generally act in ways that are wholly rational in economic terms, and this is often accounted for by reference to the symbolic meaning of property ownership and, in the case of small employers, the particularistic nature of relationships with workers (see, for example, Newby, 1977; Bechhofer *et al.*, 1974b; Deeks, 1973). Our own research very much bears these points out. Ownership of land is the preferable state for the farmer precisely because it guarantees independence of action. 'Independence' includes an element of business freedom – being able to make whatever decisions were deemed necessary without reference to a third party. No farmer who owned his land would have preferred to be a tenant, but 66 per cent of tenants aspired to ownership. Our general finding was that for the farmers in our sample, farming *means* owning land. Agriculture, in this sense, provides an interesting contrast with the rest of industry, for in agriculture ownership and control have come closer in the past 60 years. Hence hostility on the part of small farmers to City institutions is a recognition of a threat to their status as owners and their independence of action.

These points are reinforced when we consider what small farmers value most about their jobs. Two aspects of their occupations were most frequently cited, namely husbandry (that is watching crops and animals grow) and independence. The importance of husbandry reflects the greater contact which the smaller farmers have with their land: small farmers tend to be owner-operators, while the larger farmers tend to be owner-managers. In other words the smaller farmers are more involved in the mundane aspects of running a farm. This is also reflected in what small farmers least like about farming – long and awkward hours, economic pressures and bad weather. As far as hours are concerned, farmers, like other petit-bourgeois groups, work quite long hours. Over 56 per cent claimed to put in more than 50 hours per week, 41 per cent claiming to work over 60 hours per week. Economic pressures are obviously greater for most small farmers, and although all farmers complain about the weather, small farmers are also more likely to be outdoors on the land rather than in an office when the weather is bad, so perhaps their antipathy is particularly understandable. Most of the small farmers in our sample regard their activities as involving a trade-off between the autonomy and independence of being self-employed and the long hours and worry that may be involved in ensuring economic survival. In the case of small farmers, therefore, a very real tension can exist between farming as a traditional activity – a way of life – and the increasing demands of farming as a rational activity – a business which must show a profit. Inflation has tended to make this dilemma more acute than ever, yet for small farmers there is little that can be done, without adequate capital for expansion, to increase their cost-efficiency. They can only be fatalistic and 'hope for the best'. They have seen over the last 30 years the gradual erosion in the numbers of small farms and the increase in the total of large farms. They have watched as a few of their more fortunate neighbours have expanded their operations, and in some cases have felt a resentment born of powerlessness to alter their own situation and mistrust of modern trends. They have attempted to continue farming as their fathers did before them but many are wondering how long it can last. The demands of farming efficiency do not sit easily alongside the desire to farm purely for one's own satisfaction with little thought for what might be most profitable. However, for many small farmers there is no choice to be made between the traditional and the rational, if the rational requires greater investment; for they simply do not possess and cannot obtain the necessary resources. As we shall see this leads to a situation where they are equally unable to make the kinds of profit per acre that their larger neighbours regard as essential.

For most of the small farmers in Suffolk the only viable way to encounter some of the economic pressures is to obtain an alternative source of income. This has been noted as a feature of farming in upland areas (see Nalson, 1968) and among non-agricultural petit-bourgeois groups (for example Bechhofer, 1974b). Among our sample 30 per cent had 'other business interests', although in practice this represented a diverse range, from farmers with contracting and haulage businesses to one man who supplemented his meagre income from pig-rearing by doing a newspaper round for a local newsagent. Significantly, however, four out of five of the farmers who had alternative sources of income relied on these to a large extent, and spent a substantial proportion of their working week engaged in other work than farming. Consequently, we have to remember that for those farmers involved this means an extension to an already long working week.

At the end of the day, however, what a market situation adds up to is the likelihood of receiving a certain level of income with which to secure scarce goods and services in the present and future. Farm incomes are notoriously hazardous to estimate and we found it impossible to gain information reliable enough from our interviews to publish here. However, we can give some indication of general levels of income of farmers similar to those in our sample by using the data provided by the Farm Management Survey of the University of Cambridge. In 1971 average net income on farms in the survey was £17.10 per acre and this rose to £36.90 per acre in 1974. Hence in 1971 the *largest* farm in our sample would bring in £5180 and in 1974 £11,700. Since 1974 farm incomes have fallen back, but cropping farms, such as many of those in our sample, have suffered less than most. A most important caveat concerning our sample must be made here. While many of the farms we visited were marginal, most were so only in comparison with larger arable farms. Our sample fare much better on average than the pastoral farmers of the upland areas. For example, in 1974–5, the average income of *all* farms of 275–599 standard man day (smd) business size was £2353, but the mainly cereal farms averaged £6000 *for the same size of business*. Where our small farmers are at a disadvantage is in comparison with their larger arable neighbours *growing the same crops*. Take another example as an illustration: in the year ended June 1975, for a sample of farms monitored by ICI the top 25 per cent of farmers made on average £30 per acre more on winter wheat, £28 more in barley and £82 more on potatoes. Such are the advantages of scale and the ability to invest. In the same year while the Ministry of Agriculture recorded a fall in income of 0.8 per cent on farms of 2400 + smds, those between 275 and 599 smds, fell back 21.2 per cent. That is the real nature of the difference and it can only widen if current trends continue. However, it still has to be borne in mind that small farmers in East Anglia are not as a whole suffering as badly as in other areas. Less than half expressed dissatisfaction with their incomes, and only 12 per cent were very dissatisfied.

Finally, we should consider our farmers in their strictly entrepreneurial role as buyers and sellers. Here the small farmers' market situation is exceedingly complex, and we have to remember that the basic parameters are set by the state and the EEC after negotiations with the farmers' organisations (see Newby *et al.*, 1978, Chap. 3; Wilson, 1977). Beyond this, marketing depends a great deal on the nature of the product, where and when it is produced, perishability, need for processing and so on. There can be no doubt that many small farmers feel that they have enough problems producing crops and rearing animals, without having to worry about the state of the market. When markets are volatile, these problems are compounded. However, no single farmer is big enough to make any real improvement to his market situation in this respect on his own, for his contribution to the total market is so infinitesimal. And many, characteristically individualist, are suspicious of, if not hostile to, any suggestion that they should combine into groups or co-operatives.[14] Changes that could be made to improve the farmer's situation generally require capital investments beyond the means of small farmers; for example, packing and grading of vegetables for direct sale to supermarkets. Our main interest was in the extent to which farmers were sensitive to changes in the market for various products – that is, how far within the limits set by location, physical conditions, and so on, they attempted to maximise profits. As far as the smaller farmers were concerned, the results did not surprise us. Lacking any real flexibility or capital resources, they were clearly disadvantaged in the market. Altogether only 9 per cent were classified as having a high market sensitivity, and these were mainly on the larger farms. Below 50 acres no farmer was regarded as highly oriented to the market. The problems faced by small farmers who wish to take advantage of the market was well expressed by one respondent whose main crop was wheat:

> I have limited storage facilities and so I have to sell all my crop at harvest (when prices are low). I'm very well aware of the market, but I just can't act upon it . . . I have to take incredible risks to get the returns I do.

If the relatively go-ahead small farmer finds problems, it is small wonder that most simply resign themselves to their fate: 'I do what I want to do and hope for the best'. The small, lowly market-oriented farmer is almost bound to be fatalistic. For much of the time in arable farming one can take advantage of the market only if possessed of resources with which to invest in more land, storage facilities, machines and so on. Most marketing options which give the arable farmer a chance of greater profit necessitate a larger operation to make it worthwhile. Hence the growing disparity of income between the small and large farmers.

What then of the possibility of expansion for the small farmer? We asked them if they would expand if they could, and by how much. Altogether 63 per cent would have liked to expand, mainly so that they could make more efficient use of their resources, especially machinery and buildings. However, this certainly did not mean that they valued 'bigness' in farming. We asked if they thought 'bigger meant better' and it was clear for most small farmers, it decidedly did not. Quite often the hostility of small farmers to their bigger neighbours became apparent; they were suspicious of sheer size – of 'prairie farming' – and of combining many small farms into one and therefore putting small farmers out of business. At this point the tension between farming as a way of life, and farming as a rational business activity, was most apparent.

The Small Farmer as Local Politician

The importance of agriculture in the rural economy has traditionally been reflected by the dominance of farmers and farming interests in rural politics. Small farmers have played an important role in this, supporting at the parish and rural district level the political interests of the larger landowners which the latter have pursued in the administration of the county and even nationally. To this extent the small farmer has traditionally provided an essential prop of rural political stability. For this reason an important aspect of our research in East Anglia was concerned with the relationship of various categories of farmers to the local political system and this part of our analysis clearly revealed both the character of the small farmers' support for the traditional political order in the countryside, and the nature of the contradictions with which they were confronted.

Ever since 1894, local government in Britain has been organised at three levels: county, district and parish. This division of functions can be explained as the reflection of the tension between centralisation and rationalisation on the one hand, and responsiveness to local variations on the other. Centralisation, for example, is clearly necessary if a coherent strategy of social and economic development is to be pursued, but this can never be allowed to eclipse significant differences between different areas. Nevertheless, the trend has clearly been toward ever-increasing centralisation of functions, both in terms of the effective transfer of powers from local to national government and in terms of the shift of functions from lower to higher levels within local government. One manifestation of this growing centralisation and rationalisation was the re-organisation of local authorities in 1974 which created fewer, larger units of local government (see below).

From the point of view of national, or even county, government, the need to maintain responsiveness to local factors can produce problems, not least where locally elected councils attempt to pursue policies at variance with the policies of the higher authority. One vivid example from recent years was the case of Clay Cross, but to some extent the same pattern was revealed, prior to the 1974 re-organisation, in Suffolk. To draw a broad but fairly accurate generalisation, the situation in Suffolk prior to 1974 was that, in the more rural and agricultural districts (notably the more northerly rural district councils such as Hartismere), political power lay in the hands of small and medium-sized farmers, while the East Suffolk County Council was firmly controlled by large farmers and landowners. This disparity was especially marked at parish level and small farmer representation declined, the higher the authority: 33 per cent of those small farmers in our sample served, or had served, on parish councils, 7 per cent had experience as rural district councillors but none had experience on county councils. The equivalent figures for those with over 300 acres were 35 per cent, 12 per cent and 8.5 per cent. At the county level, members were (as one county councillor and landowner put it) 'more upper class . . . wealthy people with a good education and a broad vision'. At parish and district level, on the other hand, and especially in the most rural parts of the county, the smaller farmers were able to exert considerable influence, and in some cases, control. (For more details see Saunders *et al.*, 1978; Newby *et al.*, 1978, Chapter 6.) One important consequence of this was that small farmers were able to pursue policies at district level which reflected their interests but which brought them into conflict with the county authority where large farmers and land-owners, often with very different interests, had control. The implications for planning policy in particular were marked.

In order to understand this, it is necessary to note first of all that farmers shared some interests in common. Farmers as a whole tend to view their situation in Britain as that of a small, beseiged and misunderstood minority up against a vast urban-industrial population whose prime demand is cheap food. Even the large capitalist farmers, in other words, find themselves in conflict with industrial and finance capital, and their situation is probably best described as that of an 'allied' class rather than a constituent fraction of the 'power bloc'. This antagonism between capitalist agriculture and other fractions of capital (which becomes manifest in the rather broader terms of a 'rural-urban' antagonism) is revealed at the level of county government in the resolute hostility displayed by the large farmers to any industrial development in rural areas. This anti-development policy (which has been particularly marked in East Suffolk) can be explained partly as an attempt to prevent those sections of capital which have achieved dominance in national politics from extending this dominance into rural areas. But it can also be explained as an attempt to regulate local labour markets by excluding potential competitors for the pool of cheap labour which exists in rural Suffolk. Both of these objectives may be said to benefit (or at least, not to contravene) the interests of small farmers, for they too stand to lose from any intrusion of industrial capital into the local political and economic systems, especially if they employ labour.

The problem, however, is that for the large farmers and landowners, this anti-development policy constitutes part of a much broader commitment to environmental conservation. Their hostility to industrial development, in other words, is not only a consequence of their desire to retain economic and political control in the county, but is also a reflection of what is often a deep-seated and genuine desire to maintain its environmental character. This has led to the adoption of other planning policies which do not favour the smaller farmer. Paramount among these has been the refusal of the East Suffolk County Council to countenance new housing development in rural areas.

The demand for labour by agriculture has, of course, been dropping over the years, and for established large-scale farmers, this has meant there has been little difficulty in housing a diminishing workforce through existing housing stock on their estates or in nearby occupational villages. For the smaller farmer, on the other hand, the reproduction of labour-power may present a real problem, especially where an (often *the*) existing worker retires (in which case the farmer needs the house for a new worker but is faced with all the problems of eviction) or where he tries to expand his enterprise in order to keep pace with the changing economies of scale in the industry (see above). In either case, there is a need for additional housing if new labour is to be attracted.

One way in which new housing may be provided is through the local authority, and there are vivid examples in parts of rural Suffolk of district councils, controlled by small and medium-sized farmers, which have built council housing in remote areas (sometimes despite the lack of facilities such as mains drainage and the high cost of such isolated developments). A second way in which the problem may be overcome is by the farmer himself building a new tied house. But in both cases, such developments have come into conflict with county council planning policy which has been opposed to any development, housing or industrial, in rural areas.

The result, before 1974, was a series of conflicts between county and district councils. One farmer and ex-Hartismere councillor, for example, recalled:

> We did things in Hartismere a different way . . . the County Council had a terrible name in this area. They wouldn't let anybody do anything. A lot of these arty types on it – they wouldn't allow building.

And a former planning officer from another authority remembered:

> It wasn't smooth sailing at all in the old Hartismere area. The members in that area didn't accept the county policy. What they used to say was, 'If there's a sewer you can build a house'. They didn't care about scattered development. . . . You used to put the flags out if they refused anything.

The hostility of small farmers to county planning policy was widespread. It made itself apparent in all authorities where small and medium-sized farmers had undisputed control, and there are a number of examples in Suffolk of rural parish councils which have similarly consistently pushed for more housing development (not only against the county council, but also against local amenity groups which are often led by large farmers and landowners). It also made itself apparent in our interviews with farmers in the area, for although big and small farmers alike frequently expressed their concern with planning policy, three out of every four large farmers explained that they were worried about the possibility of industrial growth in the county, while the great majority of small farmers were concerned rather with the development control restrictions on the construction of houses. As a 300-acre farmer explained:

> The local farmer hasn't got such rigid ideas about preservation. He's more in contact with circumstances – more practical than the aristocratic big landowner who just wants his two and three thousand acres and doesn't want it touched.

This conflict between large and small farmers should not be under-estimated. The most important point to note, however, is that, prior to 1974, the small farmers in the rural areas were often able to assert their political interests through control of the district authority, even against the opposition of the large farmers at County Hall (and also against the newly immigrant, urban middle class).

Since 1974, however, the picture has changed. The re-organisation of local government in that year represented a marked shift towards centralisation and rationalisation, and away from local responsiveness. At the county level, three authorities (East Suffolk, West Suffolk and the Ipswich County Borough) were amalgamated into a single and much larger authority. At the district level, the old rural and urban districts were merged into a small number of new district authorities in which the rural representation was often outweighed by that of the towns. The power of the parish councils, though slightly enhanced, remained slight. The result in most cases was predictable, for although a few new districts (for example, Mid-Suffolk) retained a rural pre-dominance, in most cases the small farmer representation in district government dropped dramatically. The re-organisation provoked con-siderable opposition among the smaller farmers in the rural areas of northern and central Suffolk, and the old rural-urban antagonism remains marked in many of the new authorities, but overall there can be little doubt that 1974 marked a qualitative change in the character of Suffolk politics in which the virtual eclipse of the small farmer was the most vivid feature. As one of our respondents put it:

It's the big people who get on these councils so there's no-one left to pressure the council. It's their decisions, not the decisions of the small people. They pretend to give you a say, but what they say goes.

Of course, the big farmers have also suffered to some extent by re-organisation, most notably in their numerical representation which fell in the new Suffolk County Council to just 16 per cent. However, the big farmers have so far managed to retain control at the county level (remarkably, virtually every major county committee is chaired by a farmer or landowner), and they have, in any case, formed an alliance with the other members of the middle class, and especially the rural 'newcomers', such that the anti-development pro-conservation policy has remained intact. Indeed, recent discussions concerning the new Suffolk structure plan have only confirmed the degree of support which this policy attracts among all the dominant classes in the county. A report on the initial stages of the consultation procedure for the structure plan, for example, notes:

There is a widespread feeling that the principal issue is con-

servation. . . . A very strong consensus has emerged from the views
received that Suffolk has grown too fast in recent years. . . . There is a
very strong lobby in all quarters against development in the countryside or major extensions to villages. (Suffolk County Council, 1975,
pp. 2–3)

The old challenge from the small farmers has been dissipated.

Political Dilemmas

In his discussion of the relationship of the petite bourgeoisie to the
modern capitalist state, Poulantzas (1973) describes the former as a
'supporting class'. In this, he differentiates this class both from those
which comprise the 'power bloc' (that is the politically dominant classes
or fractions under the hegemony of monopoly capital) and from those
involved in alliances with these dominant classes. His argument is
essentially that, although monopoly capital is the dominant class, its
immediate class interests may be sacrificed by the state in order to
maintain its long-term position. In other words, subordinate classes
within the power bloc or in alliance with dominant classes are able to win
concessions from the state in respect of their support for monopoly
capital. What is crucial about the situation of the petite bourgeoisie,
however, is that its support for the state (and hence for the long-term
domination by monopoly capital) is achieved without significant
concessions being gained. As Poulantzas argues:

> The support which they give to a determinate class's domination is
> generally not based *on any real political sacrifice* of the interests of the
> power bloc and of the allied classes in their favour. Their support,
> which is indispensable to this class domination, is based primarily on
> a process of *ideological illusions*. (1973, p. 243)

The 'ideological illusions' to which Poulantzas refers consist of the petite
bourgeoisie's support of the capitalist state – and hence, it is assumed of
the dominant classes in capitalist society. For Poulantzas such support is
illusory because it is not based on the material gains which the petite
bourgeoisie hopes to achieve, but on the fear of what it stands to lose. It
therefore represents a form of false consciousness: the petite bourgeoisie
throws its support behind a form of state which corresponds to the
interests of other classes and whose interests may be inimical in certain
crucial respects to its own. The political situation of the petite
bourgeoisie therefore takes the form of a dilemma: whether to support
the *status quo* with little material reward in return; or withdraw this

support and strengthen the political forces of the working class which are often regarded as equally threatening.

Our depiction of the economic and political marginalisation of small farmers might lend some *prima facie* plausibility to such a view. However, the claim that the petite bourgeoisie are solidly 'supportive' of the dominant order must be handled with some care. Although there is a superficial unity at the political level, in terms of party political membership and voting behaviour, there is less evidence to suggest any widespread commitment to those groups and institutions believed to dominate 'the system'. Indeed, to draw a not altogether inappropriate analogy, many of the small farmers in our survey tended to regard their position *vis-à-vis* those possessing economic and political power in very much 'us-and-them' terms (cf. Lockwood, 1966). 'Us', in this case, was the 'little man' striving to earn an honest living against the predatory demands of 'them': politicians, bureaucrats, trade unions *and* big business, the urban mass of the population. Thus, although 65 per cent of the small farmers in our survey had consistently voted Conservative in general elections since 1964, and 42 per cent were party members, few harboured any 'illusions' about their fate under a Conservative administration. The policies of James Prior, the Conservative Minister of Agriculture at the time of our survey and a local Suffolk MP, were frequently reviled on account of his apparent disregard for the plight of the small farmer – policies in which the NFU were believed to be conniving. Although few farmers were directly involved there was widespread sympathy of the problems encountered by beef farmers whose sense of enraged importance had boiled over into overt political expression in 1973 in the case of the blockades on cattle imports referred to above. For the most part, however, the frustration of the Suffolk farmers remained privately expressed. One or two even went so far as to suggest that they were usually better off under a Labour government than a Conservative one (cf. Self and Storing, 1962, p. 203), but this view was expressed ruefully and with regret. They thus continued to vote for the Conservative party as 'gut Tories' even if they were 'grudging Tories' (cf. Bechhofer and Elliott, 1978, pp. 80–1). Their support for Conservatism was more emotive than calculative.

Of particular importance here is the perceived support of the party for policies designed to strengthen the state (for example, through an emphasis upon law and order) and to combat the growing power of the trade unions. Although they were almost universally opposed to interventionist government and big bureaucracies, many of the small farmers nevertheless expressed their support for 'strong government'. Recent governments of both parties were regularly accused of being too 'soft', and many of the problems currently facing the country were explained in terms of a breakdown of discipline and an erosion of respect for authority. One farmer with 180 acres observed:

> The British are too soft. There are too many do-gooders. They abolish capital punishment, and then law-and-order breaks down.

while another on 120 acres argued:

> The workers, in inverted commas, have lost their respect for management. . . . With stronger discipline, everybody would be happier.

Closely related to this perspective was a generalised disgust at what was commonly seen as the growing power of organised labour. Of particular relevance here is the fact that many of our interviews were conducted in the wake of the successful 1974 miners' strike against the Heath government; a strike which attracted some bitter criticisms from some of our informants. Indeed, in a minority of cases, small farmers expressed a genuine fear and revulsion of creeping communist infiltration in Britain and notably in the labour movement.

The hostility to the industrial working class was expressed in many ways, and it fed off familiar images and stereotypes represented in the mass media. The 'working class' was often seen as mis-named for most of its members did not seem to 'work' at all. Small farmers compared their own often arduous struggle for economic survival with what seemed to them to be a work-shy and welfare-supported industrial workforce which was ready to go on strike at the merest hint from its 'militant' union leadership. Thus, one reason why the country was in a 'mess' was that the workers were not prepared to work:

> People don't want to work. They consider the country owes them a living, but no-one owes them a living. (Farmer on 110 acres)

> The incentive to work isn't what it was. Unemployment benefit is too high – it should be a meagre living standard. A man that's able to work but isn't willing to should be pinched. It's too easy for the lazy bugger. (Farmer on 235 acres)

> It won't improve until people do an honest day's work for an honest day's pay. There's too much money wasted on social security – on those who won't work. (Farmer on 150 acres)

And this slothfulness was actively aided and abetted by trade unions which had long outgrown their usefulness:

> Our only problem is the unions. They're too powerful and control the workers. (Farmer on 75 acres)

Such sentiments were not, of course, confined to the small farmers in our sample. Many large farmers and landowners similarly berated the working class in general and the trade unions in particular as the root cause of the country's ills.

It is tempting to regard such vehemently expressed opinions as indicating support for the dominant economic and political order (of which, certainly, many of the larger farmers and landowners in our sample might be regarded as representatives). However, when we turn to the small farmers' attitudes towards 'big business' it is possible to see that such sentiments are more indicative of a fierce sense of independence and individualism, and an antipathy to *any* threat to such 'freedom' from no matter which direction it may come. Thus a majority of the small farmers in our sample were equally opposed to 'big business' – 65 per cent believed that big business was 'too powerful', most of them citing the control by large companies of the supply of farm inputs and the marketing, distribution and processing of farm outputs under today's commercial conditions. In addition, as we have already indicated, the vast majority of small farmers resented the involvement of the City institutions in agricultural landownership. The characteristic stance of the small farmer was therefore to regard himself as caught between the 'devil' of big business market dominance and Ministry of Agriculture 'red tape' on the one hand and the 'deep blue sea' of the organised battalions of the industrial working class on the other. In some situations the small farmers explicitly recognised this dilemma, of which the division within the NFU between large and small producers and between 'moderates' and 'militants' was frequently cited as emblematic. Although their political support for the Conservatives rarely wavered, as far as voting was concerned, it was because the Conservative Party came closest to supporting their cherished values of independence, hard work and thrift.

The essential ambiguity of the small farmers' class situation was reflected in their 'image of society' (see Lockwood, 1966). Asked about their views on class, 15 per cent of them (compared with 4 per cent of the larger farmers) denied that class still existed in Britain:

I don't recognise the existence of class. There's more opportunities now than in the past. There aren't the inequalities now – not really. (Farmer on 100 acres)

Class doesn't come into it at all with me. I'm just as much a working man as the lad who works with me. I'm very much a working man. (Farmer on 90 acres)

And of those who recognised class divisions, most saw them as inevitable, often desirable, and certainly legitimate. Of particular

importance here was the traditionalistic basis of many small farmers'
views on class. In other words, small farmers often recognised gra-
duations of social esteem in which wealth alone played little part. The
rapacious businessman and the *arriviste* middle class were not generally
admired, and their pretensions to social gentility were widely scorned.
Many of our respondents were keen to explain that the 'real' basis of
class was birth and breeding, and locally based members of the upper
class (and, indeed, the aristocracy) were often cited as examples of 'real
gentlemen', in contrast to the solicitors, civil servants and other
professional groups who had arrived in the countryside in recent years:

> Society is the born and bred gentleman. Yet they're often hard-hit
> financially. But breeding will always impress on them throughout
> their life. The real lady or gentleman will never put a foot wrong – not
> like someone who's risen in life through success in business. (Farmer
> on 100 acres)

> The old-fashioned rich are a whole lot better than the newly-rich.
> They understand more and don't try to put it over on you. You can
> tell a real gentleman because he'll talk to you like we're talking now.
> (Farmer on 100 acres)

> The middle class tend to be snobs. The upper class are real
> gentlemen – born and bred – they'll mix with anyone. It's like Lord Y.
> said, he'll talk to a working man the same as to a farmer. Major-
> General X. is the same – he says, 'Hello Peter' when he sees
> me. . . . Class isn't money – the upper crust might be as poor as mice
> but they're still upper class. You can distinguish between them and the
> middle class on manners. (Farmer on 250 acres)

What these views indicate is a tenacious grip on the sanctity of tradition.
The old values, the old respect, the old social order: these are the things
which the small farmers desperately try to hang on to in a world turned
upside down where the lion's share is seemingly going to the least
deserving. This adherence to tradition is important, for the close
personal knowledge which the small farmer has of his traditional social
superiors in many ways marks him off from other members of the petite
bourgeoisie in Britain. Small shopkeepers do not have the figure of the
local aristocrat to cling on to and admire; small farmers do.
   What, then, is the likely outcome of the process of marginalisation
which small farmers in East Anglia are currently experiencing? In
absolute terms, as we emphasised at the beginning of this chapter, their
economic plight is nothing like so precarious as that of small farmers
elsewhere in Britain, but the capital-intensive nature of arable farming in
East Anglia renders them no less marginal in relative terms. Politically

and socially small farmers may, in the past, have exercised a decisive supportive role in the rural class structure and to some extent this remains; but now they find themselves less confident in affirming a *status quo* in which they are becoming progressively disadvantaged and even regarded with patronising condescension by the new ex-urban professional and managerial inhabitants of the countryside. A possible result of this process of marginalisation might be the further outbreak of militantly political action, thus generating the conditions for a popular alliance with other subordinate classes against big capital. Such a prospect, however, seems, to say the least, unlikely, for the small farmers which we interviewed retained a strong sense of individualism which made them suspicious of any collective action. Given the continuing allegiance of small farmers to the Conservative Party, together with the strength of their identification with the beleaguered 'truly rural' population against the urban majority, their sense of frustration seems more likely to be aired in private and/or within the organised framework of British party politics. Only when the Conservative Party ceases to assiduously cultivate its rural vote and deny their sense of grievance of any legitimate expression will the small farmer be tempted to look elsewhere for the solution to his political dilemma.

NOTES

1. Although much the same point could be made about small farmers in Wales and Scotland, we are explicitly excluding them from this analysis.
2. 'Small' in this context, refers to the size of the business enterprise and not to the size of the holding in acreage terms. The Ministry of Agriculture adopt a 'standard man-day' classification to measure the size of farm businesses. A 'small' farm is usually considered to be one of less than 600 smds – that is it will support less than 600 average days' work for a standard man in any one year.
3. 'Efficiency', it should be noted, is measured here in terms of output-cost and not in terms of resource utilisation or energy conversion. There is a long and acrimonious debate among agricultural economists as to whether, and in what sense, size and 'efficiency' are related.
4. This area is described in Newby (1977, Chapter 2). The reasoning which lay behind the selection of this sample and its relationship to other samples of farmers in our study are described in Newby *et al.*, 1975 and Newby *et al.*, 1978, Chapter 2 and Appendix I.
5. We have chosen this figure as our cut-off point because, as we shall see below, it constitutes a significant threshold between farms which are becoming economically marginalised and those which are not.
6. It may be argued that many of our sample of small farmers do not constitute a petit bourgeois group in the classic sense – that is a stratum which owns

the means of production but which also provides the labour power in the productive process and does not extract surplus value from a hired labour force. In addition it could be argued that the wealth represented by 300 acres of farmland valued at up to £2,000 per acre places our respondents firmly in the *haute bourgeoisie* when compared with other petit-bourgeois groups in the economy.

On the first point we are constrained by our area of study. As we have already suggested East Anglia is not an area typified by petit-bourgeois farmers. Thus if we were to limit our analysis to only those farmers who employed no hired labour we would have very few cases and on grounds of expediency we have included *any* farmer with less than 300 acres. However, our justification is not *only* one of expediency, for such farmers, we argue, are being reduced to classic petit-bourgeois status by the substitution of labour by capital in modern agriculture. In addition these farmers are subjectively perceived as petit-bourgeois by themselves and by others in the locality. Similarly their wealth must be regarded in relative terms. Because land is such an important factor of production in agriculture, compared with other industries, the asset structure cannot be meaningfully compared with the manufacturing and service sectors, whose use of land is negligible (just as rates of return on capital invested are of little meaning when comparing agriculture with other industries). Once again, *within the content of the farming industry*, we feel justified in considering our sample 'petit-bourgeois'. Indeed the peculiar nature of over-capitalisation in agriculture makes this an interesting point of departure for comparison with other self-conceived petit-bourgeois groups.

7. Even in the case of those who had had non-farming occupations, virtually all had spent part of their careers in management or as self-employed businessmen.

8. A similar point is made by Deeks when discussing the findings of an American study of small businessmen (Deeks, 1973, p. 32).

9. This probably reflects the less marginal nature of small arable farms in East Anglia. It certainly contrasts with some of the findings from studies in upland areas mentioned earlier in the paper. Of course some wives had had full-time employment off the farm since their marriage. In the eight cases reported, three wives had been employers in their own right and the rest had been routine non-manual or unskilled employees. We have no data concerning the importance of wives' income to the farm family.

10. Of course, it is also in part a quirk of the life-cycle stage of most of the farmers' families in our sample. Altogether 70 per cent of farmers had some or all of their children living at home. Many of these children were too young to do any farm work.

11. We are not here making a normative statement, but a 'factual' one, of course.

12. It will not be possible to discuss in full detail all the intricacies of the market situation of farmers in what follows. For a fuller discussion see Newby *et al.*, 1978, Chapter 3.

13. Even the figure of 45 per cent might well be an over-estimate for reasons explained in Rose *et al.*, 1977. See also Harrison, 1975.

14. This finding confirms those of Bechhofer *et al.*, 1974b. Such is the problem

in agriculture that a great deal of money has been spent recently under the auspices of the CCAH trying to find out how farmers might be persuaded to co-operate.

REFERENCES

C. A. Arensberg and S. T. Kimball, *Family and Community in Ireland*, 2nd edn (Cambridge, Mass: Harvard University Press, 1968).

J. Ashton and S. J. Rogers (eds.), *Economic Change and Agriculture* (Edinburgh: Oliver and Boyd, 1971).

F. Bechhofer, B. Elliott and M. Rushforth, 'The Market Situation of Small-Shopkeepers', *Scottish Journal of Political Economy*, xvii (1971) 161–80.

F. Bechhofer, B. Elliott, M. Rushforth and R. Bland, 'Small Shopkeepers: Matters of Money and Meaning', *Sociological Review*, 22 (1974a) 965–82.

F. Bechhofer, B. Elliott, M. Rushforth and R. Bland, 'The Petit Bourgeois in the Class Structure', in F. Parkin (ed.), *The Social Analysis of Class Structure* (London: Tavistock, 1974b).

F. Bechhofer and B. Elliott, 'Persistence and Change: The Petite Bourgeoisie in Industrial Society', *European Journal of Sociology* xvii (1976) 74–99.

F. Bechhofer and B. Elliott, 'The Voice of Small Business and the Politics of Survival', *Sociological Review*, 26 (1978) 57–88.

Colin Bell, *Middle Class Families* (London: Routledge & Kegan Paul, 1968).

T. Beresford, *We Plough the Fields* (Harmondsworth: Penguin Books, 1975).

J. E. Bolton (Chairman), *Report of the Committee of Enquiry on Small Firms* (London: HMSO, Cmnd 4811, 1971).

J. Bradley, *The Small Farmer Scheme* (Exeter: University of Exeter, Department of Agricultural Economics, Report No. 144, 1963).

Peter Clery, *Farming Finance* (Ipswich: Farming Press Ltd, 1975).

Graham Day and Martin Fitton, 'Religion and Social Status in Rural Wales: "Buchedd" and its Lessons for Concepts of Stratification in Community Studies', *Sociological Review*, 23 (1975) 867–92.

J. Deeks, 'The Small Firm – Asset or Liability?', *Journal of Management Studies*, 10 (1973) 25–47.

J. G. S. Donaldson and F. Donaldson, *Farming in Britain Today* (Harmondsworth: Penguin Books, 1972).

Economic Development Committee for the Agriculture Industry, *Agricultural Manpower* (London: HMSO, 1972).

A. Edwards and A. Rogers (eds.), *Agricultural Resources* (London: Faber, 1974).

R. Frankenberg, *Communities in Britain* (Harmondsworth: Penguin Books, 1965).

Ruth Gasson, *Occupational Immobility of Small Farmers* (Cambridge: University of Cambridge, Department of Land Economy, Occasional Paper No. 13, 1966).

Ruth Gasson, 'Resources in Agriculture: Labour' in A. Edwards and A. Rogers (eds.), *Agricultural Resources* (London: Faber, 1974).

Alan Harrison, *Farmers and Farm Businesses in England* (Miscellaneous Study 62, University of Reading, Department of Agricultural Economics and Management, 1975).

E. D. Hollander *et al.*, *The Future of Small Business* (New York: Praeger, 1967).

D. Jenkins, *The Agricultural Community in South West Wales at the Turn of the Twentieth Century* (Cardiff: University of Wales Press, 1971).

James Littlejohn, *Westrigg* (London: Routledge & Kegan Paul, 1963).

David Lockwood, 'Sources of Variation in Working-Class Images of Society', *Sociological Review*, 14 (1966) 249–67.

D. Metcalf, *The Economics of Agriculture* (Harmondsworth: Penguin Books, 1969).

J. S. Nalson, *Mobility of Farm Families* (Manchester: Manchester University Press, 1968).

Howard Newby, *The Deferential Worker* (London: Allen Lane, 1977).

Howard Newby (ed.), *International Perspectives in Rural Sociology* (London: Wiley, 1978).

Howard Newby, Colin Bell, David Rose and Peter Saunders, *Property, Paternalism and Power* (London: Hutchinson, 1978).

J. D. Phillips, *Little Business in the American Economy* (Illinois: University of Illinois Press, 1958).

Nicos Poulantzas, *Political Power and Social Classes* (London: NLB, 1973).

Alwyn Rees, *Life in a Welsh Countryside* (Cardiff: University of Wales Press, 1950).

K. Roberts, F. G. Cook, S. Clarke and E. Semeonoff, *The Fragmentary Class Structure* (London: Heinemann, 1977).

David Rose, Howard Newby, Peter Saunders and Colin Bell, 'Land Tenure and Official Statistics', *Journal of Agricultural Economics*, 28 (1977) 69–75.

Peter Saunders, Howard Newby, Colin Bell and David Rose, 'Rural Community and Rural Community Power', in H. Newby (ed.), *International Perspectives in Rural Sociology* (London: Wiley, 1978).

P. Self and H. Storing, *The State and the Farmer* (London: Allen & Unwin, 1962).

Margaret Stacey, *Tradition and Change* (Oxford: Oxford University Press, 1960).

Margaret Stacey, Eric Batstone, Colin Bell and Anne Murcott, *Power, Persistence and Change* (London: Routledge & Kegan Paul, 1975).

W. Watson, 'Social Mobility and Social Class in Industrial Communities' in M. Gluckman (ed.), *Closed Systems and Open Minds* (Edinburgh: Oliver & Boyd, 1964).

W. M. Williams, *The Sociology of an English Village* (London: Routledge & Kegan Paul, 1956).

W. M. Williams, *A West Country Village: Ashworthy* (London: Routledge & Kegan Paul, 1964).

Max Weber, *Economy and Society*. Roth and Wittich (eds.) (New York: Bedminster Press, 1968).

G. K. Wilson, *Special Interests and Policy Making* (London: Wiley, 1977).

3 The Uses of the Traditional Sector in Italy: Why Declining Classes Survive*

SUZANNE BERGER

Like other advanced industrial states, Italy regards the survival of its traditional sector as a temporary if necessary evil. National plans, politicians, leaders of the major economic associations all proclaim that the future of Italy has no room for the small-scale, familial, protected economic unit. Advanced industrial societies, so the argument runs, require enterprises that are competitive, geared to profit-making, adaptable to changes in markets and technology, and structured for efficiency in production. And whatever the differences among the extremely diverse actors, firms, and classes that in Italy are usually called traditional, they all have in common a pattern of economic behaviour so different from that of the model firm of advanced industrial society that only the most radical and most improbable transformations could save them. Opinions diverge on the precise characteristics of a firm that class it as traditional – size or labour-capital ratio or productivity or management style? But for political purposes the outcome of these definitional quarrels is irrelevant, since all diagnoses and vocabularies converge on the same set of actors: the small shops, the small industries, and the small farms. This disparate group of economic firms and those who work in them are now identified by Italian political elites as traditional, unproductive, and in some sense, parasitic.

Whenever economists or politicians discuss the future of these groups, they are careful to point out the need even in advanced industrial societies for *certain kinds* of small enterprises: for the shop that caters to a special market, for the small electronics firm that is innovative and flexible, for the small farm that raises vegetables near a city, and so forth. If only small shops pooled their resources in joint enterprises; if only the peasant would switch to animal husbandry specialisation; if only the

71

small industry geared its production to the market; then they, too, would move from the camp of traditional firms condemned to disappear into the camp of dynamic modern firms on which the economy of modern Italy will be based. These and the many other reforms that are proposed for the traditional enterprise have been elaborated in abundance and generally without regard for the likely evolution of the already modern sectors of the economy. But even setting aside the dubious efficacy of many of the proposed remedies, it would appear that the vast majority of Italian small shops and farms and industries are so unlike any of the firms described as candidates for success in advanced industrial societies that they have no chance of surviving in the long run.

And yet, the evolution of the traditional sector at the end of the seventies suggests that this long run may be very long indeed. The economic crisis of the last five years, rather than eliminating small firms, has resulted in an expansion of the part of the economy in the hands of small independent property owners. The political crisis created by the failure of the old formulas of government, with the collapse of the old alliance partners of the Christian Democrats and the growth of both the Communist electorate and the Communist role in government, has, rather than diminishing the influence of the old middle classes, instead increased it. These paradoxical outcomes both reflect the same phenomenon: the interdependence of modern and traditional sectors in contemporary Italy. This essay will explore these political and economic links, for this interdependence accounts for the survival, reinforcement, and reproduction of the Italian petite bourgeoisie.

I

Which economic units are traditional?[1] A complex of firm properties – size, labour-capital ratios, market relations, productivity, management practices – might be used to describe the typical traditional firm, but statistics have not been collected and analysed with such a model in mind, so it is difficult to differentiate among Italian firms in this fashion. An even more significant obstacle to economic definition is the absence of an adequate model of the modern Italian firm. As came out clearly in interviews with young industrialists on the inefficient, 'parasitic' sector, the difficulty of establishing 'where profit ends and rent begins' is not easily resolved in the Italian context.[2] To define the 'parasitic rent' collected by inefficient firms that survive because of political protection as 'the difference between the normal profit an entrepreneur earns in a system of competitive equilibrium and the profit obtained in conditions of a different sort of market or else, sheltered by various kinds of privilege' assumes the existence of prices determined in a free market.[3] In Italy where the modern large-scale firms are well-protected not only by control over their own markets but also by the most varied kinds of government subsidies, who can define a clear economic distinction between modern firms earning profits and traditional firms living off rent?

A rather consistent political definition of the traditional sector has, however, developed. A survey of postwar economic legislation and interviews with representatives of economic groups and politicians suggest that one criterion above all shapes the elites' conception of traditional firms: that of independent small property. The large firm, no matter how labour-intensive or unprofitable or 'traditionally' managed, is not considered a traditional industry, while a dynamic modern retail business owned and operated by a single family will be grouped along with its unproductive small-shop neighbours in almost all analyses, political and economic, of Italian society.

There is, moreover, a certain economic rationale for focusing on the variable of firm size, for firm size is highly correlated with other variables in the traditional/backwardness complex, namely with labour costs, with labour-capital ratios, with the ratio of investment to workforce, with the relationship between value-added and production, with indebtedness, with propensity to produce for export markets, and other variables.[4] An economist might well argue that firm size is a very crude instrument for predicting productivity and profitability and that better information on firm performance would show that the distinction between traditional and modern firms only partially coincides with the distinction between small and large firms. But the current definition of traditional social classes as that part of the population earning a living in and from independent small property is deeply embedded in Italian legislation, in the structures of economic organisations, in the banking and loan system, and in images of the political universe common to parties of both Left and Right. Sylos-Labini (1975, Table 7.1) has estimated the Italian petite bourgeoisie, understood in this sense of small independents (*piccola borghesia relativamente autonoma*), at 16 million persons out of a national population of 54 million. Peasant proprietors are included in his definition. If all the peasants and the non-working members of the petit bourgeois families are left out of the calculation, there are 3,330,000 artisans, shopkeepers, and independents in transportation and services out of a total workforce of 19,620,000 (Labini, 1975, Table 1.1).

The degree of unanimity that unites all parts of the political class on the contents of the traditional sector of society (even if the labels on the box differ) is remarkable. Despite their different maps of society, Communists, Socialists, Christian Democrats, and Fascists would probably all agree that the relevant social distinctions are between small and medium business on one hand, and medium-large and large industry on the other; between independent shops and the self-service stores and supermarkets; between the peasant proprietors and capitalist farmers. Though the Communists see the small firms as victims of monopoly capital and hence potential allies of the workers, and the Christian Democrats see the small firms as the 'connective tissue of the economy' and hence the natural collaborators of large industry, both PCI and DC agree on who their target group is, even while they diverge in their analyses of its position in the economy and its politics.

The boundaries laid down by the parties' map of Italian society correspond to economic categories that are given separate organisational representation in the major professional associations. Within the Confindustria, there is a special organisation for the small and medium-sized industries: Comitato Nazionale per le Piccole Industrie. Within Confagricoltura, the small farmers have their own very powerful organisation: Coltivatori Diretti. Confcommercio has been until recently so dominated by traditional commerce that it is rather the representatives of big integrated commerce that have organised within the Confederation to defend their interests. In all these professional associations the organisational structure both reflects and reinforces a distinction based on firm type and scale – traditional or modern, in practice, small or large – rather than on the product manufactured by the firm or its markets (local, national or foreign) or on the firm's regional location. These distinctions (product, market and region) are important foci around which groups of interests within the economic confederations cluster. But the lines of interest they draw across the traditional-modern boundaries are rarely strong enough to pull small firms into their orbit.

The traditional social classes identified by political parties and by professional organisations have been authoritatively recognized by the state. In one case, that of the artisans, the boundaries of the category have been set by the state. Artisans were defined by a 1966 law as firms with no more than ten employees (excluding apprentices) in which members are all personally involved in work and 'work has a preeminent role over capital'. Significantly, this definition by size represented a shift from the concept of the artisanal firm as one producing particular kinds of goods.[5] Those who qualify as artisans live under a legal regime that distinguishes them from other producers: they have their own credit institutions; their taxes are calculated by a special formula; they pay reduced social insurance rates. For other groups in the traditional economy, criteria of membership have been determined on a more *ad-hoc* basis, by the eligibility requirements of particular pieces of economic legislation. The special measures of 3 July 1971 to help small and medium businesses defined as eligible for support any firm with a workforce up to 300. The distribution of investment funds proceeds according to criteria of size. The new value-added tax as well as the new fiscal system calculates taxes differently for enterprises of different scales, as reflected in their volume of trade. To these could be added many other examples of legislation which treat firms of different scale according to different rules. While criteria of eligibility for the government support offered to traditional firms are not identical, it is striking how often the rules are set in such a way as to define virtually the same constituency with the same members.

Traditional firms are not, in this sense, necessarily old firms. On the contrary, many of those considered traditional in Italy are recent creations. What makes them traditional is not their individual longevity, but rather that they have been established within a particular universe of firms with certain modes of operation and with special relationships to other groups in society. There is a constant renewal and replacement of those traditional firms that disappear – whether into oblivion or into the modern sector – by other firms operating in similar modes. The issue of death or survival is better posed as one of the rate of replacement (Bechhofer and Elliott, 1976).

II

How have the traditional groups been strong enough to ensure their survival in the modern Italian economy? Part of the answer, of course, lies in numbers. The 'precensus' of 1969 found that 94 per cent of all industrial firms employed fewer than 100 persons. This calculation excluded the half million artisanal firms employing 1.3 million people, who were counted separately (Ruffolo, 1971). The Mediocredito study of industry in 1968 used a cut-off line of 150 employees per firm to distinguish the small from the medium and large industries, and found that 45,000 out of 50,000 or 90 per cent of all Italian industries fell under the line (Mediocredito, 1972, p. 12). If to these small firms are added the 2000 medium-sized firms that employ up to 500, they account together for 55 per cent of all industrial employment in Italy and for 45 per cent of GNP. (Mediocredito, 1972, pp. 16, 24). Firms employing 501–1500 account for 13 per cent of the workforce and 14 per cent of GNP; those hiring over 1500, for 32 per cent of employment and for 40 per cent of GNP (Mediocredito, 1972, pp. 16, 24). Between 1951 and 1969 the number of small and medium firms diminished by 14 per cent but the population employed in them rose 30 per cent, increasing the percentage of the industrial workforce employed in small and medium firms by 10 per cent (Ruffolo, 1971, p. 3).

The strength of the traditional industrial firms even in the heart of the most industrialised parts of Italy suggests how misleading are the analyses of economic dualism that focus exclusively on the differences in industrial structure that differentiate North and South.[6] Even in the highly industrial region of Lombardy, the proportion of the workforce in manufacturing firms with fewer than 500 workers is *virtually the same* as the national figure (75.5 per cent as compared with 76.9 per cent). Even in the size category of small industries employing up to 50, Lombardy is not so far from the Italian national figure (37.2 per cent of total firms as compared with 45.1 per cent).[7] Similarly in agriculture, though rural exodus has proceeded more drastically in the North, still the structure of the farms that remains has preserved a large number of small units.

In no sector of the economy is the predominance of the small traditional firms clearer than in retail trade. Here the number of tiny units has been rapidly increasing since the end of the war, while the average number of inhabitants per store has fallen. These trends ran counter to those in other Common Market countries where the number of shops has been declining.

TABLE 3.1   Number of Retail Units

	1951 Census	1961 Census	1965
Food shops	316,304	385,632	427,436
Other shops	185,556	277,390	327,614
Total	501,860	663,022	755,050
Number of shopkeepers	957,617	1,332,524	1,520,000*
Average workers per shop	1.9	2.01	2.01
Number of inhabitants per shop	95	76	70

Source: Fabrizi (1967, p. 62).
* Estimate.

The appearance of supermarkets in Italy has occurred with such delay and on such a small scale that they have barely made a dent in the commercial system. As the figures on the average number employed per shop suggest, the dominance of the family-operated shop has hardly been shaken by the arrival of the self-service stores and supermarkets. As of 1968 sales made in supermarkets in Italy accounted for less than 2 per cent of all retail food sales, in contrast with 13 per cent in West Germany (1966) and 14 per cent in France (1967).[8] Once again, while there are differences between North and South, the common features of the distribution networks of both North and South are remarkable. In both cases, supermarkets are islands in a sea of tiny independent shops. Indeed only eleven Italian provinces, albeit Northern ones, have more than one supermarket per 100,000 inhabitants, a figure exceeded by all other Common Market countries (1968).[9]

In sum, in industry, agriculture and commerce, both in the North and the South, small firms employ the majority of the labour force and they produce a proportion of GNP somewhat lower than their share of the workforce, but still very high.

III

The weight of the traditional sector reflects not only the inertia and capacity for resistance of a social system that industrialised by adding a layer of large, capital-intensive, technologically advanced enterprises on top of a traditional economy, rather than by transforming the old enterprises. Rather the presence and vitality of traditional firms in Italy reveals a specific form of adaptation to industrialism, in which small independent property performs economic and political functions that are critical to the modern sector.[10]

In purely economic terms, small-scale enterprises have certain advantages that account in part for the size of the traditional sector in Italy. As Bruni (1961, pp. 51–2) suggested, small firms that are less capital-intensive may flourish in an economic environment like Italy's, with dispersed markets, high transportation costs, direct producer-client relations and imperfect competition. There are, moreover, economic advantages for large firms in maintaining or even creating around them a dense network of small firms. In some cases these small firms produce parts for the large firm that the latter does not find profitable to produce within the enterprise, either because the demand for these products is too variable to justify organising production on a large scale or else because the amount of labour involved in the production of the good is high. Other times, the large firm both manufactures a good within the enterprise and subcontracts out to small firms a certain volume of production of the good. The most highly developed case of this pattern is Fiat, which for many parts has two sources of provision: one, internal, the other external. Fiat in 1971 was estimated to deal with some 15,000 independent subcontractors (Cervi, 1971).

In a study of a community near Milan, Alessandro Pizzorno discovered that large firms often assisted some of their workers in setting up little enterprises and concluded:

In broad terms one can say that there are two reasons for the big firms to find it profitable to decentralise in this way: first, a technological-organisational factor, for in this way the firm need only organise and rationalise the main part of its productive process without taking on the burden of a wider rationalisation; second, a syndical reason, for workers inside a plant are more likely and able to organise themselves and to make demands, while the little independent producer exploits himself and a few workers, whose organisation he can easily stop (Pizzorno, 1960, p. 79).

The first of the causes noted by Pizzorno would be likely in any economy to favour a transfer of production from a large capital-intensive enterprise to a small-scale more labour-intensive enterprise.[11]

In contrast, the second cause that Pizzorno observed, namely, lower labour costs and greater labour docility in small firms, is in large measure the product of particular decisions by the Italian state and by the unions to deal with the small-scale firm in the traditional sector in ways different from those in which they tax, inspect, subsidise, and organise the large-scale firm in the modern sector. The state reduces labour costs in the small firms by taking in charge a part of the employer's social security payments, on a regular basis for artisanal firms[12] and for agricultural employers, and as a frequent instrument of conjunctural policy for other firms in the traditional sector. In July, 1971, for example, governmental measures to assist small and medium industry included a reduction of social insurance contributions amounting to 5 per cent of the employers' payments for artisanal and all other industrial firms employing up to 300. The government also helps small firms to reduce labour costs by closing its eyes to a substantial amount of cheating by small employers, who, by all accounts, get away with not paying a sizeable part of their social security bills to the state.

The presence of the unions in firms of the traditional sector is weak in most of Italy, with the exception of Emilia-Romagna. The unions have concentrated their organising efforts on workers in the modern sector. Even after 1959, when the provisions of national contracts negotiated by labour and business confederations became binding on all employers, the effect of differential degrees of unionisation in firms of different scales has contributed to maintaining lower wages in small firms. For all of these reasons, wages are lower in smaller firms in every industrial branch (see Table 3.2), and industry case studies show that essentially identical work in small and large firms earns very different wages and social benefits. For example, a study of wages in small printing companies compared with wages at a big firm showed that wages in the former ranged from 43–70 per cent of those at the latter for virtually identical work.[13] In industries where work can be given out to home workers (*lavoro al domicilio*) the differential between wages of workers producing the same product are enormous, as a study of the Modena Stocking Industry showed: 588 lira per hour for the home workers compared with 854 lira per hour for those in the factory (Commune di Modena, 1971, p. 79).

The political choices that preserve low labour costs in small firms are only one strand in a tangled net of decisions that Italian political elites

TABLE 3.2 Hourly Wages, Italy, 3rd trimester 1974: firms by size

Industrial branch	10–49 Workers		50–90 Workers		100–199 Workers		200–499 Workers		500–999 Workers		1000 plus Workers		Total Workers	
	Direct salary[1]	Comprehensive salary[2]	Direct salary	Comprehensive salary	Direct salary	Comprehensive salary	Direct salary	Comprehensive salary	Direct salary	Comprehensive salary	Direct salary	Comprehensive salary	Direct salary	Comprehensive salary
Extractive	1149	1471	1272	1657	1473	2044	1577	2265	1594	2187	1504	2062	1382	1867
Food	1046	1402	1153	1529	1233	1627	1280	1635	1380	1863	1354	1885	1222	1620
Textile, garment	942	1337	1042	1466	1085	1578	1177	1703	1218	1753	1243	1934	1106	1598
Metalworking, Transportation	1060	1459	1175	1636	1238	1753	1329	1908	1381	2054	1446	2131	1323	1914
Chemical	1171	1589	1318	1823	1438	1968	1499	2071	1641	2170	1693	2121	1562	2047
Miscell.	942	1272	1055	1431	1148	1568	1276	1764	1394	1959	1527	2307	1159	1605
Construction	1096	1441	1178	1536	1243	1637	1379	1812	1413	1936	1424	1825	1172	1542
Electricity, Gas	1626	2005	1834	2321	1823	2393	2003	2704	1729	2191	1779	2439	1779	2410
Total	1024	1381	1127	1533	1203	1662	1307	1822	1400	1996	1501	2162	1261	1761

NOTES:
1. Direct earnings include: wages paid on an hourly or other basis; piecework; special rates for overtime, holiday, and night work; incentives and special indemnities; an evaluation of payments in kind (e.g., cafeteria) and corresponding compensatory indemnities.
2. Total earnings include: holiday and vacation pay; gratuities; family payments; other salary supplements.
Source: Ministero del Lavoro e della Previdenza Sociale, Direzione generale del collocamento della Manodopera, Divisione VII, 'Indagini statistiche dell' impiego'.

have been making about the traditional sector since the end of the war. In the interstices of grand national policies for the South, the Common Market, and national planning have been secreted hundreds of decrees and laws on subsidies, tax reductions, credit institutions and so forth through which the fate of the traditional sector has been decided. Looking at the impact of these purportedly *ad-hoc* and temporary measures, it is difficult not to conclude that the survival of the traditional sector has been willed by the Italian political elites. The active support of the government, the major political parties, and even powerful groups in the advanced sector has preserved a strong traditional sector, and neither economic factors nor 'lag' are adequate explanations of the phenomenon.

No case better illustrates the importance of politics in the evolution of the traditional sector than the course of commercial legislation in recent years.[14] Since 1926 opening a shop in Italy has required a license which, depending on the size of the store, has been granted by the commune or by the prefect. After the war this system of licensing came under attack because of the obstacles it put in the way of reforming the distribution network. The opposition of local shopkeepers to supermarkets often forced the prefect to shelve applications for indefinite periods of time, apparently with the hope that either the promoters of the supermarket or the local opposition would give up the battle. Applications rejected by the prefect could be forwarded to the Ministry of Industry, Commerce, and Artisanry, where they were also likely to languish. At the end of 1971 it was estimated that some 800 applications to open large stores had accumulated in the Ministry, some of them so old that the promoters had in all probability long since given up the project. In the sixties a number of bills proposing to liberalise access to commerce were introduced into Parliament; the 1966–70 national plan called for replacing the licensing procedure with a simple registration form. The first priority of public action in the commercial sphere, the plan spelled out, must be to reduce costs, and this is best accomplished by promoting the trend toward concentration of retail units and increasing their size, by encouraging their modernisation, and by eliminating the obstacles that administrative rules put in the way of these changes. The Consiglio Nazionale dell' Economia e del Lavoro (CNEL) moved resolutions in the same sense. The preliminary project for the second national plan (1971–5) repeated the first in calling for an end to the licensing system and describing the principal goals as encouraging the development of large stores in accordance with the needs of the market and encouraging the modernisation of traditional shops.

All these soundings of the general will revealed a large measure of agreement about what would have to change in commerce in order to modernise the sector. Nonetheless, all proposals that embodied this understanding were defeated, and in the spring of 1971 commissions of the Camera dei Deputati and the Senato voted a bill on commerce, the 'Helfer project', that far from liberalising access to trade, further restricted it. Under the guise of planning urban growth, the Helfer law transfers the right of accepting or refusing a supermarket from the prefect and the Ministry down to the communal level. For the supermarket refused a permit at this point, there will no longer be recourse to higher authority. In principle, the decisions of the commune are to be taken in accordance with a plan for urban development which each commune is supposed to prepare. In fact, since the rights of the shopkeepers already in place and of their heirs are guaranteed, the law amounts to freezing the status quo.[15]

Just as astonishing as this reversion to protectionism in face of nationally proclaimed goals of commercial modernisation was the virtual unanimity with which the major political parties embraced the measure.[16] Not only the Christian Democrats and the Fascists on their right, but the Republican Party, in contradiction with its programs for the modernisation of Italian society, voted for the bill. On the Left as well, the bill received general support. The Communist Party called for rapid implementation of the legislation 'in order to block the expansion of monopolistic supermarkets and the proliferation of licenses'.[17] The bill was not even debated and voted in full assembly, but by agreement of the parties, decided in commission where the politics of the closed arena guaranteed that there would be no embarrassing confrontations with the lofty ideals of the national plan that the deputies and senators had been discussing the very same year.

That the parties protected small commerce because, with general elections approaching, they hoped to propitiate their petit bourgeois electors is undoubtedly part of the explanation. Sylos-Labini has estimated that small independent propertied groups (in which he includes peasant proprietors) constitute 31 per cent of the Italian population, 36 per cent of the Christian Democratic electorate, 42 per cent of the electorates of the DC's habitual allies, the Republicans and Liberals, and 25 per cent of the PCI-PSIUP electorate (Sylos-Labini 1975, pp. 153–60 and Tables 7.3, 7.4). But until 1976 there was very little mobility in the bases of electoral support for the various parties, and little likelihood of massive shifts in the patterns of partisan support of the petit-bourgeois electorate.[18] Just as important as electoral considerations to understanding the Christian Democrats' position on commercial reform, therefore, is their concern over controlling the rising levels of political agitation among the hard-pressed shopkeepers. Indeed, post-war governments have had little success in halting the civil violence that stems from mobilised sectors of the traditional electorate. The *qualunquismo* of the fifties, the neo-Fascist party in the 1960s, periodic outbursts of urban violence like the Reggio Calabria revolt, left and right wing *squadrismo* of the last decade, all derive much of their support from groups whose social base is small independent property. For this reason, the DC has raced to stay ahead of their competition on the right, offering subsidies and special treatment for small property at each moment of unrest in that quarter.

The Communists, too, feared the historical propensity of the traditional middle classes to support Fascism. Their vote on the Helfer project reflected, however, not only a reaction to rising support for the Fascists, but also a more long term interest in driving a wedge between small-scale firms and a modern sector dominated by large capital.[19] The long-term objective of the PCI has been to reduce and neutralise the hostility of the small independent middle class to socialism, by stressing PCI support on issues like commercial reform that pit small firms against big.

In brief, the sensitivity of the parties to the problems of the traditional sector can only in part be accounted for by electoral considerations. What leads the parties to sacrifice the interests of other groups in the population to those of the traditional sector is not only or even primarily the fear of a defection of electors. Rather they are responding to the dangers of a political and social destabilisation that might result throughout Italian society, were there any real weakening of the traditional sector. The traditional sector absorbs and digests problems that might otherwise tear apart what the political elites of all parties regard as a fragile social fabric.

Of these potentially radicalising problems none is more critical than employment. As one official of Confindustria put it: 'Unemployment or not means a certain social tension or not.' In this regard, the long-term decline in the proportion of the population in the active workforce, the number of Italians who find work only by emigrating abroad, as well as the officially unemployed, as recorded in unreliable public statistics, are all salient factors. The major increases in employment in the post-war period have been in jobs created in small and small-to-medium firms and not in the large-scale modern sector. Given the apparent incapacity or unwillingness of the large modern firms to create a significant number of new jobs, the traditional sector clearly has a critical role in keeping the numbers of the unemployed, nonemployed, and migrants at a tolerable level.

In large measure the willingness of the firms in the modern sector to accept protectionist policies for the traditional sector stems from a belief that they provide solutions on the employment front, put another way, that they are the price of a 'strategy of alliance with the small productive bourgeoisie in the task of controlling social tensions', in Pizzorno's sense. As he explains:

By providing solutions of political protection to the problem of precarious work, a solidarity was created between the small employer and the worker, since they were both dependent on a certain policy and not on the market. The complicity was shared. On one hand, the government had an interest in seeing that stability was not disturbed, and therefore, in a calculated fashion granted its protection. On the other hand, the small bourgeoisie could blackmail the government, since the latter had to help it in order to avoid the explosive situations that could result from the extreme distress of precarious workers. Out of this arose a *de facto* alliance between the small bourgeoisie and marginal social strata, and a complicity of all in a policy of protection of precarious work (Pizzorno, 1974, p. 326).

Small commerce, for example, is above all perceived as a vast reservoir of jobs that can absorb an indefinite number of individuals who either because they are new migrants to the city or because they are unemployed or because they lack skills are not yet or are no longer integrated into the modern industrial system. Even in periods of economic growth, employment in small commerce was often a by-station *en route* from agriculture to employment in industry. In periods of industrial recession small commerce serves as a 'refuge activity' (Marin, 1971, p. 70), 'an escape valve for unemployment and underemployment, thus leading the politicians to accept the idea of a commercial class that deserves to be protected and defended, because it is made up of family units' (Ravalli, 1967).

Small industrial firms and artisanal firms also mop up the labour surplus created by economic shifts as does agriculture. In the seventies it was estimated that as many men went back to the South, presumably to some kind of agricultural employment, as left Southern agriculture for Northern employment. Legislation on land tenure has preserved this cushioning function of traditional agriculture, since by protecting tenants' rights and facilitating the purchase of small property it keeps open the possibility of a return to the farm that is not an option for an unemployed black in the USA, for example, whose departure from Southern agriculture for the city usually coincides with his loss of tenure rights. Thus even where the ranks of agriculture have been severely depleted by rural exodus, still it continues to play this cushioning function in the economy. As Maggioli concluded from a study of the small agricultural sector of Lombardy: '[D]espite its minor importance in terms of the fraction of the workforce it employs, Lombard agriculture still functions as shock-absorber in the recurrent economic and employment crises that trouble our region' (Maggiolo, 1971, p. 3).

IV

It is not only the absolute numbers employed in the traditional sector that are critical for the stability of the economic system but also the traditional sector's capacity to expand or contract its labour force, in times of recession to absorb workers expelled from the modern sector, in times of growth to provide workers for the modern sector. The elasticity of the traditional firms makes them the shock absorbers of the economy. Another way of expressing it is that the traditional sector serves to reduce the costs of economic fluctuations and change for the modern sector by allowing these costs to be distributed in such a way that their burden is disproportionately carried by those who own and work in independent small property. In periods of recession like the present one, there is a progressive shucking off of costs in which each firm tries to pass on down to the next as many of the costs, both economic and social, as possible. The process resembles the children's game of hot potato, in which each participant tries to avoid having his fingers burned by getting rid of the hot potato to another player. The hot potatoes in the Italian economy are labour costs and labour agitation over dismissals. In periods of economic squeeze, the large-scale firm first tries to avoid firing any of its own labour force for fear of stirring up union agitation and attempts to reduce production by cutting off its subcontractors. Those workers that are fired from the large firms try to find work in the small-scale firms. When these latter need to compress labour costs, they resort to putting work out to home workers (*lavoro al domicilio*).

The evolution of the traditional sector in the course of the Italian economic crisis of the past five years sharply illuminates the ways in which the flexibility of the small independent firm serves to compensate for the growing rigidity of the large-scale capital intensive enterprise. One might have expected that in periods of economic trouble, numbers in the traditional sector would fall rapidly, for the resources available to the state for satisfying the contradictory claims of modern and traditional producers would be reduced, precisely at a time when increased competition for markets would be pushing less efficient producers out of business. But in fact, the picture is a mixed one: in periods of recession, tight credit, unemployment, and increased competition, major groups in the traditional sector expand. In France in the great depression of the thirties, for example, the trend towards decline in the number of tiny industrial plants with fewer than five employees, which had been in process since the turn of the century, suddenly reversed and these firms increased at least until the war. Annie Kriegel (1947, Part IV, Chapter 2) has shown how in this period in France the swell in industrial unemployment gave rise to an increase in small artisanal firms and in the numbers employed in them. Those expelled from industry set up small workshops on their own; wives sought employment to supplement their husbands' declining industrial incomes.

In Italy in the current economic crisis, there is considerable evidence of comparable shifts of production and employment: out of the large-scale, capital intensive plants into small, traditional enterprises. The decentralisation of industrial production began after 1969 in response to increased labour costs and a growing rigidity in the use of labour within large unionised factories. In the wake of the 'hot autumn' of 1969 the unions won higher wages and more power within the plant. It became increasingly more difficult for employers to lay-off workers in slack times, to introduce new technologies, in short, to manage their firms as they willed. With these new constraints, and a deteriorating – at best, uncertain – economic situation, the managers of big firms found it safer to subcontract as much work as possible out of the plant, in order to avoid hiring new workers who could not be easily dismissed and to reduce their labour costs, inflated by the new wage settlements and by social charges. The recourse to subcontracting has accelerated in the past five years. For example, a study of the metal working industry in Bologna province showed that between 1971 and 1975 the proportion of firms employing over 100 that subcontracted out work rose from 80 per cent to 98 per cent.[20] At the same time, the number of tiny firms employing fewer than twenty workers grew rapidly, and the rate of expansion of employment in these artisanal firms was higher than in any other firm size category.

Work has been transferred not only out of large, modern plants into smaller firms but out of factories altogether into the home. It seems inconceivable that work at home (*lavoro al domicilio*) could continue to play a significant role in a mature industrial economy, where the gains both from employing machinery too costly and too large to be used by an individual at home and from the concentration of workers and division of labour possible within the factory would seem to rule out the survival of a putting-out system on any significant scale. In Italy, however, at the beginning of the seventies, the Ministry of Labour estimated at least one million workers at home; the trade union estimates at that time were twice as high; and recent research suggests massive increases over the past five years.[21] While the use of home workers has always been substantial in clothing and textile trades, it is by no means confined to them. In a document prepared for the 1973 metalworkers' contract negotiation, the unions charged growing decentralisation of work in their industry as well;[22] and research in the mid-seventies on the metalworking industry in Bologna province and in Bergamo province confirmed this.[23]

Statistics on *lavoro a domicilio* are difficult to collect, since only a minority of those who work at home are registered by their employers, despite recent legislation requiring them to do so. This is because one of the principal advantages of having work executed outside the factory is that it allows the entrepreneur to escape paying various kinds of social charges for the workers as well as making it possible to pay them lower wages. However uncertain the actual national dimensions of the phenomenon, it is clear that they are substantial and expanding. In large part they account for the apparent decline in the active workforce, since a growing fraction of workers are 'irregularly' employed, hence not officially recorded as employed at all. Where official statistics report only 30–40 per cent employment, the door-to-door checks carried out in various local studies have discovered 50–70 per cent employed.[24] A recent ISVET study, directed by Luigi Frey, estimated 4.7 million irregularly employed workers.[25]

Italy is not unique among advanced industrial societies in using its small-scale traditional sector both to cushion the impact of economic fluctuations and change and to distribute their consequences in a way that shifts the burden off the modern sector. In France, for example, small commerce serves many of the same functions for society as in Italy (Berger, 1977). In Japan, the use of subcontracting has apparently allowed the large capital intensive plants to transfer uncertainty onto smaller firms in much the way that Italian firms do. What is striking in the Italian case, however, is the centrality of the links between modern and traditional sectors to the functioning of the economy and to the survival of the current political system. This centrality, which the current economic crisis has made increasingly more visible to the political elites and to major industrialists, accounts for the continuing importance of the petite bourgeoisie. The presence of a large traditional sector in Italy, whose boundaries coincide more or less with the domain of small independent property holders, has made possible a particular set of responses to industrialism and a particular kind of adaptation to economic crisis. The reliance of the modern sector on the traditional has reinforced the latter, giving it new functions and new life. The petite bourgeoisie is not simply a declining category whose electors remain significant enough to command certain concessions from the state and the modern sector, but rather, a class that controls vital institutions and resources.

NOTES

* An earlier version of this essay was published as 'Uso politico e sopravvivenza dei ceti in declino', in F. Cavazza and S. Graubard, Il Caso Italiano (Garzanti, 1974). I am grateful to the Fondazione Agnelli and the Ford Foundation for financial support of the research and to Judith Chubb, Peter Gourevitch, and Peter Lange for many rounds of criticism, counsel and encouragement.

1. For a fuller discussion of the traditional firm, see Berger (forthcoming).
2. Roberto Guala, quoted in the Confindustria publication, L'Organizzazione industriale (20 February 1973).
3. Ezio Filippone, quoted in ibid.

4. On the correlations between firm size and other factors in the traditional/
backwardness complex see for example, the study of Italian firms carried
out by the Mediocredito Centrale (1972, pp. 34–9); Bruni (1961, p. 51);
Dore (1973) also points to firm size as critical. The measures of firm size –
output, number employed and so forth are all highly intercorrelated, and
various studies have concluded that it does not matter much which is used.
On this point, see Savage (1975, pp. 92 ff.).
5. 'Artisan Enterprise in Italy', *Italy: Document and Notes*, xx (1) (January-
February 1971). See also Lutz (1962, p. 227).
6. See for example Lutz (1962), and Marzano (1969).
7. Frey (1971, Table 13). Data from ISTAT (1969).
8. *Associazione Italiana delle Grandi Imprese di Distribuzione al Dettaglio* (p.
44).
9. *Camera di Commercio, Industria, Artigianato, e Agricoltura di Parma* (p. 15).
10. In the past decade a substantial literature has appeared in Italy that explores
aspects of this general argument. Among the most interesting contributions
are Paci (1973); Labini (1975); Fuà (1976); and Salvati (1972).
11. For a development of this argument see the two chapters by Michael Piore
in Berger *et al.* (forthcoming).
12. Lutz notes that in 1959 the maximum social insurance payment that an
artisanal firm had to make for a day's work by a male was 117 lire, compared
with a 330 lire maximum in a large firm (Lutz, 1962, p. 226).
13. From a 1974 study, *Centro studi Federlibro-FLM-SISM, CISL di Verona,
Piccola azienda, grande sfruttamento*, cited in FLM (1975, p. 96).
14. On various projects for reform of commercial legislation, see Associazione
Italiana delle Grandi Imprese di Distribuzione al Dettaglio; Ariotti (1971);
and Marin (1971).
15. On the Helfer law, see *Libro bianco* and debate in issues of *Mondo
economico*, January to April 1971.
16. The new law ran counter not only to the Italian Plan goals for commerce,
but also to Common Market rules on open access to trade and professions.
The Commission in a letter signed by Malfatti expressed strong opposition
to the bill. Letter printed in *Il Sole-24 Ore* (25 July 1971).
17. These demands of the PCI appeared paradoxically in a statement against the
increases in the cost of living, *L'Unità* (18 September 1971).
18. On patterns of stability and change in electorates, see Sani (1976) and also
Sani (1977).
19. For the Italian Communist Party's analysis of and programme for small
business, see the papers and debates of a 1974 party conference, Instituto
Gramsci-CESPE (1975, vols. 1 and 2). See also Hellman (1975).
20. FLM, Sindacato provinciale di Bologna (n.d., Chapter 2, pp. 44, 53).
21. The estimates are from Antonio Molinari, report FILTEA-CGIL, FILTA-
CISL, UILTA-UIL, *Convegno Unitario sul Lavoro a Domicilio*, (Carpi: 7
February 1970, p. 2). See the arguments and research in *Occupazione,
Lavoro precario, piccola e media impresa* (Rome: Coines Edizioni,
1974).
22. See Federazione Italiana Metalmeccanici (FIM-CISL), *VIII congresso
nazionale, temi per il dibattito*, p. 3.
23. See FLM, Sindacato provinciale di Bologna (n.d.).

24. These studies are cited in Fuà (1976, pp. 32–3). See also the study of Naples reported in de Marco and Talamo (1976).
25. Cited in Di Girolamo (1977).

REFERENCES

R. Ariotti, 'Pretese corporativistiche ed esigenze di sviluppo nella programmazione del commercio', *Il Mulino*, 7/8 (1971).
Associazione Italiana delle Grandi Imprese Distribuzione al Dettaglio, *Libro bianco sulla riforma della disciplina del commercio*.
F. Bechhofer and B. Elliott, 'Persistence and Change: the Petite Bourgeoisie in Industrial Society', *European Journal of Sociology*, xvii (1976).
S. Berger, 'D'une boutique à l'autre: Changes in the Organization of the Traditional Middle Classes from Fourth to Fifth Republics', *Comparative Politics* (October 1977).
S. Berger, 'The Traditional Sector in France and Italy', in S. Berger and M. Piore, *Dualism and Discontinuity in Industrial Societies* (forthcoming).
L. Bruni, *Aspetti strutturali delle industrie italiane* (Rome; 1961).
Camera di Commercio, Industria, Artigianato, e Agricoltura di Parma, *La grande distribuzione nell 'ambito dell 'apparato distributivo alimentare al dettaglio*.
M. Cervi, 'L'Ombra della recessione sulle imprese minori: Fiat: 160 milia auto in meno', *Corriere delle Sera* (18 December 1971).
Comune di Modena, *Il Lavoro a domicilio nel quartiere Madonnina*, (1971).
R. Dore, *British Factory-Japanese Factory* (Berkeley: University of California Press, 1973).
C. Fabrizi, 'La razionalizzazione del commercio italiano in rapporto all' urbanistico commerciale', *Atti del congresso internazionale commercio e urbanistica* (14–16 October 1967).
Federazione Italiana Metal meccanici (FIM–CISL), *VIII congresso nazionale, temi per il dibattito*.
FLM, *Sindacato e piccola impresa* (Bari: De Donato, 1975).
FLM, Sindacato provinciale di Bologna, *Ristrutturazione e organizzazione del lavoro* (Rome: Edizioni SEUSI, n.d.).
L. Frey, *Le prospettive di occupazione in Lombardia nella prima metà degli 'anni '70'* (Milan: Giunta Regionale Lombarda, October 1971).
G. Fuà, *Occupazione e capacità produttive: la realtà italiana*, (Bologna: Il Mulino, 1976).
G. Di Girolamo, 'Seimila miliardi dal lavoro nero', *Corriere della Sera*, (2 March 1977).
S. Hellman, 'The PCI's Alliance Strategy and the Case of the Middle Classes', in D.L.M. Blackmer and S. Tarrow (eds.), *Communism in Italy and France* (Princeton: Princeton University Press, 1975).
ISTAT, *Alcuni risultati della rilevazione delle unità locali industriali e commerciali*, (1969).
Istituto Gramsci-CESPE, *La piccola e la media industria nella crisi dell' economia italiana* (Rome: Editori Riuniti, 1975).
A. Kriegel, *L'Evolution de l'artisanat dans le 3ème arrondissement de Paris de*

1896 à 1945 (Paris: DES memoir, 1947, unpublished).

V. Lutz, *Italy: A Study in Economic Development* (London: Oxford University Press, 1962).

C. de Marco and M. Talamo, *Lavoro nero* (Milan: Mazzotta, 1976).

U. Maggiolo, *Contributo per l'analisi e la previsione dell 'evoluzione delle forze di lavoro agricole in Lombardia* (Milan: Giunta Regionale Lombarda, 1971).

M. Marin, 'La distribuzione in Italia', *Nord e Sud*, no. 2 (1971).

F. Marzano, *Un'interpretazione del processo di sviluppo economico dualistico in Italia* (Milan, 1969).

Mediocredito Centrale, *Lineamenti dell 'industria manifatturiera italiana* (Rome, 1972).

M. Paci, *Mercato del lavoro e classi sociali in Italia* (Bologna: Il Mulino, 1973).

A. Pizzorno, *Comunità e razionalizzazione* (Turin, 1960).

A. Pizzorno, 'I ceti medi nei meccanismi del consenso', in F. Cavazza and S. Graubard (eds.), *Il caso italiano* (Milan: Garzanti, 1974).

S. Ravalli, 'La distribuzione al dettaglio', *Mondo economico* (23 December 1967).

G. Ruffolo, *Il ruolo delle piccole e medie industrie nella strategia programmatica*, (Rome, 27 October 1971).

M. Salvati, 'L'Origine della crisi in corso', *Quaderni Piacentini*, xi, 46 (March 1972).

G. Sani, 'The Italian Election of 1976: Continuity and Change', Paper prepared for the Conference Group on Italian Politics, APSA, September 1976.

G. Sani, 'Generations and Politics in Italy', Paper presented at Fondazione L. Einaudi, Turin, 1977.

D. Savage, *Founders, Heirs and Managers in France: A Business Elite in Transition* (Unpublished dissertation, Columbia University, 1975).

P. Sylos-Labini, *Saggio sulle classi sociali* (Rome: Laterza, 1975).

4 The Petite Bourgeoisie in Socialist Society

BRONISLAW MISZTAL

Questions surrounding the existence of the petite bourgeoisie in socialist society arouse considerable controversy. To avoid purely semantic misunderstanding therefore it might be as well to state at the outset that this paper will consider the following problems:

1. Is the petite bourgeoisie in socialist society a class or a stratum?
2. What are the relationships between the petite bourgeoisie and other adjacent social groupings in socialist society?
3. Does belonging to a particular social group result in the acquisition of a set of cultural features which affect people's thinking?

The Socio-Cultural Background of the Petite Bourgeoisie in Polish Society

The contemporary petite bourgeoisie undoubtedly carries the heritage of earlier periods in the development of Polish society. The present day petite bourgeoisie rests upon a different social base but its social consciousness is part of an historical tradition. Traditionally, the term 'petite bourgeoisie' did not exist and the term which was used – 'lower middle classes' – implied a certain kind of town dweller. Traditionally, the term 'lower middle class' referred to a group of people of unspecified socio-economic status who differed from the rest of society in their style of life and specific interests. We can say that their style of life went hand in hand with their wealth but we should also notice that the members of the learned professions and the more senior clerical workers, while their wealth might be equivalent only to that of shopkeepers, had a more exalted life-style (Kaczynska, 1976, p. 92). In this particular context, the lower middle class was identified by prestige based on the social consciousness of the structure of society and its economic relations.

This structure of society, and its representations in social conscious-ness, differed from historical period to historical period and also from region to region, thus giving variable meaning to the term 'lower middle class'. In the 19th century, the Polish lower middle class consisted mainly of 'small manufacturers' who were small capitalists working alongside their own employees. The so-called *nouveau riche* whose social back-ground and manners were not acceptable to the bourgeoisie and 'declining' members of the bourgeoisie, people who sold their labour but nonetheless cultivated the traditions of their former order, were also part of this social grouping (Kaczynska, 1976, p. 95).

The petite bourgeoisie in the current context, however, is to be taken as referring chiefly to all those persons holding an intermediary position in the Marxist dichotomic class model as applied to capitalist society. This dichotomic model consists of course of two social groups opposing each other; the one, working people who do not own any of the means of production, and the other, those who do not work but own the means of production. However, small manufacturers, shopkeepers, craftsmen and farmers own their means of production but also work themselves, only sometimes hiring labour in addition to their own. The term 'lower middle class' has thus included (with the exception of farmers) that petite bourgeoisie – but generally had a rather broader meaning cover-ing also clerks, teachers, pharmacists and so on (Kaczynska, 1976).

As we can see then from the historical sources, the petite bourgeoisie in the sense in which we use it here was only part of a broader group which had the character of a stratum. This lower middle class constituted the so-called intermediate stratum which occupied a po-sition in the prestige structure immediately below the intelligentsia. In the historical literature which discusses the structure of Polish society we also come across the German term 'lumpenbourgeoisie' which we could translate as 'marginal bourgeoisie'. They formed a marginal social grouping characterised by very low income, a low cultural level and little education, far less than that of the lower middle class. They had the further characteristics of lack of tradition, a strong drive towards the acquisition of wealth at all costs, and, before the war, hostility towards the state and its apparatus (Żarnowski, 1969). In the small towns the lower middle class formed the second largest group after the proletariat. According to historians, we may estimate the composition of Polish society in small towns at the turn of the nineteenth and twentieth centuries to be as shown in Table 4.1.

According to this table, the lower middle class along with the marginal or lumpenbourgeoisie accounted for 43 per cent of the population. In both these groups people of Jewish origin predominated. As must be obvious, these data are approximate referring as they do to a particular region and historical period but nevertheless they may be taken as illustrating roughly the role played by the lower middle class in

TABLE 4.1   The social composition of the population of small towns in Poland
circa 1900

Social group	Ethnic group		Total
	Christians	Jews	
	%	%	%
Social elite			
(intelligentsia and landed gentry)	9	2	11
Lower middle class	8	18	26
Marginal bourgeoisie			
(lumpenbourgeoisie)	5	12	17
Peasantry	10	1	11
Proletariat			
(industrial workers)	8	20	28
Lower working class			
(lumpenproletariat)	5	2	7
Total	45	55	100

Source: Kaczyńska, p. 111.

urban Polish society before World War II. In the period from 1918 to
1939 the petite bourgeoisie in Poland was in general affected by
economic and social change in the same way as the rest of the
population. The structure of the stratum in 1938 was as shown in Table
4.2. We can see that within the petite bourgeoisie, handicraft production
predominated. If we include the 800,000 workers employed by the
craftsmen we can see that around two and a half million people earned
their living in the manufacturing enterprises owned by the petite
bourgeoisie. In 1937 more than 30 per cent of the businesses were
shoemakers and tailors. The period of economic prosperity was reflected
in the number of newly founded businesses. In 1929 the number of new

TABLE 4.2   Economic structure of the petite bourgeoisie and the general
population of Poland in 1938

Employed in	Petite bourgeoisie	Population
Industry	1,800,000	8,099,000
Commerce	1,300,000	2,117,000
Other sectors	300,000	
Total	3,400,000	
	TOTAL POPULATION	34,849,000

Source: Żarnowski, 1973.

enterprises was 12.9 per cent greater than in the previous year, and this increased further in 1930 to 21.1 per cent above the 1929 figure.

The second major sub-group of the petite bourgeoisie were people connected with commerce. There were more than 400,000 officially registered traders, 46 per cent of them general grocers. In 1938 there were still 212,000 shopkeepers with on average 150 customers per shop.

The petite bourgeoisie was socially differentiated along two main axes. The first was ethnic. Of the 3,100,000 people working in trade and industry, 1,888,000 were Jews. Including their families they made up more than 70 per cent of all shopkeepers and tradesmen. The second axis was the economic one. A very rough estimate suggests that only one-fifth of the petite bourgeoisie enjoyed a comfortable level of income and consumption. The rest had a standard of living more like that of the proletariat.[1]

The Petite Bourgeoisie in Socialist Poland

After World War II, two major social changes affected the position and composition of the petite bourgeoisie as we have described it above. First, the new socio-economic order brought about by the national-isation of the means of production. Second, the extermination of the Jews during the war and the shifts of population which took place meant that Jews could no longer play any material part in the field of economic activity. Furthermore, the reduced circumstances resulting from the war and the food rationing system had the effect of 'equalising' consumption and thus the petite bourgeoisie existed in the social consciousness only as 'the relics of capitalism'. The social and economic development of the country was seen to depend on the labour of the rural population, many of whom were now being employed in the construction of industrial and urban centres. In the immediate post-war years then, any kind of small business was viewed with disapproval, and the mass media condemned the small bourgeois type of person.

In 1948–9 however, unsocialised trade began to flourish mainly due to difficulties in distribution which the state had to face. The administrative and financial authorities were not favourably inclined towards private shopkeepers but government officials decided that in view of the existing difficulties, small businesses should be permitted.[2] At that time one could observe the specific attitude a shopkeeper would take towards his function in society: he tried to justify the job he did. He tried to stress that small business in Poland had nothing in common with the economic forms of trading in a capitalist society and that his activity was not governed by any foreign ideology. He did this by inventing slogans such as 'a shopkeeper must be aware of the economic function he performs in our new socio-economic system'[3] or 'old forms can be inspired by a new spirit'.[4] In this way the shopkeepers emphasised that unsocialised trade was a link in the chain supplying the workers with needed basic products, and thus they tried to demonstrate their usefulness. And this conviction of their usefulness was quite justified. According to data from the Individual Trade and Services Association 'on April 4th, 1948, 135,000 enterprises applied for a license to trade. . . . In 1948 small business had a turnover of 360,000 million złotys'. In 1949 new administrative and financial regulations placed some restrictions on the private sector. At that time, almost every issue of the trade weekly magazine which was the official organ of the private sector, contained examples of revoked licences, complaints and a certain amount of legal advice.[5] On 1 April 1949 the Association, which was a kind of trade union for people working on their own account, signed an agreement settling some of the problems surrounding small business.[6] The agreement laid down the principles on which labour could be hired and committed shopkeepers to providing certain social services for their workers. In the same year, the Ministry of Finance introduced some regulations aimed at diminishing the financial standing of shopkeepers and a number of products were banned from sale in private shops. On 3 January 1953 in connection with a currency reform, prices and wages were regulated. As a result of this step, the financial position of small businesses was greatly reduced; in fact it was diminished by a factor of three as the rate of exchange was three new złotys for 100 old złotys for those employed in state enterprises and 1 for 100 for small independent businessmen.[7] That radical change revealed the attitude of the state towards the private sector and its increasing wealth which was growing faster than that of the rest of the society. From 1953 to 1955 market trading, where financial restrictions were not so strict, flourished. According to data provided by the Association, about 60 per cent of the shopkeepers wound up their businesses and went off to trade in the markets.[8] Political changes in the years 1955–6 resulted in a change of attitude towards the private sector.[9] All the regulations concerned were revised and the financial penal law was abrogated. The financial authorities were no longer able to abuse this law in order to increase taxes and subsequently confiscate funds where these special taxes were not fully paid. The law forbidding the holding of foreign currency was also abolished. This and the development of the foreign currency bank (PeKaO) gave small businessmen, particularly craftsmen, the chance to buy necessary raw materials from abroad. The regulation levying higher rents on the private sector was also abolished and the newly appointed Minister of Trade in his official announcement[10] expressed an understanding for the needs of unsocialized trade. Tax reductions, social benefits for people employed in the private sector and licence facilities were promised, and all these plans for the private sector were partly implemented in the years between 1957 and 1959.

Speculation in imported goods or in goods bought in foreign currency shops (PeKaO) however once again modified the state's attitude towards unsocialised trade for shopkeepers were profiting by the difference between the prices of goods purchased in the foreign currency shops and those sold for Polish money. The state then brought forward regulations increasing both the rent paid by small businessmen and their electricity and gas tariffs, while taxation aimed at reducing the profits of private enterprises was re-introduced.

For the next fifteen years the state in this way controlled the activity of the private sector. Finally, in 1975 it was decided once more to encourage private food shops such as bakers, butchers and so on and in addition, the state began to rent restaurants to small businessmen. Under this scheme, a businessman who rents a restaurant from the state receives fully equipped premises. His task is to employ people, to buy materials and to determine prices. Every month he is required to pay a certain amount of money to the state but he enjoys a number of social benefits and tax reductions. Thus, in its external relationships with the administration of the state, the nature of a rented restaurant is close to that of one run by the state itself, but the present arrangement relieves the state of the responsibility of maintaining close supervision. On the other hand, in its internal relations, the day to day running of a rented restaurant does not differ from that of a privately owned enterprise.

In 1976 the state permitted emigrants returning to Poland to start up a small business of their own. They are allowed to buy raw materials abroad, process them in Poland and sell them again on the foreign market, sharing their profits with the state. The year 1977 brought a further development of this *laissez-faire* policy towards unsocialised trade. People employed in state shops may now take them over and run them privately. They may also open *new* shops, restaurants and so on after making an application to the state administrative offices.

As we can see from the above account, the state's policy towards the private sector varied at different periods. It was determined by the country's economic situation, by the state of the market and by the country's financial needs. The ideological aspect of the whole problem played an important part here. At first it was believed that the socialist state could dispense entirely with the private sector. It was thought that the country would manage to avoid altogether the economic stratification of society and that it would be able to maintain an homogeneous style of life between different social classes. There was thus a tendency to restrict the conspicuous consumption of those who were better off. We may obtain a better understanding of the subsequent shifts in the attitude of the state toward the so-called private sector if we place them in the following context. We should consider first that the social structure of socialist society in Poland has not been stable in the period from 1945 to 1970 but has been in a state of continuous transition, and

the main administrative and ideological purpose of government action
has been to further the creation of the two main and basic classes of
socialist society, the workers and the peasantry. Further, official state
action was much concerned with the processes whereby the new
intelligentsia were to be recruited. The fundamental mechanisms
whereby these new groups were to be formed were on the one hand, the
manipulation of the value system and, on the other, the control of the
processes of social mobility. Education and skill therefore were to be
valued rather than money and wealth. This affected the political and
economic importance attributed to the private sector and led to
frequently shifting decisions. The chief and most specific feature of the
petite bourgeoisie in the socialist social system is, in all probability, the
fact that it is the object of direct manipulation and intervention in the
interests of state policy as this is interpreted from time to time. It must be
realised that it is not and never will be a basic stratum or grouping.
Whether or not one believes that socialist Poland could do without the
private sector at the present time, the policies of the state should not be
interpreted as a statement that this goal can never be achieved. They
simply express the view that at the present stage of economic development, and given the present composition of the social structure, it is not
necessary to demolish this peculiar grouping. But such a reform could
occur at any time, and the social role and importance of the private
sector would be replaced by state agencies. All it requires is an
administrative and organisational decision to do so. It is further
important to understand that in the period 1945–55, due to the post-war
economic problems and the shortages of goods on the market, the social
stratum of the petite bourgeoisie typified all those structural and
situational advantages that the socialist government was trying to
remove from the social stage: uncontrolled manipulation, independent
purchasing power, controversially concentrated money and wealth and
so on. During this first period, the government had to cope with an old
petite bourgeoisie formed before the war and well acquainted with the
former pre-war *capitalist* conditions for the acquisition of surplus value,
whereas now we have a new generation of small businessmen which has
grown up under the present political and economic system and chosen to
take up work in the private sector as it is presently constituted. However,
it should be noted that the shopkeepers are something of an exception
here since they constitute an older group many of whose members grew
up in the pre-war social formations.

The years 1970–7 were very prosperous for Polish society. Increasing
wealth led to some differentiation in the economic order of society as
might be expected under those circumstances. The *laissez-faire* policy of
the state towards small business was influenced by this increased wealth
and the fact that the incomes obtained by small businessmen were not
drastically different from those of other members of the society. Table

TABLE 4.3   Number of enterprises and people working in the private sector
1960–76

Year (at 31 Dec.)	No. of enter-prises	Owners and joint owners	Family members	All employees including apprentices	Appren-tices	Total
1960	147,859	150,936	13,329	86,743	43,387	251,008
1965	149,851	152,642	15,542	109,696	54,842	277,880
1970	176,313	179,653	19,862	142,509	66,339	342,024
1975	187,337	190,657	25,489	150,083	52,817	366,229
1976	188,979	192,626	26,121	152,316	50,710	371,063

Source: Central Statistical Office, 1977, p. 316, Table 5/484/.

4.3 shows the number of private enterprises and people working in the private sector in the years 1960–76. Taking 1960 figures as 100 in each case, we can see that in 1976 the number of individual enterprises amounted to 127.8 and the total number of people working in the sector to 147.8. Owners and joint owners had increased to 127.6, family members involved in the business to 195.9, employees to 175.6 and apprentices to 116.9. Thus, the number of owners has increased in proportion to the number of enterprises but the total numbers employed in the private sector have shown a higher rate of growth primarily due to a larger number of family members employed. We can see here the phenomenon of absorption; the immediate family and relatives of an individual businessman become part of the petite bourgeoisie and the private enterprise is transformed into a family unit in preference to employing people from the outside. We can only speculate on the overall processes involved but it seems likely that a son, brother or brother-in-law seeing how the business is going, makes up his mind to leave his job in the socialised sector and to start working for a family business. After a certain amount of time acquiring experience, he decides to start his own business in a similar field and the process of absorption begins again. There are a number of examples in Warsaw of private family enterprises existing close to one another which have emerged in this way. There are, however, no official data on this topic.

In the majority of statistical and sociological surveys, the problem of the contemporary petite bourgeoisie in socialist society is not considered. Generally, one talks instead of people working on their own account and not involved in farming or forestry. It is possible though to obtain some general information on the structure of and processes taking place within this social group from the official statistics. First we can consider their numbers.

Table 4.4 shows that on 30 March, 1974 a mere 2 per cent of the

TABLE 4.4　Numbers working in non-state owned and non-cooperatively owned enterprises, and total population figures, 30 March 1974

	Living from one source of income only	Living from two sources of income	Total
In the population			
Men	13,938,767	2,373,963	16,312,730
Women	15,671,749	1,651,454	17,323,203
Total	29,610,516	4,025,417	33,635,933
In the private sector			
Men	347,673	51,468	399,141
Women	270,967	28,808	299,775
Total	618,640	80,276	698,916
Supported by those employed in the private sector	295,639	42,941	338,580

Source: Central Statistical Office, 1975, Part I, pp. 10–12, Table 3.

population worked in the unsocialised sector. We may compare this with the 58.6 per cent working in the socialised sector. What is more, these figures include not only the owners of enterprises (the petite bourgeoisie in which we are interested) but also workers employed by them, apprentices and domestic servants. This latter group cannot be taken into consideration in our analysis of the structure of the petite bourgeoisie for they earn their living by selling their labour and neither own any means of production nor acquire surplus value. And this highlights another feature of the situation of the petite bourgeoisie in Poland. While they constitute an auxiliary stratum they can be tolerated and at present the amount of surplus value which can be extracted is limited. Thus, the family model of labour organisation must largely replace the extraction of surplus value or at any rate serve to satisfy the owners of small enterprises for the time being. Even the most recent discussions of the problem of the continuing existence of this stratum underline the absence of this crucial economic feature: the extraction of surplus value. The Finance Department places private industry at a relative disadvantage by levying taxes high enough to prevent the acquisition of much surplus value. The state thus takes over this surplus value and only in a few cases is it possible for people working on their own account to keep a large proportion of it. Thus, it can be confidently hypothesised that barely more than one per cent of Poland's population is able to live off surplus value generated by their ownership of the means of production. If we turn to consider the educational level attained by those active in the unsocialized sector we can see from Table 4.5 that

TABLE 4.5 Level of education attained by workers in the private sector and all those in the population economically active

	Private sector (%)	Population economically active (%)
University graduates	5.5	3.1
Some higher education	0.9	1.4
Secondary schooling plus two years training	0.7	0.6
Secondary education completed	4.4	4.5
Comprehensive education completed	9.9	8.5
Some secondary education	3.5	5.0
Vocational education completed	23.4	12.5
Primary education completed	43.2	43.3
Less than full primary education	8.5	19.5
Total	100.0	100.0

Source: Central Statistical Office, 1976b, p. 36, Table 6. Calculated from raw data.

only 48.3 per cent have a basic vocational preparation or any more extensive education, while the remaining 51.7 per cent have not been trained in any real sense for any kind of job.

As we can see from the table, if we compare those in the private sector with the general population of people economically active, then those with higher education and vocational training are actually over-represented. However, the data do also suggest that about one half of the people who are statistically included among those in the private sector are inadequately equipped with the skills necessary to run a sizeable business enterprise. Given the adverse conditions which they have to face in socialist society it is hard to imagine people so ill-prepared rising to become great private owners – members of a contemporary bourgeoisie.

These educational patterns might lead us to ask the question whether the petite bourgeoisie in Poland occupy an hereditary position. If we consider first in-flow mobility, then among every 100 people working on their own account, excluding the agricultural sector, 80.7 men and 88.0 women are working in a different socio-economic group from that of their fathers. In the economically active population at large the equivalent figures are 46.6 and 42.4 suggesting that occupational inheritance is actually much weaker in the group of workers in the private sector.[11] There is also far higher out-mobility among this group

TABLE 4.6. Children of the petite bourgeoisie* in the economically active population in 1972 by year of first job and socio-economic group of first job

Year of starting first job	Manual workers	White collar workers	Independent farmers	Petite bourgeoisie
Up to 1939	43.2	13.9	20.9	22.0
1940–4	64.1	13.7	15.4	6.8
1945–9	45.3	34.5	10.8	8.9
1950–4	46.3	42.1	6.8	4.9
1955–9	51.3	33.8	8.2	5.6
1960–4	58.0	33.0	5.7	3.3
1965–9	48.9	42.1	3.2	4.5
1970–2	54.4	41.9	1.6	2.4

* Petite bourgeoisie here refers to the self-employed outside agriculture.
Source: Central Statistical Office, 1976a, p. 84.

since 96.1 per cent of their children are mobile into another social grouping as compared to a figure of 49.9 per cent in the general population.[12] Table 4.6 above presents data on the intergenerational mobility of the sons and daughters of private owners since before the second world war. We can see that occupational inheritance has declined among this group in the post-war period at least in so far as their first job is concerned; it may be the case that they return to their father's occupation later in their working life. We can also see that mobility is consistently greatest into the manual group and that in the post-war period white collar work has become steadily more important for the children of private owners to the detriment of agriculture.

We must recall at this point that the above data do not entirely refer to people who would be classified by a sociologist as 'petit bourgeois' in the conditions of a socialist society. To what extent then are they just average figures for all those who have been put in the same category for purely statistical convenience? The Central Statistical Office states that included among those working on their own account are people owning a small workshop or shop, people who give private lessons, taxi drivers, people of the learned professions and so on.[13] It is worth remembering that all these groups constitute the 'lower middle class' in its traditional sense.

The Petite Bourgeoisie as Culturally Peripheral

We have shown that in Polish socialist society the petite bourgeoisie forms a small percentage of the population (perhaps 1 per cent), that its constant changes and fortunes depend on state policy and that it constitutes a source of social mobility due to its low social stability.

Despite the fact that so many people leave the private sector to take a job in the socialised sector and that only a very small percentage of the population is employed there, the continuing existence of the stratum leads us to suppose that there is a constant flow of new members. Unfortunately we have no official data on which we can draw to throw light on this process. We can guess, however, that there must be some factor of an essentially social nature which compensates for the disadvantages which this group suffers, and that it might take the form either of income or of culture and life-style. The social stereotype of the petite bourgeoisie still exists in the society and accordingly these two factors are seen as associated and people ascribe to those in private ownership patterns of income and consumption which they themselves would often like to possess.

There is a widely held conviction that the independent businessman has so much money that his purchasing power exceeds the possibilities provided by the domestic market. In other words, people believe that small businessmen possess all the attractive goods which are available on the market. This view is based on two simple observations. People notice that luxurious things disappear rapidly from the shops and that their prices are often greater than the average monthly salary. If a handbag costs 4000–5000 złotys which is more than the average wage (4234 złotys a month in industry in 1976) then the average Pole believes that only small businessmen could afford to buy it. The same thing goes for trips abroad organised by the travel offices. Needless to say small business *is* profitable but it is an exaggeration to believe that small businessmen have such enormous purchasing power. In the social consciousness petit bourgeois means the whole 'lower middle class', all those working on their own account and those having more than one economic source of existence. But even then the number of people possessing this really high level of purchasing power as well as the volume of such expensive products is very small if we take a wider perspective; however, there is no denying that the *visibility* of such products is high. There is another point worth making. Some possessions which people consider as the attributes of a privileged social and economic position are simply indispensible for the job the petit bourgeois does. Take, for instance, a car, still considered a luxury in Poland. For a small businessmen it is a necessary tool for the effective running of his business.

The second advantage attributed to the independent businessman is his apparent control over his work. People believe, for instance, that he can determine his working hours at will. This is clearly false and indeed nearly everyone has at some time seen the shopkeeper on his way to buy produce at the market having risen at 5 a.m. or in the evening having closed his shop, sitting down to check his bills, his papers and his accounts.

Despite all this, an image of the businessman as rich and unconstrained is still vivid in people's minds. That image is tinged with emotion. Jealousy and contempt, attraction and rejection – these are the feelings people have for the independent businessman. It is interesting, however, that the negative evaluation of the producer is coupled with a positive opinion of his products. The French are not the only ones who 'aiment le bon pain'; the Poles have a similar attitude. They appreciate shoes made by an independent shoemaker, cakes made in a small patisserie, paint from a private manufacturer and a small workshop which will repair the car. They believe that these do a much better job than their equivalents in the public sector. That is why markets flourish in many Polish towns and small shops have their regular customers.

The next thing we must consider is that there is today, among a broad stratum of the lower middle class a certain kind of culture together with a particular brand of morality which has emerged at its base. In Poland it is referred to as 'lower middle class culture and morality' but it is associated particularly with the traditional petite bourgeoisie from which people are convinced it came. This is only partly true. Middle class culture emerged in Poland with the arrival of capitalism, that is to say in the first decade of this century. We take it to have embraced several elements; the ideology of making a quick fortune through trade and industrial activity was the first. This ideology also stressed an almost philanthropic attitude of the whole class toward the rest of society. Thus the owner of a house renting rooms to the poorest people stressed that he did it to provide a lodging for the poor, thus taking on himself a social burden. The other elements in the stereotyped culture of the traditional petit bourgeois had several facets – economic rationality affecting interpersonal relations, ignorance of loftier values and hypocritical piousness hiding the real passions beneath.

In present-day Polish society, many of those features have undergone certain changes. The ideology of getting rich quick has fallen on stony ground. State policy towards the unsocialised sector has been in constant flux for the last thirty years. The tax system, the state of the home market and financial principles have changed. And as a result, a new type of small businessman has emerged: a chameleon. He constantly changes the rules of the game, adapting himself to the changing situation, altering his field of activity, responding to the needs of the market. Thus a new and different ideology has emerged, stressing adaptability to rapid change, a full awareness of the social situation and the ability to survive. Despite a certain disapproval felt by Polish society towards the small businessman that element of his culture is accepted as a peculiarity of this group. No longer does the group claim any philanthropic role and the shopkeepers I have interviewed stressed that the private sector, exhausted by its present function is fading away in the face of generally improving socio-economic conditions. If we relate this to the statistical data we should bear in mind that shopkeepers are somewhat atypical, still traditionally minded, having entered the stratum before the war; there are no new recruits to this occupation now. The growth of the private sector comes from a growing number of private firms and restaurants.

Nor does the interpenetration of economic and personal relations serve to distinguish this social group any more. Certainly, many elements of the petit-bourgeois morality have been frequently criticised as reflected in modern literature, films and satire. The result of this is, however, often contrary to what one might expect. For instance, a popular bi-weekly radio programme, broadcast for almost twenty years, presented two characters, the one a manager of a middle-sized office and the other his employee, one Mr Malinowski. The first was a naive, straightforward and somewhat stupid man often ridiculed by Malinowski, who was shy, cruel and hypocritical. Surprisingly it was Mr Malinowski – in many ways the symbol of petit-bourgeois morality – who became more popular with the public. Mr Malinowski, an established member of the socialist system, became the darling of contemporary mass culture. His cultural pattern has taken over from that of the small businessman before the war: today's lower middle class culture is founded on activity, independence, a dual standard of honesty and an interest in one's own pocket.

Conclusion

To sum up, we can draw the following conclusions about the role played by independent businessmen in contemporary Poland. First, they constitute a vestigial social group, a stratum not a class and a stratum whose position in the social structure is becoming more and more marginal. Secondly, the difficulties placed in their way have resulted in a new type of small businessman who fights for his survival. The existence of the private sector is no longer an ideological threat to the socialist society as is shown by the way the state supports certain forms of activity, for instance, by renting restaurants. Nor is it a threat as far as income inequality is concerned for incomes are diversified in Polish society anyway and the petite bourgeoisie is too small to be of importance.

The other aspect of the problem may cause a certain surprise, even perhaps anxiety. The culture of the petite bourgeoisie which is of a peripheral character has survived, albeit changed in various ways and it has penetrated the new middle class of lower-grade clerks.

When we speak of the petite bourgeoisie in socialist society we should bear in mind that there are potential theoretical and practical difficulties. Cases of true bourgeois activity, though they do occur, are very rare indeed. The renting of restaurants, cafés and other state owned enterprises of this kind to private individuals will continue to develop. The culture, however, which has survived in its peripheral form and is now taking root in the soil of the middle class can perhaps be more correctly viewed as 'the culture of the middle class'.

NOTES

1. All data referring to the inter-war years come from Żarnowski, 1973, pp. 228–263.
2. See the account by Hilary Minc of the National Congress of the Unification of Political Movements, 1948 in *Tygodnik Handlowy* (Trade Weekly) *Yearbook* (1949).
3. *Tygodnik Handlowy*, No. 8 (1949) p. 1.
4. *Tygodnik Handlowy*, No. 9 (1949) p. 3.
5. *Tygodnik Handlowy*, Nos 6-9 (1949).
6. *Tygodnik Handlowy*, No. 22 (1949).
7. According to the decision of the government on the so-called 'regulation' of prices and salaries from 3 January 1953.
8. *Tygodnik Handlowy*, No. 7 (1955) p. 7.
9. *Tygodnik Handlowy*, No. 14 (1956) p. 7.
10. *Tygodnik Handlowy*, No. 19 (1957) quoting the statement by Minister Lesz on Private Trade.
11. Central Statistical Office, 1976a, p. 33, Table 4.
12. Central Statistical Office, 1976a, p. 37, Table 7.
13. Central Statistical Office, 1976a, p. XIV.

REFERENCES

Central Statistical Office, *Spis ludności i mieskań metoda reprezentacyjna* (Sample Census of People and Flats) (Warsaw, 1975).
Central Statistical Office, *Zmiany struktury i ruchliwość społeczno-zawodowa w Polsce* (Changes in Social Structure and Social Mobility in Poland) (Warsaw, 1976a).
Central Statistical Office, *Spis ludności i mieskań metoda reprezentacyjna* (Sample Census of People and Flats) (Warsaw, 1976b).
Central Statistical Office, *Statistical Yearbook* (Warsaw, 1977).
E. Kaczynska, 'O drobnomieszczczaństwie ziem polskich' (On the petite bourgeoisie of Poland – historical analysis), *Dzieje Najnowsze*, viii (1976).
J. Żarnowski, *Społeczeństwo Polski miedzywojennej* (The society of pre-war Poland) (Warsaw, 1969).
J. Żarnowski, *Społeczeństwo drugiej Rzeczypospolite* (Warsaw, 1973).

5 The Petite Bourgeoisie and the New Middle Class:

Differentiation or Homogenisation of the Middle Strata in Germany

FRANZ URBAN PAPPI

Introduction

Many sociologists think that the trend towards a middle-class society is characteristic of modernisation. True, sociological catch phrases such as 'class-society in the melting pot' (Geiger, 1949) or *nivellierte Mittelstandsgesellschaft* (Schelsky, 1965) have worn thin in the past 25 years, but the developmental dynamic supposedly lying behind them is not automatically considered to be wrong.

Some elements of the diagnosis are thought to be right, even by authors who are in no way committed to a consensual view of society. Thus, Narr and Offe, for instance, claim that status inconsistency and 'inconsistent dispositions of interests' (cross-pressures), expanding as industrialisation proceeds are responsible for the fact that 'collective identity in the sense of class identity' does not come about. 'Socially heterogeneous structures of communication in the spheres of work as well as non-work make the consolidation of a political conscience difficult' (Narr and Offe, 1975, pp. 35–6). Only in their choice of terms do some authors give the thesis of levelling an emphasis different from that of the consensus theorists. Here, we should mention Enzensberger (1976) who postulates the cultural hegemony of the petite bourgeoisie in European societies. Using an odd definition of the petite bourgeoisie as 'the class, which is neither nor', he claims that it is self-evident 'that the European proletariat in its forms of living and aspirations is marked by the culture of the petite bourgeoisie'. The grande bourgeoisie which shrank a great deal because of the economic process of concentration has had to give over to the petite bourgeoisie its function as the class whose life style was to be emulated.

When in the title of my paper I explicitly refer to the petite bourgeoisie and the new middle class, terms which were coined in the nineteenth and early twentieth centuries, I wish to suggest that the homogenisation which is attributed to the entire society did not occur, and failed to occur precisely in the centre of the so-called middle class. These doubts about the *nivellierte Mittelstandsgesellschaft* do not only refer to the overstated literary versions but also to its form in professional sociology.

With the advancement of survey research after World War II, and the strong influence of American sociology, the clearly differentiated class divisions of European sociologists were replaced by a hierarchic rank ordering. If the middle strata were to be differentiated further, one would do this using aspects of social status to create the lower, middle and upper middle classes. This practice, used in social research even today, is rendered problematic here by recalling a question which engaged social science discussion in Germany until the end of the Weimar Republic.

In the first part, therefore, I will present an historic perspective of the subject. In the second part I will branch out from the concrete groupings and talk about principles of class structuration by which social classes in economic and/or prestige terms can be generated from the social relations between occupationally and economically defined statistical categories. Finally, in the third and last part I will try to produce some theoretical statements about the developmental dynamic towards differentiation or homogenisation within the middle strata, and attempt to substantiate them empirically.

The Middle Strata in the Phase of Industrialisation

Terms such as 'bourgeoisie' and 'proletariat' were introduced as catchwords into political rhetoric and social science by socialists. The term 'petite bourgeoisie' also takes its special meaning from this discussion. With growing industrialisation and in the course of increasing class struggles, this 'class in between' was to be destroyed between the two antagonistic classes. The Communist Manifesto talks about the small middle classes, the small industrialists, merchants and rentiers, the artisans and peasants, whose downfall into the proletariat is forecast. In contrast to the peasants Marx and Engels talk of the petite bourgeoisie when they speak about the remaining groups of the small middle classes. In the Communist Manifesto, however, the term 'petite bourgeoisie' is not simply neutral but, by this time, it is already being used pejoratively as, for instance, when petit-bourgeois socialism is described as a variant of reactionary socialism.

The term *Mittelstand*, however, is tantamount to a revaluation of these very same groups of self-employed artisans and merchants. According to Wilhelm Heinrich Riehl this term 'is apt, looked at from different viewpoints and with regard to its content. We would like to understand it in the higher and prouder sense that the bourgeoisie (*Bürgertum*) forms the centre, the very core of modern society' (1930, p. 110). All radii of social life would meet in this centre (p. 224). When Riehl criticises the retreat into privacy, 'the stupidity towards any social interest', as the social illness of the bourgeoisie, he does not associate it specifically with the petite bourgeoisie but with a generalised philistinism. The term petite bourgeoisie is simply to be taken in the sense of small trade. This is sometimes accompanied by the 'autocracy' of the old guild system when, for example, 'the butchers and bakers burden the buying public by following their comfortable and long-established practices of trade' (p. 204).

The Marxist thesis of extinction partly accounts for the increasingly pejorative connotations of the term 'petite bourgeoisie' in contrast to *Mittelstand*. In view of the 'iron law' of growing economic concentration, the desire of this social grouping to remain independent inevitably seemed irrational. True, the predicted downfall did not occur, but in political discussion the thesis of extinction played an important part, especially in Germany. For Geiger the German movement of the *Mittelstand* at the end of the nineteenth century is only a confirmation of Marxist prognoses. 'Didn't the cries for help of the middle class prove that it saw itself in danger of being destroyed between the fronts and that on the struggle of the two major classes hung the fate of the third one? Anti-Marxism in political praxis confirmed the social theory of Marxism' (Geiger, 1949, p. 97).

Essentially, the economic situation of the craft and retail trades developed similarly in various European countries. What was different was the ideological interpretation and the willingness of the governments to pursue an active *Mittelstandspolitik*. In Germany, Anti-Marxism as a reaction to Marxist revolutionary rhetoric may have played an important part in the ideological interpretation of the situation. It is noticeable that before 1914 in Germany, in contrast to England, there was a politically influential movement of the middle-class with independent ideological elements (Gellately, 1974).

The self-employed artisans and retailers did not find themselves in the same objective economic situations. Many artisans had to compete directly with industry in an unequal struggle whose outcome Marx had predicted. At the time of the Great Depression lasting from 1873 to 1896, many gave up their businesses. After the Depression, such enterprises went through a phase of consolidation; larger workshops of artisans which were not in direct competition with industry were in the main able to survive. The same growing demand which favoured the retailers was profitable for part of the artisans' trade. In the German

Reich, the number of small businesses increased from the beginning of the 1880s until World War I (cf. Pesl, 1926, p. 104).

That is not to say that individual retailers were not in danger. Individual insolvencies and the existence or even the growth of an economic grouping are not incompatible. In the period before World War I some authors assert that the number of retailers grew even quicker than the favourable conditions warranted (cf. Gellately, 1974, pp. 28– 57). The number of economic openings compared to the number of firms wanting to take advantage of them was of course inevitably less favourable in times of crisis. This seems to apply particularly to the retail trade, as in times of crisis some previously dependent employees go into business on their own. Thus, for the Weimar Republic, Geiger can talk of a 'founding time for small traders' with the consequent growth of 'proletarianised' existences in trade.

In this paper we can start from the null-hypothesis of 'the stubborn almost incomprehensible persistence of the stratum in all industrial capitalist societies . . . ' (Bechhofer and Elliott, 1976, p. 75). We can presume that the decline of the self-employed in the Federal Republic in the period between 1950 and 1970 was essentially caused by the fact that the proletarianised self-employed became employees.

In the period of the Kaiserreich the feeling of uncertainty among all the petite bourgeoisie concerning their own economic future which stemmed both from the objective realities of trade and from their subjective experiences, led to a large number of defensive measures. The best documentation can be found in the history of interest organisations (*Verbandsgeschichte*). Most relevant for our purposes are the attempts to found a homogeneous ideological movement of the *Mittelstand*. This ideology has often been described (Geiger, 1967; Lepsius, 1966; Winkler, 1971). The *'Puffertheorie'* which depicted the *Mittelstand* as a balancing power between the antagonistic classes was directly political in its aims.

These ideas can be directly linked to National Socialism (see for example Wehler, 1969), but one should not forget that these conclusions stem from research on the history of interest organisations which tells us more about the leaders than the members. Recently, voices have been heard warning us not simply to take over the interpretive schemes of contemporary politicians of primarily conservative leanings, without questioning and checking them (Blackbourn, 1977).

The attempt of the conservatives in Germany to create a mass base in the *Mittelstand* with the help of these ideologies – remember the 'Kartell der schaffenden Stände' shortly before World War I – showed the greater importance of the middle class in Germany than elsewhere. In Great Britain, at any rate, retailers for instance have been virtually overlooked in official politics before and after World War I (Gellately, 1974).

The ideology of the *Mittelstand* which is used in the political struggle may have strengthened the desire of the private white-collar workers and officials to belong to this middle class. Organisational mergers of the self-employed and parts of this new middle class, however, were not successful in the long run. The economic interests of the old and the so-called new middle class very quickly diverged. First the technical employees organised themselves into their own trade unions and no longer in '*Standesorganisationen*' and then the employees in trade gave up the idea of '*Harmonie-Verbände*' (Speier, 1977, pp. 124–44). Despite these differences of economic interest, this self-classification as *Mittelstand* on the part of white-collar workers was not merely the false class consciousness of a 'stiff-collar proletariat'. What they had in common were their claims to social acceptance. In his dissertation – written in the last years of the Weimar Republic, but published only in 1977 – Hans Speier argues that this wish for social acceptance is an essential cause of the white-collar workers' identification with the *Mittelstand*. Thus, Speier took over Weber's distinction between economic classes and prestige classes. The peculiarity of the white-collar employees in the Weimar Republic consisted in the fact that they were not accepted as a prestige class of their own, but had to borrow prestige from other classes such as the old middle class.

Speier remarked, quite rightly, that the class theorists ran into difficulties, 'when they wanted to understand the peculiarities of the white-collar in contrast to the blue-collar workers'. Theorists of the *Mittelstand* however, lacked the methodological means to explain 'what white-collar employees and workers had in common socio-economically' (p. 18). At first sight the conventional interpretation of the objective developments seemed to show that the *Mittelstand* theorists were right. Neither Marx's prognosis of the extinction of the old middle class nor his predicted homogenisation of the proletariat came about. It was a particular problem for orthodox Marxists when the 'stiff-collar proletariat', in spite of their class situation, did not want to become supporters of a socialist policy. 'Class theory explained the middle class behaviour of the white collar unions by their "false consciousness".' But how did it explain the false consciousness itself? (Speier, 1977, p. 87).

To sum up the historical development of the self-employed petite bourgeoisie and new middle class in Germany, one might venture the thesis that the development of the idea of the *Mittelstand* owes its essential impulses to Anti-Marxism, which had its origin in a reaction to Marxist revolutionary rhetoric. The fact that in Germany in general the idea of estates survived longer than in France or Great Britain, is due to industrialisation beginning later and to the late introduction of freedom of trade (*Gewerbefreiheit*). After industrialisation commenced, the objective development of the various economic and occupational groupings was generally the same as in other industrial societies. But before one can make statements about differentiation and homogenisation in the middle classes, a sociological gap must be bridged. So far we have not explained how more comprehensive social groups arise from economic and occupational categories. Was the ideology of the *Mittelstand* merely an idea existing only in the heads of the functionaries of the diverse-interest organisations?

The Structuration of Class and Status Group Relations

With Max Weber and Hans Speier, we encounter two sociological concepts, social classes and status groups which emerge out of the variety of economic and occupational classifications. Status groups are aggregates which successfully lay claim to a special evaluation (Weber, 1922, p. 180). An important question therefore is, whether one permits a juxtaposition of different evaluations or requires a clear hierarchy of social groups according to a uniform criterion. Thus, Speier adopts the stringent second alternative when he wants to speak of a 'society' (*Gesellschaft*) as comprising the entire population only if 'either there is a single monopolistic value principle or if there is a recognized rank order of value principles' (1977, p. 91). In accordance with his stringent criterion, in the Weimar Republic different 'societies' with incompatible evaluations were juxtaposed.

When Speier stresses at the same time 'that German society was a capitalist society in the period of the Weimar Republic' (p. 90) he entirely changes the frame of reference. The capitalist character of a society does not result from current value systems, but solely from the antagonistic distribution of the means of production. In a development of Marx's idea of classes, the objective class situation is to be understood as control over economically usable resources, whether in the form of power over the means of production or in the form of occupational qualifications or manual manpower (cf. here the term 'market capacity' in Giddens, 1973, p. 103). Social classes only come about when the use of resources on the market results in more durable coalitions.

Problems such as these concerning the sociology of status groups and classes cannot be solved here. The aim of this chapter is rather to work out clearly the conditions for the formation of classes and status groups, especially for the petite bourgeoisie and the new middle class. As this theoretical analysis is of course not without underlying assumptions, we will state them here in the form of postulates.

We start by asserting the primacy of the social division of labour. Irrespective of its possible causes, we will describe this division of labour as the differentiation of knowledge and abilities which are demanded on the labour market in form of occupations. The coordination of individual occupational skills with units of production can thus no longer be carried out exclusively by way of ascription. Behind the market mechanism is the development of generalised conceptions about the usefulness of occupations, which at the same time makes these occupations the most important links for non-economic status evaluation. Thus, occupations become the starting point of status group as well as of class formation.

The social division of labour on the demand side is joined by the further principles of the legally institutionalised organisation of labour in manufacturing firms, and the power to dispose of the products of labour. In capitalist societies both are linked to property rights over the means of production. A secondary aspect of the organisation of labour is the existence of legally guaranteed prerogatives for the holders of particular positions in the firm.

As the division of labour increases the differentiation of the positions can be empirically captured in occupational classifications. The further principles of the organisation of labour can be approximated by the variable 'class of worker' (*Stellung im Beruf*), which is customary in Germany.

With occupation and 'class of worker' as variables, significant units can be defined economically and to some extent even socially. More comprehensive social groups such as status groups and classes can only be built out of social relations which link these units. Classes form out of coalitions and collective conflicts, in the exchange of economic resources. Status groups are formed via affectually positive relations among the basic units, so that it comes down to consolidations of interaction zones on the one hand and a hierarchic order due to non-mutual choices on the other hand (see Table 5.1). The above can be exemplified with block models (see White *et al.*, 1976; Breiger, 1978). Where an antagonistic class structure can be inferred from social relations, occupations with similar interest profiles are combined into two confronting coalitions without connection with one another, and in the event of conflict they will fight against each other and not among

TABLE 5.1   Class structure: status group structure

Antagonistic class structure				Status group structure
Instrumentally				
Positive relations		*Negative relations*		*Expressive positive relations*
1	0	0	1	1 0
0	1	1	0	1 1

themselves. In the status group structure the emotionally positive relations lead to closely connected groupings – the ones in the diagonal – and to a hierarchic order in the sense that the higher rank does not replicate the choices of the lower rank to the same degree. Here we have a strong criterion of hierarchy which is inferred from the actual behaviour one to one another of the members of the different status groups. It is a weaker criterion if one requires only that the ranks differ according to some measure of their social status, for example the average occupational prestige of their members.

In so far as theoreticians ever see the problem of status group and class structure in terms of the social relations of the units one to another, they focus on one kind of relation only. According to Giddens, processes of social closure in mobility chances lead to the reproduction of common life-experiences from generation to generation, and thus generate social classes as identifiable collectivities (1973, p. 107). According to K. U. Mayer, 'the family and inter-family relations are the basis of the formation of status-group solidarity . . . , which crystallizes around a common style of life' (1977, p. 60). Here, the patterns of inter-marriage between the occupational groups become of paramount importance. Other authors give preference to the structural principle of friendship choices (see Laumann, 1973; Pappi, 1973). We lack both a theoretical starting point as well as a method with the help of which the variety of structural principles can be put into order.

Theoretically we must postulate that both types of structure should be demonstrable in the daily interaction of a society. How useful would an historical explanation of the mobility chances of certain occupational groups be if these were irrelevant for the behaviour of the members of classes or status groups one to another? As a primary principle of structuration for *social classes*, we therefore suggest the instrumentally positive relations which form between occupational groups through common memberships in interest groups and the instrumentally-negative relations of strikes. For the structuration of *status groups*, we first suggest as constitutive elements – friendship choices – which may be mutual or not; that is to say they will not always be symmetric. Mobility chances form structuration criteria of a somewhat synthetic character causing the formation both of status groups and social classes. Thus, occupational mobility will tend to lead to structures of *classes* because of its greater dependence on the labour market, and marriage mobility will tend to lead to structures of *status groups* because of the dependence of the marriage relationship on aspects of prestige.

With the help of this theoretical starting point and the method of block-modelling we can ascertain the place of the petite bourgeoisie and the new middle class in the class and status group structure of the Federal Republic. Here we shall report the results of such an analysis.

The starting units of this investigation were 17 occupational groups, which were constructed by combining the 7 major groups of the International Standard Classification of Occupations with the variable 'class of worker' (self-employed, state officials (Beamte), non-manual employees, manual workers). Two groups can certainly be included in the petite bourgeoisie: the small self-employed in trade and service, and the self-employed craftsmen. Among the initial categories used, the peasants and the freelance professionals are further examples of the self-employed.

Certainly, the office clerks would *a priori* be included in the new middle class, as would be the employees in trade and service and the employees among the professional, technical and related workers. The bulk of production and production-related workers were included in the analysis as skilled, semi-skilled or unskilled.

Methodologically, the problem is to combine the 17 starting groups into fewer units according to the criterion of resemblance over several social relations. The result forms an *empirical* classification. The cell frequencies of the respective 17 × 17-tables are very unevenly distributed. The rows and columns are to be permuted in such a way that so-called zero-blocks are generated, that is, whole regions in the table with very small frequencies.[1]

For the Federal Republic, not all the necessary types of social relation for class and status group structures were at my disposal. Therefore, the following analysis confines itself to the proximity between occupations in terms of membership in trade unions and occupational organisations, of the inter-generational mobility of men, of the marriage mobility of women (occupations of father v. occupation of spouse), and of the intra-generational mobility of men (first v. present occupation).

Their similarity in terms of these four types of relations, gives rise to the following groupings of occupations: (A) professional, technical and related workers, in so far as they are employed; (B) the employees in offices and service including foremen (Werkmeister); (C) the self-employed in the professions, in craft and in trade, and (D) the workers as a whole including the peasants. These groupings are to be seen, of course, in the light of the relations used. For instance, the fact that the peasants are seen as part of the working class is to be traced back to the use of mobility tables, for the sons of peasants generally decline to the working class if they do not take over their parents' farm, and this transition is not infrequent, even in a peasant's normal occupational career. That the petite bourgeoisie are joined together into one group, including the self-employed professionals, is the result of the matrix of union and occupational association membership. All groups of *employees* are connected to one another by varying levels of *Deutscher Gewerkschaftsbund* (DGB) memberships. The connection of the self-employed professionals with the employed professionals through special *occupational* associations does not suffice to surmount the split

TABLE 5.2   Block models

Inter-generational mobility of men					Marriage mobility of women			
	A	B	C	D		A	B	C	D
A	1	0	1	0	A	1	1	1	0
B	1	1	1	0	B	1	1	1	0
C	0	0	0	0	C	1	1	1	0
D	0	1	1	1	D	0	0	1	1

Intra-generational mobility of men					Structure of interest group membership			
	A	B	C	D		A	B	C	D
A	1	0	0	0	A	1	1	1	1
B	1	1	1	0	B	1	1	0	1
C	0	0	0	0	C	1	0	1	1
D	0	1	0	1	D	1	1	1	1

with regard to trade union membership. The group which overall we described earlier as new middle class breaks down into two blocks; the generally academically trained professionals in block A and the rest in block B. This separation also reflects a classification of prestige, so that the employees in offices, trade and service (block B) constitute that part of the new middle class which has approximately the same prestige ranking as the petit bourgeois occupations (block C).

The structures of classes and status groups are better seen in block model diagrams than in verbal descriptions. These diagrams reflect in condensed form the relations between the four blocks of (A) salaried professionals, (B) the new middle class in a narrower sense, (C) the petite bourgeoisie and (D) the workers. The status group structure as a rough dichotomisation of society into a working class and a middle class is most clearly expressed in the marriage mobility of women. A middle class, well connected in itself, is distinguished from the workers, while women coming from workers' families still have a more than proportional chance to rise up to the petite bourgeoisie. Thus, we get the form of hierarchy typical of the relations between status groups.

If we look at the structure of interest group membership as the best approximation of the tendencies towards class formation, then we can see that the 'lower' new middle class and the petite bourgeoisie, which occupy about the same rank as far as prestige is concerned, are the only groups which are not accessible to one another. The economic interests of these two groups emphatically exclude a class connection.

The inter- and intra-generational mobility of men make the structural affinities within the middle classes visible. The lower new middle class (block B) is, if we judge exclusively by the pattern of the ones and zeros, in a lower position than the salaried professionals, (block A). On the other hand, within the middle class the petite bourgeoisie is relatively isolated.

In order to be able to make a statement regarding the status group structure as unequivocal as that concerning the class split in German society, we need to consult the pattern of friendship relations. Data about friendship choices in the appropriate occupational coding are at our disposal only for a small German town. A separate block-model analysis of the data for these friendship choices of men and women results, apart from insignificant deviations, in the same block-classifications as the one we have just discussed above. For men, for instance, we get the following pattern of friendship relations between salaried professionals and the petite bourgeoisie:

Friendship choices of middle-class men in a small German town

	A	C
A	1	1
C	1	0

This is the pattern which Breiger (1978) describes as 'centre and periphery'. The centre of the professionals is well connected in itself, and on its part chooses the petite bourgeoisie periphery in the same way as it is chosen by it. But within itself the periphery has no social coherence. The class split of the middle strata and the hierarchical classification within the new middle class in a broader sense (blocks A and B) is joined by a third structural principle, namely the peripheral social position of the petite bourgeoisie.

Differentiation or Homogenisation of the Middle Strata

The observed status group differentiation and the class division within the middle strata provide little indication of any tendency towards homogenisation. Up to now, however, we have a description of the situation which does not necessarily tell us anything about developmental tendencies. If we want to establish the development of greater differentiation or homogenisation we first must state the criteria by which these changes are to be assessed.

Here we differentiate between three types of processual change. First, the size of the different classes and status groups can change; secondly, the kinds of relationship between the units can change; and thirdly, the consequences of the status group and class structure for the behaviour and attitudes of the members can change.

Marx's prediction of the decline of the petite bourgeoisie into the proletariat is a developmental thesis of the first type. Generally, we can understand changes in the occupational structure as a consequence of three processes: industrialisation, bureaucratisation and professionalisation. The growth of the working class in the phase of industrialisation was followed by the growth of clerical occupations due to increasing bureaucratisation and the growth of scientific and technically skilled tasks in the course of the professionalisation of work. These processes led to a relative decrease of the older occupations; they did not lead to large parts of these occupational groups disappearing *in toto*. Homogenisation of the middle strata in line with this first type of change would mean a progressive increase in the size of the new middle class relative to the petite bourgeoisie. Homogenisation in this trivial sense is indeed to be found.

In the literature, changes in the relationships between occupational groups have most frequently been described in terms of typical channels of mobility. Thus, for instance, it was claimed that up to the Weimar Republic the middle and upper white-collar positions were occupied by persons of petit-bourgeois origin, whereas today they would primarily be filled from lower white-collar positions. This statement seems to be right insofar as nowadays clerical and sales workers do indeed have overproportional access to the more prestigious professions, whereas these careers are denied to the petite bourgeoisie as well as to the workers.

Homogenisation according to this second criterion would mean that the diagrams for the three sectors of the middle class would increasingly be filled with ones. As we have seen though this holds only in the case of the marriage mobility of women. The conditions of the labour market do not seem to be promoting further homogenisation within the middle classes. Instead it might be supposed that the barrier to mobility between the petite bourgeoisie and the new middle class has been strengthening since World War II.

The statements about homogenisation or differentiation most frequently refer to the third type of processual change distinguished here: a levelling between the different status groups and classes as far as attitudes and behaviour are concerned. In the course of increasing modernisation, it was predicted that traditional occupational milieux would progressively disappear.

In Germany, the share of the petit bourgeois occupations has decreased since World War II. If one supposes that this decrease was primarily caused by the movement of those with proletarianised modes of life to the expanding white-collar sector, it suggests anything but a tendency towards homogenisation in the middle strata. This latter hypothesis, however, only applies to those attitudes which are centrally identified with the class split in the middle strata, and these are primarily political attitudes. A petite bourgeoisie which, shrunk to 'normal' size, prospers economically is likely to give stronger support to conservative economic and social policy opposing welfarism, than would an economically weakened petite bourgeoisie, which itself was in dire need of subsidies.

If we investigate the voting behaviour of the new middle class and the petite bourgeoisie, this can be confirmed. In the past 25 years, the new middle class has associated itself politically more and more with the working class, so that the difference from the petite bourgeoisie, which overwhelmingly votes for the Christian Democratic Union (CDU), becomes bigger and not smaller (see Pappi, 1976).

Whereas political attitudes directly depend on the economic situation of social classes, in other areas of life such as consumer behaviour, for example, this dependence cannot be given such theoretical underpinning. The marking out of special styles of life is primarily a phenomenon of status group differentiation. Since, according to our results the petite bourgeoisie cannot in any way be defind as a status group, because it lacks the necessary social cohesion, it consequently cannot embody a uniform style of life which would provide a frame of reference for other classes.

On the other hand, the new middle class has changed internally since World War II. The numbers of sales and service workers, employed in small firms, decreased in favour of clerical workers and above all in favour of professionals and semi-professionals. The prestige and social dominance of the professionals is likely to lead increasingly to emulation of their whole style of life. If, however, the remains of a petit-bourgeois tradition are to be cultivated by another class, then it is most likely to be by the workers. As far as consumption is concerned, if we paid more attention to the differences of style then to the mere ownership of consumer goods and durables, we would be able to find sharper differentiation beneath the allegedly levelled mass culture. Thus, if we consider living-room furniture, for instance, we can show that members of those professional occupations typical of the post-industrial society tend to prefer modern styles, whereas the petite bourgeoisie, as well as many of the workers and certain parts of the new middle class, are oriented to the past (See Pappi and Pappi, 1978). To the extent that the structure of the new middle class changes, new differentiations arise which isolate the petite bourgeoisie somewhat less than political attitudes which, in accordance with economic class situation, lead to sharp cleavages. But clearly, these new contrasts and similarities in styles of life cannot be described by the catchword – 'homogenisation'.

Summary

At the beginning I mentioned a popular practice among empirical social researchers of working with clearly hierarchical classifications of strata. In view of the results presented here, it is difficut to understand this practice. A middling position on indicators of social status, measured one way or another, simply does not tell us enough; it tells us neither about the structure of relations between the strata, nor about the many aspects of social behaviour. In Germany, the middle classes are strongly differentiated within themselves. The differentiation of the petite bourgeoisie and the new middle class is an economic class division highly relevant for political behaviour, and the differentiation between professionals and the rest of the new middle class is an important division of status groups. Nowadays, as far as status groups are concerned, the petite bourgeoisie, not socially homogeneous and cohesive in itself, is to be found on the periphery of the middle strata.

In Germany, the petite bourgeoisie were the first to discuss questions concerning the middle strata. In defending itself against the Marxist theses, the new middle class thought it best to claim social honour by associating itself with the *Mittelstand* movement and with the ideological connotations of that term. But even in the Weimar Republic this connection was already problematic, as white collar employees developed a more positive orientation to the trade unions. After World War II, this political division was soon accompanied by ideological and cultural separation. The new middle class is no longer in the position of borrowing its values (*wertparasitar*), (Speier, 1977). As the labour force has become more professionalised, the new middle class has developed a rationale for its own social importance and finally separated itself from the old German *Mittelstand* ideology.

NOTE

1. To get rid of the size effect the original frequencies were not used as inputs to the block-model analysis, but the interaction terms after having removed the marginal effects with the program ECTA by Leo Goodman (1970). These interaction terms were then dichotomised, the threshold value being $= 0.50$, and used as input data to a version of CONCOR (cf. Breiger *et al.*, 1975) written by Clyde Mitchell and C. Payne of Nuffield College, Oxford.

REFERENCES

F. Bechhofer and B. Elliott, 'Persistence and change: The Petite Bourgeoisie in Industrial Society', *European Journal of Sociology*, XVII (1976) 74–98.

D. Blackbourn, 'The Mittelstand in German Society and Politics', *Social History*, 4 (1977) 409–33.

R. L. Breiger, 'Toward an Operational Theory of Community Elite Structures', *Quality and Quantity*, 12 (1978).

R. L. Breiger, S. A. Boorman and P. Arabie, 'An Algorithm for Clustering Relational Data with Applications to Social Network Analysis and Comparisons with Multidimensional Scaling', *Journal of Mathematical Psychology*, 12 (1975) 328–83.

H. M. Enzensberger, 'Von der Unaufhaltsamkeit des Kleinbürgertums: Eine soziologische Grille', *Kursbuch*, 45 (1976) 1–8.

T. Geiger, *Die Klassengesellschaft im Schmelztiegel* (Köln and Hagen: Verlag Gustav Kiepenheuer, 1949).

T. Geiger, *Die soziale Schichtung des deutschen Volkes* (Darmstadt: Wissenschaftliche Buchgesellschaft, 1967; 1st edn., 1932).

R. Gellately, *The Politics of Economic Despair* (London: Sage Publications, 1974).

A. Giddens, *The Class Structure of the Advanced Societies* (London: Hutchinson University Library, 1973).

L. A. Goodman, 'The Multivariate Analysis of Qualitative Data: Interactions among Multiple Classifications', *Journal of the American Statistical Association*, 65 (1970) 226–56.

E. O. Laumann, *Bonds of Pluralism: The Form and Substance of Urban Social Networks* (New York: Wiley, 1973).

M. R. Lepsius, *Extremer Nationalismus*, (Stuttgart: Kohlhammer, 1966).

K. U. Mayer, *Fluktuation und Umschichtung: Empirische Untersuchungen zu Strukturen sozialer Ungleichheit und Prozessen sozialer Mobilität in der Bundesrepublik Deutschland* (Unpublished 'Habilitationsschrift', Faculty of Social Sciences, University of Mannheim, 1977).

W.-D. Narr and C. Offe, 'Wohlfahrtsstaadt und Massenloyalität: Einleitung', in W.-D. Narr and C. Offe (eds.), *Wohlfahrtsstaadt und Massenloyalität* (Köln: Kiepenheuer and Witsch, 1975).

F. U. Pappi, 'Sozialstruktur und soziale Schichtung in einer Kleinstadt mit heterogener Bevölkerung', *Kölner Zeitschrift für Soziologie und Sozialpsychologie*, 25 (1973) 23–74.

F. U. Pappi, *Sozialstruktur und politische Konflikte in der Bundesrepublik: Individual-und Kontextanalysen der Wahlentscheidung* (Unpublished 'Habilitationsschrift', Economic and Social Sciences Faculty, University of Cologne, 1976).

F. U. Pappi and I. Pappi, 'Sozialer Status und Konsumstil: Eine Fallstudie zur Wohnzimmerreinrichtung', *Kölner Zeitschrift für Soziologie und Sozialpsychologie*, 30 (1978) 87–115.

L. D. Pesl, 'Mittelstandsfragen, (Der gewerbliche und kaufmännische Mittelstand)', in *Grundriss der Sozialökonomik, Section 9, Part 1* (Tübingen: Mohr (Paul Siebeck), 1926).

W. H. Riehl, *Die bürgerliche Gesellschaft*, 11th edn. (Stuttgart and Berlin: Cotta'sche Buchhandlung Nachfolger, 1930).

H. Schelsky, 'Die Bedeutung des Schichtbegriffs für die Analyse der gegenwärtigen deutschen Gesellschaft', in H. Schelsky, *Auf der Suche nach der*

Wirklichkeit: Gesammelte Aufsätze (Düsseldorf and Köln: Diederichs, 1965, first published, 1953).

Hans Speier, *Die Angestellten vor dem Nationalsozialismus* (Göttingen: Vandenhoek and Rupprecht, 1977).

M. Weber, *Grundriss der Sozialökonomik, Part 3: Wirtschaft und Gesellschaft* (Tübingen: Mohr (Paul Siebeck), 1922).

H.- U. Wehler, *Bismarck und der Imperialismus* (Köln and Berlin, 1969).

H. C. White, S. A. Boorman and R. L. Breiger, 'Social Structure from Multiple Networks. 1. Blockmodels of Roles and Positions', *American Journal of Sociology,* 81 (1976) 730–80.

H. A. Winkler, 'Der rückversicherte Mittelstand: Die Interessenverbände von Handwerk und Kleinhandel im deutschen Kaiserreich', in W. Rüegg and O. Neuloh (eds.), *Zur soziologischen Theorie und Analyse des 19 Jahrhunderts* (Göttingen: Vandenhoek and Rupprecht, 1971).

6 The Petty Commodity Producer in Third World Cities: Petit-Bourgeois or 'Disguised' Proletarian?

CHRIS GERRY AND CHRIS BIRKBECK

The definition of class according to the nature of the relations of production has traditionally centred on the distinction between the bourgeoisie and the proletariat, a focus which has involved the identification of concepts which are in direct contradiction – the private ownership of the means of production by a privileged minority and the necessary sale of labour power by the majority. This situation is mirrored in the essentially antagonistic relationship normally existing between the two classes, which finds expression, at least in theory, in the ideologies of each class. Whilst the division between bourgeois and proletarian may be used as the foundation of class analysis, it does not take account of the complexities of class formation which may exist at any stage in the development (or, indeed, the overthrow) of capitalism. The dissolution of 'pure' ownership of the means of production into separate but closely related functions of possession and control (Wright, 1976, pp. 21–6) and the consequent existence of more complex technical relations of production (for example the functions of foremen, supervisors and managers) is evidence that there are some jobs – perhaps the majority in advanced industrial society – which combine within the individual, elements of both the classical bourgeois and proletarian roles in the production process. Additionally, there may be persons who are self-employed and who appear to lie outside the principal sphere of large-scale capitalism. How to classify those workers who do not easily fit into the two-fold class division, has been something of a problem for social scientists. Not only is it difficult to identify the precise nature of the relations of production within capitalism, but also the analysis of ideology has proved particularly intractable. Confusion has arisen out of the failure within the analysis of class formation to identify and attach sufficient importance to both the economic and the politico-ideological components of the process. How are we to explain the existence of a 'proletarian' who votes for a party of the right? How are we to navigate the theoretical currents generated, on the one hand, by those who see embourgeoisement and on the other by those who identify proletarianisation as the dominant trend in contemporary class formation?

It is in the context of these conceptual problems that the debate on classes and class formation in under-developing countries assumes particular interests, for, if such problems confound social scientists in the study of advanced capitalist society, then it must be said that they increase when attention is turned to the Third World. There, we are confronted with an economic and social formation which is markedly different in composition. In certain circumstances it may even be misleading to employ the term 'capitalist mode of production' (Kitching, 1977, pp. 56–9). Nevertheless, for the purposes of our analysis, we take the view that many underdeveloped economies will be characterised by capitalism, but a capitalism distinguished by several features. On the one hand it is linked in a highly dependent way with the developed capitalist economies, and the commanding heights of the economy are normally controlled by foreign capital. On the other hand, the structure of employment is also different. Not only is the sectoral distribution of the working population much more heavily weighted towards agriculture, but there is also an apparent shortage of capital, and a marked structural inequality in the distribution of that capital and great unevenness in its accumulation. Foreign capital, as well as the majority of that originating from the relatively small indigenous capitalist class, is largely dedicated to relatively capital-intensive production. As a result, the creation of well-remunerated employment opportunities in 'western-style' enterprises is limited in comparison to the growth in the size of the working population. In Colombia, for example, during the 1960s the active labour force was growing at a rate of not less than 200,000 per year, whilst by contrast agriculture could only provide 30,000 new jobs per year, and the modern manufacturing sector 10,000 new jobs per year. The rest of the labour force '. . . has been absorbed in construction, handicrafts and services, often somewhat artificially – or has not been absorbed at all' (ILO, 1970, p. 34). This would appear to be a familiar descriptive schema for most Third World countries.

The results are well known: a relatively small working class, and, whether we accept the dictates of labour surplus theory or not, a sizeable portion of the labour force who appear to be 'forced' into creating their own jobs with very scarce capital resources, 'primitive technology', and little enterprise. The artisan and the street trader are perhaps the classic examples of this and the following is a not untypical view of the way in which this employment is generated:

> Entrance to the occupations in question is open. Most of them require little or no skill and also little or no capital. They thus provide a natural entry point for migrants from the country, who win a precarious foothold in the urban economy by crowding into petty trade, services and other small-scale activities. Overmanning of these activities contributes to low output and income per worker. (Reynolds, 1969, p. 91)

In addition, it has been usual to conceptualise this development as somehow dualistic – the 'traditional' and 'modern' sectors, the 'formal' and 'informal' sectors, the 'firm-centred' and 'bazaar' economies – and in the same way low income employment opportunities are often referred to as the 'marginal' occupations, 'underemployment' and even the '*lumpenproletariat*' (Fanon, 1967, and Cohen and Michael, 1973). Rather than accept these dualist interpretations, and for reasons which will become apparent during the development of our argument, we prefer to use the term 'petty commodity production'.

In referring to petty commodity production we make no *initial* attempt to characterise that production as something essentially separate or different from the rest of the economy. It is used in the first instance as a descriptive term for those workers who apparently fall 'outside' the major axis of capitalist production and/or market relations.

The principal focus of this paper is therefore the way in which we might make a class analysis of petty producers. There is a considerable body of literature that might be drawn upon for this task, for social scientists have never been content to posit a simple two-class structure, rather they have attempted to take more account of the complexities of reality. In this sense we think particularly of the literature on the petite bourgeoisie, for, at the level of appearances at least, petty producers would seem to have much in common with the notion of a petit-bourgeois stratum. Nevertheless, the concept is somewhat problematical, in that the various ways in which the term has been and is used have obscured rather than clarified analysis. Indeed, as is often the case in social science there seems to be no agreement about what might constitute a petite bourgeoisie.

Bechhofer and Elliott (1976, p. 76) have defined the petite bourgeoisie by its 'occupational base', rather than by directly analysing the relations of production. By this method the petite bourgeoisie are defined as the owners of small enterprises, using a relatively low level of technology, and employing a small and weakly differentiated labour force. Whilst this approach may take some account of political reality in that particular occupations may have specific political leanings, the lack of an analysis of the relations of production clearly invites ambiguity. In particular, we see that he who is being defined is the small, low technology capitalist. How are we to identify the class boundaries between, for example, the economically powerful capitalist who uses relatively low-level technology, and small capitalists who employ expensive, technically advanced means of production?

A second approach has been that of Poulantzas (1973), who argues firstly for a petite bourgeoisie that is defined by its ownership of capital, its control over the production process, and the fact that it does not employ the labour power of others. This is called by him the 'traditional petite bourgeoisie', and is clearly differentiated from the petite bourgeoisie of Bechhofer and Elliott by its emphasis on the self-employment of the producer and the fact that no direct recourse is made to the purchase of the labour-power of others.

In addition, Poulantzas identifies a group which he terms the 'new petite bourgeoisie', and this is composed of those managers, technicians and other white collar workers in large enterprises who have some control over the productive process, and who may be subject to exploitation to a more limited extent than the classic proletariat.

This analysis has been subsequently taken further, and considerably modified by Wright (1976) who, whilst accepting the existence of a traditional petite bourgeoisie in accordance with Poulantzas' definition, would nevertheless argue against the notion of a 'new petite bourgeoisie'. Although the theoretical validity of the concepts of bourgeoisie and proletariat will not be disputed here, we should not always expect to find them clearly outlined in reality. In particular Wright stresses the importance of distinguishing between 'economic ownership' and 'possession' when considering the ownership of the means of production, and the consequences that spring from this. Thus, in criticising the work of Poulantzas he comments that:

> . . . in his analysis of the working class, any deviation . . . from the pure working class criteria . . . is sufficient for exclusion from the proletariat; in his analysis of the bourgeoisie, on the other hand, it is necessary to deviate on *all* criteria in order to be excluded from the capitalist class. In neither case is the possibility allowed that positions within the social division of labour can be objectively contradictory. An alternative way of dealing with such ambiguities in the class structure is to regard some positions as occupying objectively *contradictory locations within class relations*. (Wright, 1976, p. 26. Emphasis in original)

For Wright, therefore, there are three classes in society: the bourgeoisie, the petite bourgeoisie and the proletariat. He identifies three groups of

FIGURE 6.1. The relationship of contradictory class locations to the basic class forces in capitalist society

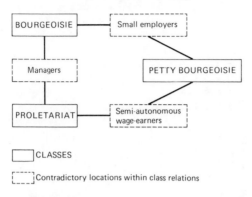

Source: Wright (1976, p. 27)

workers who are conceived as being in contradictory class locations between these classes: managers, small employers and semi-autonomous wage earners.

Put at its simplest, Wright is arguing that there are many jobs which combine elements of both the bourgeois and the proletarian, and we should take account of this in class analysis. Whilst we are in agreement with Wright's conclusions, we are led to ask if they go far enough, particularly in the maintenance of the term petite bourgeoisie. This is essentially for two reasons. Firstly, because as we hope to show from our own evidence, the concept of self-employment embodied in Wright's term 'petite bourgeoisie' may be found far less frequently than is apparently the case. In particular, there may be many 'self-employed' who in reality are little more than semi-autonomous employees. Secondly, as both Poulantzas and Wright stress, class analysis must rest not only on economic criteria, but also on political and ideological criteria. Wright suggests that the concept of contradictory class locations allows for the existence of competing and contradictory elements within the political development of the worker – a process which may itself be subject to particularly rapid change. Hence, those in contradictory class locations may or may not be supportive of capitalism. Taking the argument to its logical conclusion, we may be just as correct in speaking of the 'grand' proletariat as the petite bourgeoisie. Similarly, the economic characteristics of the traditional petite bourgeoisie do not necessarily imply a political stance in total accord with bourgeois values; indeed very often the continued viability of petit bourgeois economic activities has required a political stance to be taken which was in direct conflict with the policy preferences of the bourgeoisie.

TABLE 6.1 Contradictory locations within class relations

	SUBSTANTIVE SOCIAL PROCESSES COMPRISING CLASS RELATIONS			JURIDICAL CATEGORIES OF CLASS RELATIONS		
	Economic ownership	Possession		Legal ownership		Wage labour
	Control over investments, resources	Control over the physical means of production	Control over the labour power of others	Legal ownership of property (capital, stocks, real estate, etc.)	Legal status of being the employer of labour power	Sale of one's own labour power
Bourgeoisie						
Traditional capitalist	+	+	+	+	+	–
Top corporate executive	+	+	+	partial	–	minimal
Contradictory location between the proletariat and the bourgeoisie						
Top managers	partial/minimal	+	+	minimal	–	partial
Middle managers	minimal/–	partial	partial	–	–	+
Technocrats	–	minimal	minimal	–	–	+
Foremen/line supervisors	–	–	minimal	–	–	+
Proletariat	–	–	–	–	–	+
Contradictory location between the proletariat and the petty bourgeoisie						
Semi-autonomous employees	–	minimal	–	–	–	+
Petty bourgeoisie	+	+	–	+	–	–
Contradictory location between the petty bourgeoisie and the bourgeoisie						
Small employers	+	+	minimal	+	minimal	–

+ = full control,   minimal = residual control,   partial = attenuated control,   – = no control
Source: **Wright** (1976, p. 33)

To have a stake in capitalism does not automatically mean that one will support the particular brand of capitalism offered by one's economic and political masters. To class all those who may not be proletarian as bourgeois is, we feel, a gross oversimplification of a complex reality, and to allow for this variability we need a class analysis which encourages more disaggregation (and thus a dialectical approach) rather than the monolithic (or should it be duolithic?) formulation so often encountered in the literature.

In this paper, we will be examining these problems in the context of underdeveloped countries. Our discussion will be confined to urban areas, although the analysis may offer a point of departure for the examination of the class locations of other groups such as the peasantry. We will attempt to show that many of the apparently 'self-employed' (and hence apparently 'petit bourgeois') members of the labour force are not in fact self-employed at all, and that there often exists a considerable degree of contradiction in their corresponding class locations. In particular we will use empirical evidence from Senegal and Colombia, where our own fieldwork has taken place. Our aim is to review the characteristics of petty producers, their relations over time with the dominant mode of production and specifically the relationship with contemporary capitalism. Following this, an attempt will be made to clarify their class location, and finally to suggest guidelines for the analysis of their ideological positions.

Petty Commodity Production: Characteristics and Evolution

For many years the conventional dichotomy of 'traditional' and 'modern' sectors of the less developed economy constituted a comfortable framework within which to examine the trajectory of economic growth. More recently, this formulation has been up-dated and has quickly gained international acceptance. The 'informal sector', as 'traditional' economic activities have now been renamed, is currently seen as a potential engine for achieving self-sustained economic growth in underdeveloped economies (ILO, 1972, pp. 4–8, 21–2, 223–32, 503–10). Probably the major point of criticism of the current use of the 'formal–informal' sector dichotomy, is that it takes as its basic philosophy the proposition that *only* capitalist growth will lead to real economic and social development, and that strategies aimed at removing the imperfections in the distribution of benefits from growth can be successfully implemented without altering the existing structure of ownership of the means of production. Perhaps capitalism has the monopoly of the most profitable resources in the underdeveloped economies, but there is no reason to suppose *a priori* that capitalist relations of production have the monopoly on development.[1] The conventional approach also tends to isolate and characterise sectors within the urban economy of underdeveloped countries without examining in any detail the basis for the differentiation and the nature of those relationships, whether these latter be actual or potential.

In order to assess the class composition of petty commodity production, it is first of all essential to define it. When referring to that group of activities normally seen as lying outside the principal spheres of capitalist production in underdeveloped economies, we shall use the term 'petty commodity production' (PCP). For the purposes of this paper, we will define PCP as a distinct economic form, found in the context of several modes of production (feudal, capitalist or socialist). PCP is normally subordinate (though not necessarily lacking in power to take initiatives), dependent (though this does not preclude the existence of asymmetrical 'two-way functionality' between PCP and its dominant partner) and transitional (though periods of stasis and regression are always likely). Alison Scott (1977, pp. 1–2) sums up the characteristics of PCP as follows:

> Three elements are crucial to the definition of PCP: (a) production of commodities for the market . . . (b) small scale production include volume of output, size of work-force, size of capital and level of technology . . . PCP [is] referred to (by Marx) as the 'pygmy property of the many'. (c) ownership of the means of production by the direct producer. For Marx the foundation of PCP is the fact that 'the labourer is the private owner of his own means of labour set in action by himself'.

The subordinate nature of PCP only comes to the fore once a specific and generalised mode of appropriation has been established within a society. When a particular mode of production is establishing its overall control, PCP may play a decisive role in providing the dynamic of transition.

Looking at PCP in a historical context, it appears that this economic form co-exists and interpenetrates with a succession of dominant modes of production, employing the latter as the principal means of its reproduction (Scott, 1977, pp. 4–5). Despite this impressive historical pedigree, PCP has never formed (and almost by definition cannot constitute) the economic base of society. Some social formations such as Australia, New Zealand, the settler economies of Southern Africa, and the Eastern seaboard of North America have relied substantially on PCP during the initial stages of their modern development, but very quickly the rudimentary economic form has both been superceded and has superceded itself within the dialectic evolution of early capitalist accumulation (Amin, 1973, pp. 320–5). The reason for this lies in the nature of PCP, since the principal conditions for its reproduction and survival are supplied by the dominant mode of production in any given conjuncture. Whatever this dominant mode happens to be (feudalism, incipient or mature capitalism, or socialism), its preferential provision of markets, either in PCP's favour or to its detriment, its characteristic form of surplus appropriation and its specific social and spatial division of labour, ensure that its transition from simple reproduction to accumulation is predicated upon the transformation of its paternalist relations of production into those of the dominant mode of production. In short, this implies that if it is to break out of its cycle of simple reproduction, and engender a spiral of accumulation, PCP must transform itself into something else. What PCP has transformed itself into in the past, and what the future may hold for it, largely depends upon the nature of its dominant 'partner'. Petty commodity production, as an economic form, will now be examined in its historical context, with respect to several different modes of production. In the first instance we will summarise the role of PCP in the development of European capitalism, and this will be followed by a more detailed analysis of PCP in the context of the underdeveloped economy, using the example of Senegambia in West Africa.

The roots of PCP can be traced back to small-scale subsistence agriculture of pre-feudal society. Similar agricultural activities still dominate the economies of Third World countries. Then as now the dominant force in production was the (extended) family unit, and thus relations of production tended to be patriarchal and personalised. PCP in this agricultural context provided the basis for feudalism and the breeding ground for hereditary privilege. As feudalism evolves, a part of PCP relocates itself in the emerging urban areas, constitutes itself into guilds, and grasps the possibilities of capitalist accumulation. PCP becomes stronger and begins to constitute a threat to the dominant feudal order. Eventually, it becomes the vehicle by which this order is overturned (at least in Europe). As capitalism gains ever more control over the means of production, and as the principal means of accumulation becomes concentrated in manufacturing and particularly trading, rather than the ownership of land, the remaining elements of PCP fall under the direct or indirect subordination of capital.

Following its industrial and technological revolutions, the capitalist mode of production can be characterised as 'mature'; at the international level, capitalism has moved from its competitive mercantilist phase to one in which trans-nationally active capital systematically causes an augmented flow of surplus to move from the colonies and semi-colonies to the advanced capitalist economies, following the contours of an uneven capitalist development previously established through direct political domination. The position of PCP in the developed capitalist economies in this period, though constantly changing, is largely characterised by chronic crisis: more than capable of subsisting in the era of mature capitalism, and often capitalising on periods of crisis within large scale capitalism, PCP finds itself supporting but rarely able to make any substantial inroads into a capitalism which exhibits an unprecedented degree of monopoly. Advanced industrial capitalism has progressively and proportionately less need of labour within the process of direct production, and its periodic crises force some workers and large numbers of petty commodity producers into unstable employment situations. Some former wage workers shift into self employment in service occupations; some small businessmen are actually able to take up labour expelled from larger enterprises. The growth of subcontracting, franchising and out-working gives the appearance of an extremely high turnover rather than unprecedented growth in self-employment. However, much of this self-employment is but thinly disguised wage labour, enabling large-scale capitalist enterprises to shift both responsibilities and, as a consequence, production costs onto ostensibly independent operators. If *petit embourgeoisement* is seen to be the dominant change now taking place in the working class of the advanced capitalist economies, in the Third World we tend to encounter, on the contrary, a process of concealed proletarianisation. Thus, the future prospects of development for the petty commodity producer appear to be ambiguous, to say the least. Ideological commitment to independent economic activity remains strong, whilst the trend in the objective environment of PCP progressively weakens independence and steadily reduces the likelihood of a future transition to capitalist accumulation. Yet even with the declining statistical probability of such a transition, ideological mechanisms rooted in the bourgeoisie and often disseminated through the media are allowed full play within the sphere of PCP: even if bootstraps capital accumulation is restricted to certain narrow avenues (for example high-risk, high-technology lines such as electronics; new forms of service activities and so on), one or two success stories are sufficient to motivate many thousands of aspiring entrepreneurs to enter the fray in spite of the doubts one might reasonably have about the continued independence of a successful small scale business. Nevertheless, PCP may offer 'independence' and some income stability even if substantial progress is not made. The all-consuming search for 'success' may not be characteristic of all operators within petty commodity production.

Just as there exists considerable disagreement over the class position and evolution of the peasantry in Third World countries, there is often heated debate over the use of the term 'feudalism' to describe the relations of production prevailing in many parts of the now underdeveloped world prior to European colonial expansion. Amin (1973, p. 9) characterises the West African societies in this period as being based upon a:

tributary mode of production in which the continuing existence of the village community was juxtaposed with a social and political apparatus of exploitation, based upon the extracting of tribute . . . . We can distinguish two forms of this – early forms and evolved forms, such as feudalism, in which the village community loses its right of landed property to its feudal masters, with the community continuing as family groups.

In the Senegambian region of West Africa, the petty kingdoms were highly inegalitarian, with the individual's rank determined by that of his family. In the Kingdom of Waalo, on the present-day borders of Senegal and Mauritania, society was divided into three hierarchised and hereditary segments – noble freemen, caste-organised freemen and slaves. Each of these segments was internally hierarchised, so that freemen status encompassed both the most privileged members of the royal court, who enjoyed the benefits of hereditary power and property, as well as the freemen of the village communities, who were little more than peasants commanding minimal political power and having no real rights of inheritance. Tribute was extracted by the King through community-level representatives, who effectively managed the village usufruct on his behalf. The concentration of power in the hands of village patriarchs and the appropriation of agricultural and artisanal surplus through them by the royal family considerably reinforced social inequality (Barry, 1972, pp. 77–105; Diop, 1972, pp. 13–66).

Until the arrival of the Portuguese in West Africa, local non-agricultural production (namely, artisanal activities) was closely connected with and dependent upon subsistence agriculture and the political structure which dominated the village communities. For the majority of village craftsmen, complete specialisation was unheard of: normally the rural smith, woodworker or weaver was also an agricultural producer (albeit on a smaller scale than his fellow villagers). His craft activities helped to fulfil the subsistence requirements of the community, in return for which he could acquire the additional foodstuffs he was unable to produce himself. Nevertheless, such craft activities were specialised in as much as they were undertaken by well-defined social groups organised along caste lines, such that each member of the group could trace both his ancestry and his occupation back to a common origin.

The origin of these castes appears to lie in the manner in which ethnic groups, conquered during a period of expansionism on the part of a political kingdom, were integrated into the dominant social and economic system: forced to undertake specific activities as slaves, and often diluted by other ethnic groups, village craftsmen were not permitted to marry outside their occupation, a situation which did not change, even after the caste-organised producers became freemen. Caste activities were regulated through a caste-chief and his immediate subordinates, all of whom were usually nominees of the King. In general, non-agricultural producers in Senegambian society could be categorised as either low status, occupationally specific freemen (usually of slave origin), or the even lower status domestic slaves, who would assist freemen in all their activities, agricultural or otherwise.

The European slave trade introduced foreign commodities into the economy in a very dispersed manner. It is unlikely that their impact was significant upon the levels of production of the local craftsmen: in some ways, they may even have acted as a stimulus to the local production of certain articles. However, after the region had been politically dominated by European colonialism, and the volume of trade between Europe and Africa (in both directions) increased substantially, a process of narrowly defined evolution began among these individuals who had specific craft skills. As the coastal towns grew, and administrative control of the whole of French West Africa was transferred from the small coastal colonial town of St Louis to the rapidly growing commercial centre at Dakar, rural–urban migration commenced. Initially, the major attraction was employment in the construction of military and transport infrastructure, which automatically gave certain 'modern' skills to a small but growing section of the population. The growth of the urban population also required the availability of goods and services at prices and levels of quality acceptable to the African population. Thus, small producers and traders quickly followed in the wake of the migrations which accompanied the evolution of a capitalist labour market.

At this point it is important to make a distinction between what were essentially 'traditional' artisanal activities pre-dating the penetration of capitalism, such as weaving, smithing, leather-work and so on, and those which owed their existence to the establishment of certain elements of the capitalist system in the colonies, such as masons, mechanised tailors, vehicle mechanics, shoe-shine boys, construction workers and the like. These two forms of activity should by no means be identified with a crude 'traditional–modern' dichotomy. In some respects, the former have modernised their means of production to a considerable extent, in the face of market competition from manufactured goods of European origin (Le Brun and Gerry, 1975, p. 28) whilst the latter are often engaged in production processes in which the level of technology is quite rudimentary, despite the apparently modern materials which are worked up or used (for example vehicle repairs, brickmaking). Many of the small-scale, own-account petty producers presently working in the cities and towns of underdeveloped capitalist countries acquired their skills in capitalist wage employment, and, deliberately or otherwise, have since become self-employed. In Dakar, for example, it has been calculated that between 55 and 70 per cent of own-account vehicle mechanics and furniture makers respectively had spent more than one half of their previous working lives in wage employment (Le Brun and Gerry, 1975, p. 22).

Despite the surprisingly high level of skill existent in many sectors of PCP, there are extremely potent forces which retard any growth strategy which might evolve within this part of the urban economy, resulting out of the dominant position held therein by the capitalist mode of production. The avenues of expansion and capital accumulation available to PCP are largely determined by the extent to which capitalism has established its hegemony over the principal production processes in the economy. There is also a tendency for the institutional means of capital accumulation to be controlled by the largely foreign-owned and/or dominated enterprises, usually through the indigenous ruling class. The impact of *mature* capitalism on PCP is considerable; however, it is not directly comparable to the relationship between *early* industrial capitalism and PCP in the European Industrial Revolution. Whilst the latter could incorporate sections of PCP, and extract surplus by forcing longer working hours on the labour force, the former eschews the necessity of incorporating more labour by introducing labour-saving machinery and advanced technology, and is thereby able to greatly increase its rate of surplus-appropriation.

In summarising the evolution and consequent impact of PCP, we might focus on the multiple connotations of the word 'petty'; though some Marxists prefer the term 'simple', the previous formulation at least hints at the historical changes that have occurred in PCP's trajectory. As the direct outcome of the development of a primitive division of labour, and the concentration of early crafts within the household rather than in the community at large, PCP in its rural context provided a fertile medium for the development of feudalism. In this sense, 'petty' implies both *small-scale and original.* In its later urban context, PCP was an important source of entrepreneurial advantage, if not of large-scale capital accumulation: in this respect, 'petty' might be thought of as meaning *embryonic* or *incipient* with respect to the evolution of a bourgeois class and a capitalist mode of production. Later still, with the constitution of an advanced and mature capitalism, PCP plays both a material and an ideological role: the former is to support capitalist industry materially, whilst allowing a considerable transfer of the burden of responsibility and cost to the lower echelons of production and distribution hierarchies; the latter is to convince a large section of the economically active population that only the maintenance and reproduction of the capitalist system offers them the chance of material well-being and the promise that the hardest-working and most in-novative will reap the rewards of their past sacrifices and hardships. In short, the word 'petty' here has a double meaning: in material terms it means *small, gap-filling, exploitable* and *cost-absorptive.* But all of this has only real relevance to the capitalist mode of production which PCP faithfully serves; in ideological terms and as far as the capitalist mode of production is concerned, it means *insubstantial* and *insignificant* (though not without usefulness) *vis-à-vis* the system it supports. To those who constitute the focus of this ideological strategy, it implies future growth potential.

The contemporary situation of the majority of petty producers in underdeveloped capitalist economies has been succinctly summed up by Williams and Mutebile (1978) as follows:

> petty commodity producers provide inputs which the capitalist firms are unable to produce profitably. These include cheap food and consumer goods for employees of capitalist firms (and the state which services them), thus reducing wage costs and inflating the salaries of managerial staff. Petty producers . . . maintain the reserve army of labour, which limits the bargaining strength of organised labour, thus, reducing wage costs and ensuring a flexible supply of labour to capitalist employment. They provide opportunities for additional earnings, and the possibility to employees of establishing themselves as independent men. They provide the (protected) market for the products of capitalist firms. Far from being displaced by capitalism, petty commodity production (including peasant agriculture) is essential to the neo-colonial form of capitalist production.

Thus, far from being an isolated, exclusively traditional and self-contained economic form, petty commodity production, its production process and its labour force, is inextricably related to the capitalist mode of production not only at the local and national but also at the international level.

Relations of Production and Contradictory Class Locations in PCP

Whilst PCP is clearly linked to the development of capitalism, our discussion up to now has been predicated on an implicit acceptance of the relative ease of defining what actually constitutes PCP in reality. In fact, that task becomes very difficult immediately we are confronted with the complexity of the labour market and employment structure in any Third World city. At the level of appearances, the tendency would be to classify the majority of petty producers as self-employed. The range of occupations which might normally be identified with the 'petite bourgeoisie' is therefore extensive. Aside from the small shop-keepers, tradesmen and embryonic entrepreneurs, there exist large numbers of individuals who make a living by using their own labour power in the production or provision of commodities for the general public. These one-person operations do not involve the wage employment of others, and quite rarely involve even the use of family and/or child labour. Individual families may engage in a number of separate individual activities: for example the father may be a shoe-shiner, the mother a market trader, and the children may earn small amounts as lottery ticket sellers. Such one-person activities involve the production of goods or the provision of services, often requiring inputs purchased in the capitalist market. Since no labour other than that of the individual operator is involved it appears that he or she is both capitalist and worker, though perhaps 'lumpen-capitalist' might be a term which reflects the low level of capital, incomes, technology, and expansion possibilities normally associated with such activities. Nevertheless, the relations of production can be considerably more complex than this superficial analysis would suggest, as the following example, drawn from an interview with a Dakar woodcarver, shows:

> Arriving in Dakar in his early teens, D. was taught the basic skills of wood carving by his uncle. After his period of apprenticeship, he did not have sufficient savings to establish himself as a journeyman. Eventually, the uncle withdrew from direct involvement in the business, and D. took on the additional responsibilities of supervising the workshop and training the apprentices. Soon he became convinced that his uncle was exploiting him, and decided to use his small amount of savings to work independently elsewhere. He first of all rented space in a large workshop in which a master carver and his wage employees produced masks and statues for the tourist trade. The master carver supplied D. with wood at the beginning of each month (on credit), and the latter paid for the raw materials when he had sold the month's output. With this arrangement, D. was able to save considerably more than he had done when manager of his uncle's workshop, even though the credit arrangement meant that he lost a fixed proportion of his profit on each article sold. D. planned to save as much as possible and establish his own workshop at some future date. When the master carver instructed his workers in the sculpting of a new model, D. was able to pick up new ideas for his own merchandise. When the master had need of a particular model which was out of stock, D. would supply the article if he had one available. If customers asked for a model which the master was unwilling, incapable, or too busy to produce, these orders were passed on to D. Wood of the best quality was never in short supply, because the master carver had excellent contacts with the Dakar wholesalers, and, indeed, owned a small warehouse of his own. (Gerry, fieldnotes, January–March, 1974)

Thus, in a single workshop, we find a complex of relations of production ranging from incipient capitalist relations between the master craftsman and his wage workers to the paternalist relations of co-operation between the young carver and the master. This co-operation could very easily develop into a more advanced form of capitalist subordination, if for example the young carver's credit relationship with the master were to become too onerous relative to the demand for his output. This is the classic manner in which credit relations are transformed into sub-contracting and/or piece-work. Speculation aside, it is not at all clear that the relationship between the young carver and the workshop proprietor falls into any of our conventional categories: not only are the relations ambiguous, but also in a process of formation. Whether the young carver becomes a capitalist himself, or is absorbed into the wage labour force is immaterial. What is clear, however, is that the average petty commodity producer in similar circumstances, has little chance of making the transition (assuming he so desires) from the simple reproduction of his existing conditions, to the 'dizzy heights' of small-scale capitalism.

It is therefore of crucial importance to examine the relations of production in order confidently to identify particular workers with specific and analytically relevant employment categories. In taking such a step we are in fact considering the *types* of enterprise in the urban economy, since the terms self-employment and wage labour refer not simply to different categories of employment, but contain implicit reference to different kinds of productive enterprise, or more specifically to different relations and forms of production. The complexity that we have noted implies that a comprehensive analysis of the relations of production of a worker should involve at least the following three strategic variables: the self-employed worker, for example, is defined as the owner of his means of production, as having control over the productive process, and as being the sole appropriator of the surplus generated by the enterprise. In contrast, the wage labourer exhibits exactly the opposite characteristics. There are many workers, however, who work under apparently different and *intermediate* relations of production. The number of variants likely to be encountered is great, but, for the purposes of illustration, we have selected one detailed example – the garbage picker of Cali, Colombia.[2]

Garbage picking is one of the lowest status jobs to be found in Cali, Colombia's third city, giving employment to an estimated 1200–1700 people. The majority of garbage pickers would, if asked, classify themselves as self-employed – indeed they have no contract, written or verbal, with any company in Cali or the rest of Colombia. Twenty years ago garbage picking was almost exclusively concerned with the collection and re-cycling of goods, such as clothes, shoes, cutlery and jewellery which passed directly into the low income commercial network for consumption in low income households. Since that time the development of industry—both in Cali and elsewhere – has created a diverse and expanding market for industrial raw materials that can be recuperated from the city's domestic garbage. Of these, the most important is paper, which can be used in various forms to make cardboard and tissue. In addition there are also markets for scrap metals, bone, plastic, bottles, glass and cloth, so that today the garbage picker devotes most of his time to the collection of these materials, either on the municipal garbage dump or in the streets of Cali.

The work itself requires various means of production. Most important is access to the garbage itself. Under Colombian law it is not clear who is defined as the legal owner of garbage. The Colombian Environmental Protection Code, however, gives each municipality the right to organise its collection of garbage, together with transport and disposal, as well as the right to control others engaged in those activities. Where garbage is dumped on private land, it appears that the owner of that land becomes the owner of the garbage (Sfeir-Younis, 1977). Despite the legal complexity, it is very apparent that the garbage picker has no legally guaranteed access to the garbage, but rather depends on the municipal authorities and land owners for the right to 'possess' that garbage. There may well be occasions when this right is denied (Birkbeck, 1978).

In addition to access to the garbage, there are certain tools and equipment necessary for the successful sorting and transport of recuperable materials. At the lowest level there is a need for sacks in order to pack the materials. Those garbage pickers who work on the streets will usually buy their own, but those who work on the garbage dump will borrow them from the dealers in waste material. Whilst on the dump there is no necessity for a handcart, in the street it is highly important for raising productivity by allowing more material to be carried at any one time. Such carts, however, cost between 500 and 1 000 pesos according to the quality of construction, and such amounts of money are often not available in terms of savings or credit to many garbage pickers, but dealers in the waste materials. Ownership of the means of production is thus a complex issue. Whilst the garbage pickers may have *de facto* access to the garbage, it is not legally theirs. In addition they may be forced to depend upon others for the tools necessary to carry out the job effectively.

Control over the productive process demonstrates similar complexity. Since the pickers are not officially employed by any company, they can decide whether or not to work, at what times to work, where to work and what to collect. Hence, for example, it is not uncommon for a picker who has earned a lot of money in one day to take the following day as a holiday, or for a picker to concentrate on collecting paper because it is his preferred material. It is perhaps this aspect of the job which most creates the illusion of independence for the worker – the feeling that he is working for himself. Nevertheless, it is the needs of the industrial raw materials market which sets important limits on the nature of his work. Not only does this market specify the different types of materials that are to be collected, but it also stipulates the form in which they are to be collected, and whether or not they are to be sorted in some preliminary fashion before sale.

The final variable concerns who actually appropriates the surplus generated by garbage picking; it is perhaps this factor which contributes most to the contradictory nature of the economic status of the picker. An adequate analysis of the generation and appropriation of this surplus requires an investigation of the way in which recycled materials are linked to the productive process. As we have pointed out, the market for recycled raw materials has been principally created by the large industrial consumers, who represent the final buyers of these materials. The garbage pickers are thus essentially working for these industrial consumers, but they never sell materials to these, but to any one of a number of intermediaries. It is usual for these intermediaries to be legally independent enterprises, but quite often with some capital finance from the factories themselves or from other larger dealers. Each of the intermediary enterprises and all of the garbage pickers are paid according to the volume of materials that they produce, which clearly categorises garbage recycling as piece work. The market is thus organised hierarchically shown in Figure 6.2.

Prices for raw materials are always determined from above. At the

FIGURE 6.2. Relationships between the garbage picker and dealers in waste paper.

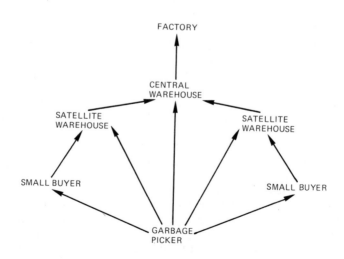

level of the factory the main consideration is the price of raw materials on the national or international market, together with the degree of competition for local recycled materials. The latter always command a substantially lower price than raw materials. The price for recycled materials becomes lowered as it passes down the chain of intermediaries and each leaves as large a margin as possible to cover costs and to generate profits. The garbage picker has no bargaining power whatsoever in this economic system. Indeed, in the waste paper industry it has been argued that prices to the picker could be raised by 30 per cent with no ill effects for the factories.

By his sales to any of the three kinds of intermediaries outlined above, the garbage picker is directly linked into the industrial system as a pieceworker. The wage he earns is a result of prices which are set, not with any idea of generating a subsistence wage, but in view of considerations of the availability of raw materials at any particular moment. Indeed, in times of industrial recession, prices may fall to ridiculously low levels, and the pickers will be forced to select other materials which have a relatively higher price. The income of the garbage picker is thus to a large extent determined by the prices commanded by recycled raw materials, and these prices represent nothing more than the price of the labour power of the garbage picker at any particular time. The surplus generated by garbage picking is appropriated in the first instance by the various intermediaries who deal in waste materials, and more importantly by the factories through raw material substitution in the productive process. The garbage picker is thus little more than an industrial outworker. Rather than being easily classified as either petit bourgeois or as a member of the proletariat, his socio-economic condition, both in terms of relations of production and ideology, embodies elements of both bourgeois and proletarian.

In view of our theoretical discussion of the work on the petite bourgeoisie, we are thus led to conclude that the garbage picker occupies an objectively contradictory class location in the urban labour force in particular, and in Colombian society in general. Additional examples of the contradictory class locations which exist within PCP in underdeveloped capitalist economies are summarised below, in order that we might give some wider impression of the magnitude and variation of the phenomenon:

> We encountered a case where a tiler worked as a wage earner for his own employees whenever they had work and he had not; nevertheless, the relations of production had left their mark in terms of status and remuneration, for he demanded and received 5000 francs a day, whereas he only paid them 3000 francs for the same work. (Le Brun and Gerry, 1975, p. 25)

An illustration of the tendency for small capitalists to emerge outside the ranks of petty producers, is provided by the relationship between Government contracts for commodities within the productive capabilities of petty producers, the entrepreneurs who situate themselves between contractor and producer, and the petty producers themselves. Such entrepreneurs have gained a quasi-monopoly of contacts and information relating to Government and private sector contracts, despite their often considerable ignorance concerning the production processes required to fulfil these contacts. They are able to use their accumulated wealth to secure valuable contracts which they then subcontract to petty producers unacceptable to the government or private enterprise as legitimate contractors. . . . These intermediaries' accumulated wealth and/or business and personal contacts permit a transfer of surplus to take place from the petty producer, and forms the basis for their own enrichment without physical involvement in the production of commodities. (Gerry, 1978)

There are traditional petty producers who are more or less subordinated to commercial capital. A striking example is the case of the weavers at the Artisans' Village in Dakar, an establishment created by the state who . . . produce for individual tourist's orders . . . , local petty commerce and for large orders negotiated by the Senegalese Artisans' Board (a public institution which manages the Village). The prices asked for these large orders are usually unknown to the weavers, and the remuneration . . . is annually fixed by the Board. Initially, guaranteed prices and supplies of raw materials were arranged, and no workshop rents were asked. More recently, the guarantees have been suspended and the weavers forced to purchase their thread on the open market at double the price which obtained when the Village was created. Workshop rents have also been imposed. A certain number of master craftsmen and their apprentices have left, either to return to their villages as artisan-peasants, or to attempt to re-integrate themselves into urban independent weaving . . . . (Le Brun and Gerry, 1975, p. 21)

In Colombia, the sale of lottery tickets and other forms of bets (on horse racing, on the results of lotteries etc.) is normally effected through street vendors: neither *loteros* (who sell lottery tickets), nor *chanceros* (who take bets on the results of State lotteries) working in Cali, are recognised as wage employees, and under normal circumstances, would be officially classified as 'self-employed'. In spite of this official viewpoint, both types of street vendor are little more than highly dependent commission agents working either for a public institution (in the case of *loteros*) or private companies (in the case of *chanceros*). In fact, the term 'commission agent' is just a euphemism for piece-work employment in the sphere of services rather than within the direct production process. (Gerry, fieldnotes, Summer 1977)

The degree of differentiation outlined here has important implications for the analysis of the mass of apparently self-employed working poor in underdeveloped countries. This differentiation consists of:

1. the particular sphere of the capitalist system with which small enterprise has its strongest connections;
2. the degree to which capitalist relations develop within a specific activity (whether imposed from above, or initiated 'boot-straps fashion' from below).

The linkages and connections may be different for workers in apparently identical situations: an ice-cream vendor may be provided with a cart by an ice-cream company, and may receive a commission based upon his daily sales, another such worker may rent a cart, making the ice-cream himself. Yet another vendor may have built the cart himself and may make the ice-cream at home using equipment purchased from previous savings. This latter seller, if business goes well, may start to increase the size of his business, and take on wage labour to either make the ice-cream or sell it. Clearly we are not confronted by three identical situations but by:

1. A direct wage worker, whose status as such may or may not be recognized by his employer.
2. A disguised wage worker, the rent of whose handcart will be determined by the average productivity of street sellers of this sort, much in the same way as land rent is calculated by the rural landlord on the basis of the fertility of the land. Into this category fall all workers who occupy objectively contradictory class locations, such as the garbage pickers described above.
3. A self-employed worker, or lumpen-capitalist, who may become an incipient 'boot-straps' capitalist if his business expands.

Thus we can now make some tentative conclusions about the economic bases of class formation among petty producers in the Third World. First, and perhaps most importantly, it is clear that many apparently self-employed workers in reality are little more than disguised wage workers. Hence the particular pattern of class formation among these workers will be complex, for their contradictory class locations will make them particularly prone to conflicting and changing ideologies. Second, and as a corollary to this, the truly self-employed is a much smaller group than we would have at first imagined. We have preferred to call them lumpen-capitalists rather than petits bourgeois since we cannot envisage them as enjoying anything like the same possibilities of accumulation that are presented to the true capitalist class, nor can we see how their ideology will necessarily be equivalent. By implication, we place disguised wage workers in the same category as managers, and semi-autonomous employees, in that their class locations are contradictory. The resultant pattern of classes and class fractions will depend not only on the balance of presented forces, both economic, political and ideological, but also upon changes in the character of petty commodity production over time. The nature of these changes and their consequences, though of considerable interest and importance, lie outside the scope of this paper.

We have seen that there exist certain problems in identifying and subsequently analysing unambiguously the relations of production under which individuals and groups work. This is especially the case in underdeveloped capitalist societies. But relations of production are only one determinant of class location which shape the historical course of class formation at the economic level. In order fully to appreciate the dialectic of class formation, we must examine with equal rigour (if possible) the politico-ideological level.

The concluding part of this essay will focus upon some of the major factors influencing the development of ideology among the numerous 'non-proletarian' workers in underdeveloped capitalist countries. What we have to say is indicative and speculative, since it is based on a relatively small sample of case-studies. It is intended to bring to the surface some of the issues we feel are central to an understanding of the process of class formation.

Ideology, Class Formation and PCP

When we speak of ideology in relation to class formation, we are effectively concerned with the way in which different classes can be distinguished according to their conceptions of, and the political action based upon, the objective relations of production which constitute their political and economic environment. These conceptions may be diametrically opposed, convergent and/or reconcilable according to the historical conjuncture. We feel that the most rigorous way of conceptualising this is to link the formation of ideology directly, though not uniquely, with the objective relations of production. Since the characteristics of the latter under capitalism are such that there is an inherent conflict between the owners of the means of production (the bourgeoisie) and the sellers of labour power (the proletariat), we may conclude that the ideologies of the two groups will also be in fundamental opposition, thereby identifying classes both in terms of production relations and ideology. Ownership of the means of production would imply strong attachment to the maintenance of private property, the concept of individualism, and the ethic of work. The need regularly to sell one's labour power would perhaps lead to a belief in collective action, the dissolution of private property and privilege, though in this respect we are pre-judging the effect that the dominant ideology may have on the evolution of subordinate ones, since those who directly lend their support to the maintenance of the *status quo* could be said to possess a bourgeois ideology, whilst those who are openly critical of it do not. But it is not always easy to reconcile the ideological positions of particular groups with their location in the objective relations of production. On the one hand there are those who, despite an apparently unambiguous position in the relations of production, possess an ideology more normally associated with another class location. The best example would be the proletarian who, for one reason or another, prefers deliberately to support capitalism. In reality however, this type of apparent anomaly is relatively infrequent, and of less importance than the ideological orientations which characterise contradictory class locations, since the latter may be far more pervasive than a mechanistic application of class categories and relations of production would suggest. In view of the preceding discussion of the extent to which many class locations in the Third World could be deemed contradictory in character, it would be helpful to mention Wright's comments (1976, pp. 39–40) on the ideologies of individuals in such positions:

> The extent to which the political and ideological relations enter into the determination of class position is itself determined by the degree to which those positions occupy a contradictory location at the level of social relations of production. The more contradictory is a position within social relations of production, the more political and ideological relations can influence its objective position within class relations.

We find ourselves in basic agreement with this conclusion. When class location is objectively contradictory, it becomes increasingly prone to varying ideological currents. If a person's job combines elements of both the classical bourgeois and proletarian (such as that of the manager or foreman) then the corresponding ideology is also likely to contain a corresponding and probably asymmetrical combination of those elements.

Within large-scale capitalism in the Third World, the mechanisms contributing to the formation of ideology are fundamentally little different from those which are found in the developed countries: often the former may be nothing more than the extension of the latter. Even so, the process of class formation in Third World countries, and the class composition of the corresponding societies, should not be mechanistically derived from that prevailing in the developed metropolitan economies. The hierarchisation of the productive process in its social manifestations results in the creation of a large number of jobs that are contradictory in their class locations. Neither manager nor workshop supervisor is unequivocally bourgeois or proletarian, but a mixture of varying degrees of both. Whilst many workers may identify themselves strongly as proletarian (indeed syndicalist and political action are often strongest in the sector of large scale capital), they may be objectively and in some cases deliberately supportive of capitalism. Whilst it is usual for the ideology of those in middle and senior management positions to be dominantly bourgeois in nature and to become increasingly so as their stake in the productive process gets larger, their role in the process of production itself may not be unambiguous. By promoting and rewarding selected individuals, the uppermost echelons of management (the 'real' capitalists) ensure the continued success of the capitalist production process. A production supervisor, for example, may receive relatively higher wages, and be accorded a higher status in the company, for helping to ensure that production is maximised and continually on schedule, and that the optimum surplus is extracted from the workers. In turn he may well come to realise that his relatively privileged position is dependent upon the existence of a body of workers whom he can supervise. If he is not to lose his more enjoyable and better remunerated job, then he must begin to think in positive terms about the 'benefits' of the present system under which he operates. Yet he is also exploited by those above him, and indeed may feel this very strongly from time to time. In part this is allayed by his gradual incorporation into the 'responsibilities' of the company. He begins to understand more about the problems facing the owners of the establishment, and worries about the solving of production problems and the meeting of deadlines. The confidential information that he is given makes him feel increasingly at one with the interests of the company. In this way a contradictory location can produce an ideology apparently at odds with the real conditions under which the person ensures his or her subsistence. Workers not directly active in the production process may be the subjects of similar ideological ambiguity: policemen, teachers, administrators, technicians and social workers all sell their labour power, yet do not generally see themselves as working class. They are required to uphold and/or reproduce the dominant values of capitalist society, in return for which they are rewarded with a social status which may or may not be reflected in the remuneration they receive. As Frank (1975, p. 87) comments:

> Though the exploitative two-class structure persists, the upper class or bourgeoisie diffuses to some members of the lower class or proletariat

some of the benefits of the former's exploitative position and gains. Without transforming these recipients into a part of the bourgeoisie itself, these economic, political and cultural pay-offs permit the bourgeoisie to obtain the co-operation of the recipients in the exploitative process and even to attenuate or even eliminate opposition to the exploitation. . . . The creation or existence of these strata, and the upper and lower ones with them, serves to perpetuate the exploitative class structure. They enlist more members of the system into the exploitative process, give these . . . an interest in maintaining it – though they themselves are exploited – and serve to substitute a stratification consciousness for class consciousness.

Or as Hodges (1960, p. 258) suggests:

> The intermediate group that gains most from indirect exploitation consists of skilled and professional workers who do not directly or indirectly produce articles of necessity. . . . Generally speaking, the tendency of this group is to favour the economic and spiritual authority of the capitalist. Although exploited themselves, many members of this group indirectly exploit other workers by an amount greater than the value of their own labour power. In addition, they tend to strengthen their economic position through periodic investments of a portion of their surplus. . . . Although most investments of this kind are on a small scale, the amount tends to be compound, thereby further tying these workers to the system of exploitation.

The kinds of workers described by Frank and Hodges (rather than those we have examined) have been called by Poulantzas (1977, p. 115) the 'new petite bourgeoisie'. This term may not however be helpful. It implies a static concept of class and an unwillingness to incorporate the concept of class-in-formation into the analysis. Whilst there are powerful mechanisms involving status and income differentials which encourage the absorption of bourgeois ideology by those in contradictory class locations, these may break down, and produce an opposite reaction. In Colombia, for example, recent strikes amongst school teachers suggest that they are unhappy both with their status and with their pay. It is clear that the ideology of those in contradictory class locations may well change over time, not only because of modifications in their own circumstances, but also as the fortunes of other workers change.

On the other hand the use of the term 'new petite bourgeoisie' is confusing because of its inaccuracy. First, it suggests that those who are not owners of the means of production, but who are nevertheless supportive of capitalism, have essentially the same ideology as the 'true' bourgeoisie. In fact, from time to time, there may very well be clashes of interest between different groups of 'non-proletarians'. Second, the term suggests too much ideological similarity with the 'traditional petite bourgeoisie'. Perhaps we need to break away from the old terminology in order to adequately analyse the ideological position of those who do not see themselves as proletarian, and yet may not be entirely in accord with the interests of the 'true' bourgeoisie.

For those workers who fall somewhere outside the sphere of direct capitalist relations, there exist other mechanisms which may help to obscure the objective relations of production under which they operate. The two groups that are of most interest in this context are those that we have described as disguised wage workers and lumpen-capitalists. In many ways the two are in a similar position – their upward mobility is blocked, in one case because they are part of a wider system of wage-labour and exploitation, and in the other because their market is either habitually that of the very poor, or deals only in commodities of a relatively low value. However, the differences are also clear: whilst the former are fully integrated into capitalist relations of production within the sphere of production itself, the latter are structurally excluded from such relations and are only subordinated to capitalism within the sphere of circulation. In such circumstances, their corresponding ideologies may have the tendency to be quite dissimilar, even though the possibility of ideological convergence should not be ruled out.

Among disguised wage workers in particular, there is often the illusion of independence. This may be a result of the operation of a piece-work system (as in garbage picking) or may result from the fact that the worker uses credit in some way, or rents his necessary equipment. This apparent independence is enhanced by the fact that the hours and location of work are normally variable, according to the predilections of the individual, rather than that of a supervisor or manager of some sort. This aspect of independence may remain relatively untouched, even after the production process has become subordinated to externally imposed capitalist relations of production, as in the case of sub-contracting (Le Brun and Gerry, 1975, pp. 27–8). Whether truly independent or not, such low income workers may well be in a position where, irrespective of their subjective evaluation of the probability of 'upward social mobility', they are in no position to influence their own situation. Garbage pickers and lottery ticket vendors, for example, operate at the bottom of a shifting and complex hierarchy of intermediaries, which may obscure the real nature of their relationship with the factory or distrbuting agency. Indeed, in many cases, such workers may only be aware of a small part of the hierarchy in which they operate. Additionally, they are rarely involved in the production or circulation process of only one firm. Thus, they cannot focus their disaffection on any but very general causal factors. In this sense, collective action and organisation only springs up in a fragmented and disjointed manner within a particular production process. Such action is also inhibited by the fact that most of the occupations which can be described as either disguised wage work or lumpen-capitalist activities, require that workers operate in isolation from and in competition with each other. Artisans, mechanics, shoe-shiners, street sellers and garbage pickers, spread themselves far and wide over the city, and do not often come into contact with each other, except for the relatively few who have formed 'professional associations'. As a result, little discussion of mutual problems takes place and collective action is the exception rather than the rule.

A second feature common to the position of these workers is the essentially unprotected, insecure and unstable nature of their work. The occupations commonly found on the streets of Third World cities are usually subject to official regulation and persecution. To return to the example of garbage picking, those who habitually work at the dump are not even assured access to the work. Thus, their major preoccupation is with the *right* to work, not with the *conditions* of work, and this is evidenced in their manner of political organisation (Birkbeck, 1978). Their ineligibility for social security payments means that the necessity to work is always present; irrespective of circumstances, the worker is forced to worry about where the next meal will come from rather than reflecting on the fundamental reasons for his predicament.

These factors make for a highly complex ideology-forming environment in which petty producers spend their working lives. In Colombia, for example, practically every low-income worker is quick to point out that *estamos en la olla* (literally, we're in the pan). Yet this may be nothing more than the truth: the worker is poor; what prevents political action to alleviate the situation is the failure to pose the fundamental question 'why?', and/or to get any reasonable answer. The experience of adversity does not necessarily lead to the attribution of blame, even less the development of a conscious feeling of being exploited. Our experience suggests that the majority of workers who could be described as disguised wage employees or lumpen-capitalists, would tend to have as complex and contradictory an ideology as the objective circumstances in which they work.

There exist potent processes which reinforce the belief in capitalism, and this situation has its origins in two separate but related factors: a belief in individualism, and the myth of the miracle. The basic tenet of individualism is the idea that one's economic situation can be remedied by one's own efforts, the corollary of this being that only oneself is to blame for adversity. This belief is exemplified by such common statements as 'the rich man is he who eats less' or 'life is not expensive, it is just that we do not know how to live it', and given concrete subjective form by the existence of a few successful individuals who have emerged from the ranks of the urban working poor.

In all occupations there are classical examples of people who have succeeded materially, and whose upward mobility (measured either in terms of status and esteem, or in terms of the role played in a production hierarchy) becomes a model with which the less and least successful would almost automatically identify their own possible futures. A classical example of the ideological 'beacon' provided by an individual success story, is that of the Senegalese capitalist Ndjouga Kebe. An uneducated boy from a poor background, he is said to have worked relentlessly to amass his initial capital, which took him to Zaire, where he made his fortune. On his return to Dakar, he was able to finance the building of hotels, luxury apartments and latterly has become prominent in banking. Such a story acts as a 'beacon' guiding all small entrepreneurs, who believe that if Kebe could succeed, hope exists for others. Hard work, resilience and perseverance are the key to success: a shoulder kept to the wheel today is a shoulder on which some fine garment may one day be worn. The statistical improbability of such success being achieved by a particular individual (gifted or otherwise) is masked by the belief – encouraged by the State, the media and the ruling class – that hard work brings its own rich rewards. For the mass of the labour force in Third World cities, however, hard work brings nothing more than survival.

Thus for a disguised wage worker to become an intermediary agent, or 'informal' foreman, or for a lumpen-capitalist to rapidly expand his business by employing others, increasing output, etc., would constitute in the eyes of others evidence of the *success* rather than the *failure* of the economic system. The prejudicial effect that a colleague's success may have on one's own position often goes unnoticed. 'Successful' individuals are often characterised as hard-working, skilful and ingenious – the implication being that if they apply themselves to the task, anyone can achieve success. Equally so, the reverse is true: business failure will be attributed to some personal deficiency. People will say of the failed man that he drank too much, he was too interested in women, or that he became lazy and complacent. The possibility of the economic system itself constituting the cause of his downfall is normally ruled out.

Yet the mobility of the 'successful' few is conditional upon the stagnation of the many, and all the hard work and ingenuity in the world will do little to change this. How can the harsh reality of the situation be reconciled with the predominant individualist ethic? The problem may be solved by the intervention of the myth of the miracle. The miraculous is known to happen to certain individuals on a regular basis, through some windfall gain, the winning of a lottery prize or a football pool, or some chance occurrence, as in the following example from Dakar:

The interviewee, widowed with a son and two daughters, was required after the death of her husband to marry his younger brother. The marriage only lasted a year, but she was permitted to keep the family house in trust for her children. She had a relative who worked as a customs official on the Senegalese–Gambian frontier, who procured the necessary documents for her to pass freely over the border as a petty trader. A friend of the deceased husband offered to finance her first trading expedition. She purchased cloth, jewellery, perfume and cigarettes in Banjul and was able to return to Senegal without paying customs duties, thanks to the help of her relative. With her accumulated profits she was able to buy successively larger amounts of merchandise. On one trip she had a stroke of luck. The Senegalese customs men had seized a number of radios, which they were selling off to traders. She was thus able to increase her profits considerably. On her next visit, she took advantage of an even greater and more fortuitous occurrence: a customs official offered her what was apparently a large box of printed cloth at a reasonable price. On the other side of the border, she decided to examine what she had bought. Beneath the top layer of cloth, she found 25 transistor radios, which the official had failed to discover. These two unforeseen gains (referred to by the smuggler almost as constituting divine intervention) were instrumental in permitting her to accumulate sufficient capital to purchase a second-hand taxi, acquire all the relevant permits and papers, and hire a driver. She now conducts her 'trading' activities on a relatively large scale and is able to send her two daughters to a private secondary school. She also employs a maid to look after the house while she is away on business. She wants to ensure that her children all have a future, which from her viewpoint means a profession and an inheritance (both paid for out of her profits). Relatives occasionally come to borrow money, but her close kin are now few in number, and, due to pressure of work, she is not often at home. (Gerry, fieldnotes, January–March 1974)

On other occasions, the 'miracle' which has the potential to change an individual's life, to transport him or her from poverty to affluence, is of a more supernatural character, as the following example illustrates (Birkbeck, fieldnotes, 1977):

Don Colo owns a small shop in one of Cali's poorest neighbourhoods. One day, not too long ago, he was walking on the outskirts of the city and felt the call of nature, so he went into a banana plantation at the side of the road. Having no paper, he used the leaves of a nearby plant, and, on returning home, realised that his ring was missing. In bed that night, he dreamt that the loss of the ring was related to the plant, the leaves of which he had used that day. The following day he returned to the plantation, gathered some of these leaves and brought them home.

He rubbed the leaves over his daughter's gold ring and it became rubbery and malleable. He realised that he had found the long-lost legendary plant the Indians had used to work their gold with such delicacy. He could in turn become a legend. Yet he has not, due to his fear of divulging his secret, his fear that someone else will take advantage of it, and make the fortune that should be his.

This latter story is of interest not because its contents are necessarily false, but for what they show about the psychology associated with the myth of the miracle. The miracle is something that happens to the individual, and it is something that can only be enjoyed by him or her. To confide with a fellow-worker or friend would be to lose any real chance of gaining from the miracle. In a similar way the garbage picker may miraculously find a wristwatch or some other piece of jewellery during his daily work, whilst the lottery ticket seller may find a client who will buy nearly all of his tickets, or the artisan may be offered a large and lucrative contract. Virtually every low income worker awaits a win on the lottery, football pool or some other windfall. The great willingness of these workers to invest in gambling suggests that for them the odds against winning the lottery are no greater than odds against some less 'premeditated' miracle occurring. Lotteries not only raise revenue for the Government, indeed in some countries they are the primary source of funds for social expenditure such as health facilities, but they may also be instrumental in strengthening the idea that the capitalist system can at times bring forth unexpected prizes. Finally, the miracle requires the worker to harvest its possibilities himself. This reflects the very prevalent feeling that one's fellow worker is not to be trusted, and, that the way to pull oneself up does lie in individual effort. All attempts at co-operation are apparently doomed from the start and, thus, should be avoided. Whilst this may be a realistic attitude for the low income worker, it has surely developed partly out of the system under which these workers are forced to operate. Capitalism is at its most divisive at the lower end of the scale, and yet here, paradoxically, its strongest supporters-in-principle are to be found. In addition, much State and media propaganda designed to encourage the 'small businessman', either through credit programmes, the extension of training and consultation services, or through banking schemes, is to be found in underdeveloped countries. It is doubtful that these policies result in any major improvement in the economic position of the majority of such workers, and yet the active support of such activities by the State serves a major ideological function in suggesting that with a little bit of help from its friends, the small business can not only succeed, but may even represent the very backbone of the economy.

Outside the network of direct capitalist relations, the picture is complex. The disguised wage worker is in a contradictory class location and yet tends to be supportive of the capitalist system. The lumpen-capitalist on the one hand is an independent worker and the owner of his own means of production, yet on the other hand has few chances of material progress. His ideology will be moulded by both of these factors, though the 'recipe' will almost certainly change over time, according to the historical conjuncture, both as it affects the system as a whole, the class composition of society, the trajectory of class formation, and the individual. There are important and powerful mechanisms operating within the international economy which generate support for the capitalist system. Indeed, it may be appropriate to see the politicians, administrators and entrepreneurs of underdeveloped capitalist economies as constituting little more than the co-opted petite bourgeoisie of an internationally active capitalist class.

At grassroots level, the working poor in Third World cities are encouraged to feel that they have some control over their own work and destiny; independent labour not only has value but as a future. The miracle may be just round the corner. The end product of this message is the creation of a number of ideological variants each of which is supportive in its own way of the capitalist system. There will be a number of such variants precisely because of the different objective relations of production under which the various fractions of the urban working poor operate. It may not be helpful to term all those in contradictory class locations the petite bourgeoisie of underdeveloped societies. Some, indeed many may be 'pro-capitalist', and yet from time to time may perceive their interests to be quite clearly at odds with those of the indigenous ruling class. Here we are not only referring to politicians, senior civil servants and the like, but also to the multitude of public and private sector functionaries and technicians, who service the machinery of capitalism in its Third World operations. The reason for their support lies in the material benefits, status and power which accompanies, in varying amounts, their specific roles in the capitalist division of labour. Those who, in Frank's terms, are co-opted (though not fully adopted) by the bourgeoisie, are placed in a relatively privileged position *vis-à-vis* the officially-recognised proletariat, the disguised wage-workers and the lumpen-capitalists.

On the other hand, there are many who do not have this sort of 'capital', namely a stake in the system of exploitation. The 'pygmy property' (Marx, 1970 vol. I, p. 762) (whether in the form of a disguised wage or lumpen-capital) of the mass of the urban working poor permits the majority of them to do little more than reproduce their existing conditions. Far from having a viable stake in an exploitative system, in many cases they constitute the objects of exploitation, producing valuable surplus from which the 'co-opted ones' are in part re-munerated. In other cases, petty commodity producers are either neglected or actively persecuted by the authorities, a process which itself can often indirectly facilitate the general process of surplus-appropriation.[3]

We may conclude, therefore, that the principal common denominator linking the so-called 'new' and 'old' petite bourgeoisie is constituted by their interest in the benefits which they believe capitalism can directly or indirectly afford them. Where the difference between them lies (and it is a significant difference) is in the nature of the capitalism of which they would wish to be a part. In effect, the 'best interests' of the co-opted workers would be served by the maintenance of the mature, corporate and internationalised capitalism which is their master. The petty producer, whether disguised wage worker or lumpen-capitalist, requires a return to the liberal, *laissez-faire* and highly individualist capitalism of the past. Pygmy property is thus compromised in that, rarely able to make the ideological leap to radical political action, it tends to lend its support to the parties of corporate bourgeois property – the very mode of production which blocks its development.

Conclusion

The issue of class and class formation in the Third World is undoubtedly complex. In this paper we have been able to do little more than raise certain questions, and attempt to match theory with what we know about reality. We began with the proposition that, despite the utility of Marxian concepts of class, an analysis made with reference to (a) a specific historical conjuncture and (b) a particular social formation, must use those concepts in a manner which responds to the Marxian method and not to a dogmatic and presupposed universalism. The notion of a 'petite bourgeoisie' is problematical, firstly because it does not allow that workers might have contradictory class locations, and secondly because it tends to locate all workers deemed not to be 'true' proletarians in the camp of the bourgeoisie, with the corresponding ideology and objectives.

In our consideration of the evolution of capitalism in underdeveloped countries in general, and the corresponding forms of employment in particular, we argued that petty commodity production was, and remains, intimately linked to the development of capitalism. Additionally we have disaggregated petty producers into three types: direct wage labourers, disguised wage workers and the truly self-employed. Most petty producers are not therefore petit-bourgeois. Nevertheless, in our considerations of the politico-ideological factors in class formation, we argued for the existence of powerful factors at work which tend to make many of these people supportive of capitalism. But one can 'support' capitalism in many ways – deliberately, unwittingly, unwillingly. To class as one all those who do so, we feel, is not only a theoretical error, but also an oversimplification of an exceedingly complex reality.

For Frantz Fanon (1967, p. 103), petty producers among others were perhaps the key to revolutionary political change:

> It is within this mass of humanity, this people of the shanty towns, at the core of the lumpen-proletariat that the rebellion will finds its urban spreahead. For the lumpen-proletariat, that horde of starving men, uprooted from their tribe and from their clan, constitutes one of the most spontaneous and most radically revolutionary forces of a colonized people.

For us the analysis is very different. The 'people of the shanty towns' are not a lumpen-proletariat, nor do they constitute a 'radically revolutionary force'. There is no doubt that they are the victims of exploitation and inequality, but there is also no doubt that if we wish to achieve a clearer understanding of their political formation and behaviour, then our analyses will have to be substantially more sophisticated than we have been accustomed to make them.

NOTES

1. See for example, the economic achievements of China, Cuba, North Korea.
2. Research conducted by the authors in Colombia was financed by the Ministry of Overseas Development.
3. (a) Producer and/or traders can be harassed out of prime locations.
   (b) They can be denied access to a market which has become of interest to large scale capitalism.
   (c) The value of taxes, licences, permits and bribes may also constitute leakages out of the petty commodity producers' circuit.

REFERENCES

S. Amin, *Le développement inégal* (Paris: Maspero, 1973).
S. Barry, *Le Royaume de Waalo: Le Sénégal avant le conquête* (Paris: Maspero, 1972).
F. Bechhofer and B. Elliott, 'Persistence and Change: the Petite Bourgeoisie in Industrial Society', *European Journal of Sociology*, XVII (1976).
C. H. Birkbeck, 'Self employed Proletarians in an Informal Factory: the Case of Cali's Garbage Dump', *World Development*, 6 (1978) 1173–86.
R. Cohen and D. Michael, 'The Revolutionary Potential of the African Lumpenproletariat: a Sceptical View', *Bulletin of the Institute of Development Studies*, University of Sussex, 5 (1973).

M. Diop, *Histoire des classes sociales dans l'Afrique de l'ouest: le Sénégal* (Paris: Maspero, 1972).

F. Fanon, *The Wretched of the Earth* (Harmondsworth: Penguin Books, 1967).

A. G. Frank, *On Capitalist Underdevelopment* (Bombay: Oxford University Press, 1975).

C. Gerry, 'Petty Production and Capitalist Production in Dakar: the Crisis of the "Self-employed"', *World Development*, **6** (1978) 1147–60.

D. C. Hodges, 'The Anatomy of Exploitation', *Science and Society* (1960).

International Labour Office, *Towards Full Employment: A Programme for Colombia* (Geneva: 1970).

International Labour Office, *Employment, Incomes and Equality: A Strategy for Raising Productive Employment in Kenya* (Geneva: 1972).

G. N. Kitching, 'Modes of Production and Kenyan Dependency', *Review of African Political Economy*, 8 (1977).

O. Lebrun and C. Gerry, 'Petty Production and Capitalism', *Review of African Political Economy*, 3 (1975).

K. Marx, *Capital* (London: Lawrence & Wishart, 1970).

N. Poulantzas, 'On Social Classes', *New Left Review*, 78 (1973).

N. Poulantzas, 'The New Petty Bourgeoisie', in A. Hunt (ed.), *Class and Class Structure* (London: Lawrence & Wishart, 1977).

D. G. Reynolds, 'Economic Development With Surplus Labour: Some Complications', *Oxford Economic Papers*, 21 (1969) 89–108.

A. Scott, 'Notes on the Theoretical Status of PCP' (University of Essex: mimeo, 1977).

A. Sfeir-Younis, 'Institutional Arrangements and Economic Development: Access to the Solid Waste Economy', World Bank, Urban and Regional Economics Division, 1977.

G. Williams and T. Mutebile, 'Petty Commodity Production in Nigeria: a Note', *World Development* (1978).

E. O. Wright, 'Class Boundaries in Advanced Capitalist Societies', *New Left Review*, 98 (1976).

7 Artisanal Bakery in France: How it Lives and Why it Survives

DANIEL BERTAUX AND ISABELLE BERTAUX-WIAME

What the Anglo-Saxons call 'French bread' is found, in fact, all over Latin Europe; it is the ancestral form of bread, compared to the industrial food wrapped in a shroud of cellophane which is sold in the supermarkets of the Western world under the somewhat euphemistic label of 'bread'.

This industrial 'bread', which accounts for almost all the bread in the United States and in Canada, is also produced and sold in Europe, including Latin Europe. For the time being, however, it does not account for more than 10 per cent of the market but its share is slowly growing. The day will come perhaps when it will be the turn of Frenchmen to eat this food. Come that day and it will become very clear that 'French' bread was not specific to France or any other geographic area, but to a particular *mode of production*.

While industrial 'bread' is the product of capitalistic relations of production, what is called 'French' bread is the product of *artisanal* relations of production. And it is called 'French' only because France is indeed, among the industrial countries, the only one which still retains a large sector of small, 'pre-capitalist' family production; the peasantry, the small shopkeepers, and the artisans together still amount to about 20 per cent of the active population.

Why is it so? That is to say, why do the artisanal relations of production in general and those of the production of bread in particular, survive in France? Are they nothing but 'survivals' soon condemned to disappear? And if this is so, how come these 'survivals' have lingered so long in France, and not elsewhere? On the other hand, if one argues with Claude Servolin and others that these 'pre-capitalist' relations of production are in fact functional, even in the midst of a capitalist

155

economy because they allow the low cost production of certain types of goods (like poultry, milk or pork) whose production is difficult to industrialise, then one has to face the question: why have these 'functional' relations of production disappeared elsewhere in the industrialised world?

After studying the artisanal bakery for several years, I have come to answer these questions by changing their terms which, despite their Marxist guise, give off a strong smell of functionalism. How can we 'explain', or rather describe in depth the reasons for the massive scale of artisanal bakery in France without having to resort to functionalist circularity? This is the topic of this paper.

I

France has now about 52 million inhabitants and 50,000 bakeries; one bakery for one thousand people, this is the average ratio. And it means, quite obviously, a very decentralised scattering of small, independent bakeries. In official statistics, small bakeries are included in the 'commerce' category. However, a big difference between bakeries and most other shops is that the bread, before being put on sale, is firstly *made* on the spot. Not only bread but also cakes, croissants, and so on are *produced* by the baker (who is by training and function, an artisan rather than a shopkeeper) and by his workers, when there are any. The shopkeeper here is the baker's wife, and the couple is the real economic unit, man as artisan, woman as shopkeeper, and the bond of marriage between them functioning somehow like a relation of production.

The 50,000 bakeries employ about 80,000 workers, and this says a lot about the small size of most bakeries: on average they employ less than three workers. What is more, 40 per cent of these 'workers' are under 20 years old, they are in fact *apprentices* (aged 15 to 17) or young workers aged 18 or 19. The age-pyramid of the male population is quite unusual; it has a tremendously large base, composed of these young men. Such a structure means that most of them leave the trade some time between 20 and 25, that is soon after returning from military service (which is compulsory for all men, starting at age 20 and lasting at least one year).

To indicate with rather more precision the structure of this branch of trade, we have to use detailed statistics, the most recent of which date from 1962. In this year, the total number of bakeries was 48,000. Of these, 13,000 did not employ anybody other than family members. The husband at the oven, the wife at the cash register, maybe a child helping to sell on Sunday mornings or market days, or a young girl from a neighbouring family working there as a non-registered salesgirl: this was all the labour power of these very small bakeries. Out of them, 5500 made and sold bread only, not pastries, which means that the profit they were making was quite low. We have visited some of these bakeries; you will find them in those villages whose young population is migrating to the cities; you find them in cities in those old areas which used to have a dense network of shops, corresponding to a very dense population.

In the large cities the new 'middle-class' population has left for the green suburbs, the working-class population has been kicked out towards housing projects in white and grey suburbs. The network of shops remains, slowly deteriorating. Its small bakeries are inhabited either by an old couple who vegetate towards retirement, or sometimes a young couple whose husband, a former bakery worker, is now trying to become a self-employed baker. A shop with such poor trade is all he could afford to begin with as a self-employed baker.

In 1962, 28,000 bakeries still employed only one or two persons, usually one worker and either an apprentice or a salesgirl. And if one adds the 5700 bakeries employing from three to five persons and the 13,000 without employees, the total comes to 46,700, that is almost the totality (97 per cent) of the bakeries. In the midst of an industrialised society, the existence of such a scattered branch of production looks like a socio-historical aberration.

The remaining 3 per cent of the total (1300 bakeries with more than five employees) employ 45,000 persons, which means 40 per cent of the *salaried* workforce of the bakeries (in 1962). It seems huge, but this percentage is misleading because the artisans and their wives should also be included in the workforce; taking this into account, the largest bakeries employ no more than 20 per cent of the total workforce.

Not all these bakeries are of the industrial type. Actually most of them are large *boulangeries-patisseries*, making not only bread and *viennoiserie* (*croissants*, *petits pains*), but various kinds of cakes and pastries, which require much labour. The number of really *industrial* bakeries was small in 1962 (thirty-three establishments employing more than twenty persons, out of which four employed more than 100, and one more than 500). In 1978 their number is still small, and their share of the bread market is under 20 per cent.

As far as we know, there has not been any drastic change since 1962. For instance, the number of bakeries has remained stable; in fact it increased between 1962 and 1966 (from 48,000 to 55,000), thus following the increase of French population at this time. Their number has been diminishing since, but quite slowly (53,700 bakeries in 1970, 51,000 in 1977).

According to our research, this overall decrease is the result of a double movement. On the one hand, many of the poorest businesses are closing down for ever, either in deserted villages or in the depopulating districts of cities. In this last case, it is not without interest to note that more often than not, what has taken the place of the small bakery is the branch of a bank. The biggest banks considerably developed their national network of offices during the sixties; they liked to buy bakeries, not only because they could put the safes in the basement previously used for the oven and making of the bread, but also because bakeries are usually extremely well located; besides if you are in the habit of walking to a place every day to buy bread, it will be easier to persuade you to go there every week to get some of the money the bank is kindly keeping for you.

On the other hand, new bakeries have been built, not in cities but in newly developed suburbs. Since the fifties, these have popped up in the outskirts of every city, where the housing projects align their slabs and towers in a muddy no-man's land. The bakeries which have been built there are of a larger type than usual; but while they employ ten to fifteen persons, and make bread for 10,000 to 20,000 people, they produce the same type of bread as the artisanal bakeries, using the same process of production. Although the product of a new form of urbanisation, these 'new' bakeries are not the beginning of a passage towards industrialisation. On the contrary, they mean that the artisanal form has adapted itself to the new suburban forms.

How is it that among all the capitalist countries France is the only one (though perhaps we should include Italy) in which bread is still made and sold through *artisanal* relations of production? When we asked this question, we got the same unanimous answer:

C'est parce que les Français aiment le bon pain!

How obvious, how plain, how simple: the French like good bread! True enough; but what about the British, or the North Americans, who also liked 'good bread' we may think; that did not prevent the small bakeries from being forced out by the bread factory.

Now it could be argued that in the *culture* of the French, food occupies the central place. This is a well known fact and we can all presumably testify to it; besides, it is verified by comparative surveys. Not only do the French spend a larger part of their income on food, but they also spend much more *time* eating. Comparative time budgets are extremely revealing. While, for instance, East Germans eat quite quickly and at both ends of the work day, Frenchmen stop for one to two hours at midday. It is almost as if while other industrial nations eat during the pores of the workday, the French work during the interval between one meal and the next. But does this actual need for 'food' (or rather, for meals, meals as social events) have any social force? No doubt, the French used to like good wines, good poultry, good cheese and that did not prevent all these foods from becoming food products, industrialised, standardised, homogenised; dead things. Still the French eat them, albeit with a grimace.

Bread, however, has resisted so far. Its very *shape* may indicate this, in a surer way than statistics. For when foods pass from an artisanal mode of production to a capitalist one, their form changes (and also, unfortunately, their content). Every capitalist good must adapt to the necessities of *stocking* and *transportation*. As a mass-produced good, it becomes standardised; its quality becomes invariable (or invariably poor). In North America, the bread which is sold and eaten is more than industrialised bread (you can produce fresh bread in factories, but you cannot stock it or transport it too far); it is 'capitalist' bread, a stabilised product in a cellophane envelope; it is canned bread.

Given the distinction between these two types of bread, the 'artisanal' and the 'capitalist', each one corresponding to a wholly different mode of production, what is the reason for the disappearance of artisanal bread in most industrialised countries, and for its persistence in France? We do not believe it can be explained by the taste of the French people; rather it is this taste which is a consequence of the persistence of artisanal bakery. But neither is it to be explained by 'structural' features which hold only as *ex post facto* explanations. We find it more adequate for the processes we have observed to think of this survival as the result of a continual *fight* by the artisanal form of production, against the attempts by large financial groups (and especially flour mill owners) to take over the huge market for bread.

This fight is not mere hypothesis. In fact, since the beginning of the century, there have been several attempts to establish factories making industrial bread. Most of these attempts failed. It is the discovery of these successive attempts which led us to the hypothesis of a constant fight against a *potential* enemy (we shall come back to it); and it is in the context of this fight that the taste of French people as consumers may be playing a key role. For, every time there was a possibility of choice between artisanal and industrial bread, the consumer chose the first one, thus ruining the hopes of the 'industrialists'.

It seems that the financial groups which look for the takeover of the bread market have drawn their lessons from earlier failures, and have incorporated in their definition of the situation a clear understanding of the necessity to break the back of small artisans *before* industrial bread is promoted on the market. Artisanal bread, which we are tempted to conceive as a luxury good sold at a mass-production price, is too competitive; it has to be suppressed by noneconomic means. But how to do it?

A variety of strategies have been tried. During the fifties for instance, a series of articles appeared here and there, in ladies' journals and in the newspapers, arguing that bread makes you fat. What was advised by (usually American) dieticians was to substitute rusks for bread. Pretty soon this idea that bread is bad for your body silhouette became common knowledge (note in passing the existential contradiction between gastronomy and slenderness, the pleasure of eating and the pleasure to please; the target of the campaign against traditional bread, young women, had been quite carefully chosen).

Reacting at last to what appeared to be a carefully planned campaign, the Syndicat de la Boulangerie (Bakers' Professional Union) asked some nutritionists of high scientific reputation to establish objectively whether or not it was true that bread was making people fatter. Their report, which we have every reason to consider as fair and independent, pointed to the falsity or at least, inconclusiveness of most arguments against bread. But if these conclusions comforted the bakers, they did not reach the public at large. Good science, as we know, usually makes bad reading.

Fresh bread was saved, probably, by a move in another field, far more efficient in the long run than the ideological one: the material field of bread itself, as a thing. For it was precisely during the same historical period (the fifties) that the bread changed its shape; that a shift was observed from the one-pound loaf to the crusty *baguette* (half-pound loaf). More crust, less crumb. In the big cities, the urbanised public turned massively towards the *baguette*; those bakers who had first introduced the *baguette* (it meant a change in the technique itself) had so much success that the others followed. In shifting the image of bread from bread-as-crumb to bread-as-crust, and thinking they were merely following 'the taste of the public', the bakers quite unconsciously won the fight. The huge propaganda which had been put about in favour of rusks against bread (bread-as-crumb) was thus warded off, and its effect may appear retrospectively as having prepared the emergence of the *baguette*, bread-as-crust, the new strong point of the artisanal bakery. We should add, though, that for all the bakers we have interviewed, this shift in the form of bread is seen purely as a result of a change in 'the taste of the public'; the interpretation drafted above is ours.

During the sixties, it seems that another massive attack was launched by industrialists against the artisanal bakers of Greater Paris. We have heard the following story, which we have been unable so far to check completely, but which we believe to be true in its broad lines. In 1966, the largest flour-milling group in France, which has the near monopoly of supplying flour to the Greater Paris area (nine million inhabitants at the time), decided to try taking over the market for bread. Plans were drawn up for a huge bread factory to be built in Paris itself, close to the river Seine. Banks and, it seems, government officials, were backing the project. But first of all, it was necessary to weaken the artisans. So, one day, without warning, small bakers were told by the flour-milling company that flour would henceforth be delivered in full truckloads only. As many of the bakers had neither the storage capacity nor the volume of sales corresponding to full truckloads, they found themselves in great trouble. What could they do?

After one week of panic, they found out that some small mills were still functioning in the rural regions surrounding the Paris area. These mills were on the verge of closing down, as they were only working at 20 per cent of their capacity. They were, of course, extremely happy to accept the orders of the small bakers, and thus to reach full capacity. After one month of groping about, it appeared that the new network could quite possibly function smoothly. The big flour-milling company understood it had lost the fight; it went back to its previous policy of retail delivery, lowered its prices to get back its former customers, and put the plans for the factory back in the safe where they are waiting for the next opportunity.

It seems to us that this story, which shows how the relations between big flour-mills and small artisans may sometimes take on the character of an open war, reveals the hidden truth of the *normal* daily situation of artisanal bakery. While it may seem at first glance that this sector lives the peaceful life of a charming anachronism kept alive by the complicity of 50 million bread-loving Frenchmen, in fact, the latent covetousness of the great agro-industrial firms for the market of the bread makers makes the survival of artisanal bakeries problematic, and forces an everyday struggle against the potential enemy. But because the threat is latent, because the enemy is invisible, the struggle is not recognised as a struggle; it is conceived simply as the usual way of life in the trade. A hard way, certainly, but *c'est la boulange!*, as the bakers say with resignation.

II

This characterisation of bakers' hard work as a kind of militancy, of the taxing rhythm of life in the trade as a sign of chronic mobilisation of all its members, is again our own interpretation. It may be wrong; but the facts on which it is based will remain. When collecting life histories, we always asked about the length of the working day, at each different period of life. The results were quite amazing. Before the last war, the working 'day' of a baker, which ended at around seven in the afternoon, quite commonly began not at eight in the morning, or at six or four, but at midnight, and sometimes even earlier! You had to prepare the dough for the first batch; then, while it was rising, you could sleep for two hours. Then the oven had to be warmed, which meant first cutting wood, lighting up the fire, and so on. When the oven was clean and hot, the first batch was cooked (at around two in the morning); the following batches were prepared and cooked during the rest of the night and the morning, up to noon.

At noon the baker and his employees had lunch (they sometimes fell asleep over their plates while eating), and went to bed for a couple of hours. But around four, the baker would wake up the young apprentice, load the loaves in the cart, and start going round the countryside, bringing bread to the farms. Coming back two hours later, they would have a quick dinner and go back to sleep until eleven or midnight, when they would start the whole process again.

Before 1936 the bakeries *never* closed; they were open every day of the week, and Sunday too. It meant that the 'workday' we have just described was repeated day after day, week after week all year long. As for the feast days, for the bakers they were the worst; while everybody else rested, extra work had to be put in baking cakes. Imagine the kind of life it meant: sixteen hours of work for the baker, and as many hours for the young apprentice (aged 13 to 16); twelve hours at least for the adult worker. And the baker's wife was sitting behind the counter for twelve hours, day after day, week after week, every day of the year. It seems another world – and so it was.[1]

In 1936, by State decree, it was decided that all bakeries would close for one day in the week. In most villages and city districts, it made the situation even worse. Bakers did not want to close the shop when the competitor's bakery across the street was kept open. Thus, all bakers of a given area closed on the same day. As a consequence, the customers would buy twice as much bread on the day before closure, which meant that the baker and his worker(s) had to make twice as much bread on the night before (it is called *le doublage*). As they used the same tools and manpower, it required twice as much work, and the 'workday', instead of ten hours in a row, lasted twenty. The rest day was used to try to make up for the lack of sleep and enormous spending of energy. But it could not prevent the body, and especially the heart and the nerves, from wearing out.

The situation has changed since then, but not as much as we might think. Fuel heating has replaced the wood fire and the dreary task of cutting and drying wood. Machines have replaced hand labour in a number of operations, not only for kneading (this was done as early as 1914, because of the lack of labour due to World War I), but also for dividing the dough into pieces, for weighing each piece separately, for putting them into the oven and getting them out of it. Now the usual work 'day', actually a work night, will start around three or four in the morning and will last no more than nine to ten hours. But it still means 54 hours a week of night work, not counting the *doublage*. Besides, due to mechanisation, you have now to work faster; 'now we always run', say the old bakery workers who can compare the two epochs.

The law, actually, does not allow the artisan to employ a worker for more than 54 hours a week but in fact we never met anybody working *less* than 54 hours. Most workers worked longer hours (one aged 63 was doing 72 hours a week). Extra hours are paid in cash 'under the table'. They never appear in written documents, which means that here as in many other places, oral sources are *more* reliable than written ones.

The law also forbids artisans employing the apprentices entrusted to them before six o'clock in the morning. Concessions may be given permitting work to begin at four o'clock. But most of the apprentices we interviewed got up at two in the morning and sometimes even earlier. Apprentices almost invariably have a room in the same building as a bakery and when the baker gets up, he wakes up the apprentice. And the 'night' begins. Several apprentices told us they were working 14 hours a day . . .

III

In all this, the bakers' wives do not have the best part either. They have to keep the shop open from eight in the morning (seven, in working class districts) to eight in the evening, sometimes without interruption (usually the shop is closed from one to four). To this work as a shopkeeper, six days a week – work which by the way gives no salary, no social rights whatsoever, and no property right either – they must add the work of any housewife and mother. The closing day is used not for rest or leisure, but in making up for the accumulated backlog of cleaning, washing, shopping . . .

Bakeries are family businesses, which means that they are production units in which both husband and wife invest their energy. But the key role is played not by the baker, but by his wife. In the competition between small bakeries, the appeal of the baker's wife plays a greater role than the quality of the bread, which does not vary very much from one shop to the other. Small shops have a personality of their own, and customers choose them (or abandon them) according to this.

Besides, an 'imprudent' wife can very quickly ruin her husband. When a young couple start with their first bakery, it is all too easy for the wife to fall into the illusion that the money which comes into the drawer of the cash register belongs to the family, and to spend it. But, comes the end of the month, and they have to pay the bills for flour, fuel, the taxes included in the bread's price; the drafts on the loan which has set up the business have been spent; bankruptcy is near.

Finally, a baker simply cannot be a baker without a wife to act as cashier. He has to get somebody behind the counter and it has to be his wife. A wife is a woman you can trust, and one you do not have to pay. If a young baker had to give a salary to a cashier, and had to run the risk of being cheated by her, he just could not make ends meet. When a baker dies, his wife may hire a bakery worker to do his job; we have seen such cases. But if the wife dies, or if she leaves her husband, the baker has to close the shop immediately (to find another wife takes some time). Thus, he will lose his customers, hence the greatest part of the value of the goodwill. What happens usually, in this case, is that he becomes a bakery worker until he can bind another woman to him through the bonds of marriage.

IV

But why is it that the artisanal form has survived up to this day? What gives it the strength to survive? And, if it is true that it is the tremendous amount of work which is put into the bread by all the personnel of the bakery, why is it that these people accept working so hard? Or rather – considering that bakers and bakery workers have *always* worked hard – why is it that they continue to accept such conditions of life, while the world around them has changed tremendously and allows much more time for enjoyment? To understand their reasons, which are so existentially anchored that they can hardly articulate them, one has to understand who they are. It took us some time to discover it.

Today's bakers are not born bakers; this is the key discovery. Once said, it seems quite simple. In our research, however, everything pointed in the opposite direction. The historical study we made of the bakery indicated that the trade had always been transmitted from father to son. Not only before the 1789 Revolution, but a century later, the only way to become a baker was to be born the son of a baker. The professional organisation of bakers (their corporation before 1789, their syndicate later) saw to it that no baker's hand, no bakery worker set up his own business – except in the rare case where it was a baker himself who, having had as an apprentice and then as a hand, a young man whom he had totally under control, decided to leave him his own business, perhaps by marrying him to his daughter. If this fortunate man was not a baker's son biologically, he was one through education, plighted faith, and (most often) marriage.

As for the present times, no statistics of the social origins of bakers were available. Neither could we get to know them through a representative survey. In fact, we tried to make such a survey; we worked out quite a detailed longitudinal questionnaire. But we could not get the bakers to answer it through the mail (the first attempt was quite conclusive on this: shopkeepers being distrustful of everything which comes from the State, they catch the scent of more taxes and systematically play 'dead'). And we were unable to interview several hundred bakers.[2] Actually it was difficult to interview bakers at all. As soon as Daniel, who started this research, introduced himself as a State paid research worker involved in research about 'bakery' (not bakers!), a kind of invisible iron curtain was drawn between him and the baker. Long experience has taught shopkeepers that State curiosity, whatever form it takes, ends up with one and the same content: more taxes. After the warm welcome of bakery workers, the coldness of bakers was especially disconcerting.

Some attempts to get around this difficulty, like sending charming feminine co-workers or trying to get the support of the professional organisations of bakers – were slow to bring results. The solution to this thorny fieldwork problem was found by chance. Isabelle, who is an historian by training, had become interested in this research and started to study the economic and social history of the bakery. Then one day, as we were on holiday in the Pyrenees, both of us went to see the village baker. First, of course, we met the baker's wife, and asked for an interview. She was rather surprised and got her husband to come up. 'What do you do this research for' he asked – as usual. So we explained that being husband and wife, we worked for . . . 'Husband and wife?', interrupted he. 'So you are working like us – *en couple*. Only we are making bread, and you are making . . . research? You are some kind of artisans like us, is that it?' Both couples looked at each other and some process of mutual identification, some non-verbal, human communication happened. And it solved our problem. After that, we either conducted the interviews as a couple or if Isabelle went alone, she was careful to mention that this research, although financed by the State, was also a family thing. This, plus the belated help of the professional union, allowed us to gather about forty life history interviews with bakers and bakers' wives.[3]

Once we had started to interview bakers, we realised that a number of them (most of them actually) were not bakers' sons, but former bakery workers who had become self-employed at an early age (25 to 35). Then we met the secretary of the professional union of bakers in a southern *department*, and this woman who had occupied this position for 25 years was of great help to us. Together we examined the cases of 180 bakers she knew personally, and it appeared that more than two-thirds of them had not in any way inherited their bakery; they were self-made men.

This discovery was puzzling. Most bakery workers we had interviewed had told us that they had thought about becoming self-employed, but that it was impossible: where could they find the 100,000 Francs (£12,000) necessary to take up even one of the smallest going concerns? It was pretty obvious that, given their workers' salaries, they could not save much, and that saving up to £12,000 was completely out of the question. It was also obvious that no bank would ever risk loaning money to a bakery worker, who had no property to offer as security.

So the mystery remained. We tried to ask bakers whether other bakers they knew had been bakery workers before, but this question proved meaningless. *Every* baker, even a baker's son, has been an apprentice first and then a bakery worker for several years. The real question is whether, when setting up his own business, the bakery worker who becomes a baker may 'mobilise resources' (that is, get funds) from his relations, or not. But this is the kind of thing which remains confidential.

V

It took more fieldwork, more life stories and interviews with a retired business broker to get the whole picture. The hidden social mechanism which allows some bakery workers to become self-employed works as follows. Take an old couple who want to retire. Suppose they have no son, no nephew or daughter to whom they could pass on the business. Their problem is to put a *baker* in their business, and nobody else; because only a baker will buy the goodwill at its real value. For, what makes up the value of a given bakery? It is not the machinery (usually worn out), nor the walls (which, in cities at least, do not belong to the shopkeeper, but to the owner of the building). It is the *goodwill* itself, that is the several hundreds of customers who are accustomed to come to *this* bakery to buy their bread. It is a set of relations to a given population.

Now a hairdresser or a cloth retailer will not want to buy this set of relations; they have no interest in it. Only a baker will pay for it.

If the baker's trade was still a good trade, as it was for centuries, the sons of bakers would have chosen this profession and one of them would be ready to take over his parents' business. If not a son, then a daughter – married to another baker's son, or to a bakery worker. But the baker's trade is not what it used to be. There are complex, historical reasons for this; but the declining appeal of the trade is obvious. So, most bakers orient their sons away from the trade; instead of putting them into bakeries as apprentices at age 14, they want them to go on with their studies and become commercial workers of some sort freed from hard manual work; or maybe state employees with easy jobs and with good pensions attached to them. Similarly, bakers' wives will advise their daughters to avoid marrying a shopkeeper – they speak from experience.

So, when the time for retirement comes, they do not find any baker's child to take over their business; neither their own nor the children of their colleagues. Thus, they have no other choice than to turn to the only type of men who are willing to take over the shops – young bakery workers.

These young men started to learn the trade early in life. If they have accepted all the hardships of apprenticeship and night-work, long hours and low pay (the salary is by the hour, and although the work is skilled, it is paid at the rate of unskilled labour), it is because they have lived with a project at heart – becoming self-employed. Actually it is the bakers themselves who continually tell their apprentices and young workers, *quand tu seras patron* . . . (when you are on your own), and this sentence is crucial in making these young men accept the hardships of the profession. If they considered themselves as *workers*, they would not accept things that they do accept as future bakers. In fact, when they get back from military service, where they have met industrial workers and realised that they are better paid and have a better life, working during the daytime and only nine hours per day, they all follow the same line of reasoning: 'either I become self-employed, or I quit'. And indeed, many do quit, as the curious age pyramid of the profession demonstrates.

There is, however, a catch: these eager young men have no money. Most of them come either from poor peasant families, or working class families (we checked this by examining the social origins of 200 apprentices in Paris and through our interviews in the Pyrenees); it is those families who live on the verge of poverty who bind their sons to a baker at 14, thus getting rid of the boy altogether (the baker gives him room and board). No loans can be expected from these families.

So it remains to the retiring baker to lend money *himself* to the young bakery worker. The usual arrangement is as follows: both agree on the value of the goodwill (based on the amount of bread sold in one month); the new couple steps in and repay this sum in eight years. It means, of course, very hard work for the young couple and a very low standard of living for a number of years. It also means a tremendous risk for the retiring couple. Imagine that the young couple have some weaknesses and that customers abandon the shop one after the other. Thus, the value of the goodwill will go down day by day. We have witnessed such a case; in six months, because the young baker's wife used to close the shop at midday to have some time to herself, because she was not always good-humoured, the largest bakery in a small town lost half of its customers to another bakery and the retired bakers lost most of their savings (actually they lived upstairs and the old baker, unable to stand the rapid decline of his bakery, soon died).

As shown by this example, the success or failure of the young couple (and the risk taken by the retiring couple) rests mainly on the shoulders of the young wife. A bakery worker, after ten years in the trade, can be trusted to make at least average quality bread. But what about his wife? She has never been a shopkeeper before. Will she do well? This is the riddle that the retiring couple has to solve. And it is extremely interesting to observe the practices of the two couples during the crucial period of *passage*. Pretending to show to the young lady how to behave as a *boulangère*, the experienced woman will also check her spontaneous reactions and try to uncover her fundamental values. There is still time to cancel the whole thing if the young lady appears to react too strongly to what she is discovering; the grim reality of a baker's wife's daily life.

VI

What is this daily life? First, very long hours of work – as mentioned earlier. The shop has to be kept open five and a half days a week, including Sunday morning. Opening time is eight at the latest, but seven in many places; workers and employees going to work in the morning want to buy fresh bread for their lunch. Closing time is eight in the evening – again everybody wants fresh bread for dinner. The symbolic aspect of fresh bread is well expressed through the fact that in many towns or villages, even if the bakery is closed (after 8 p.m.), people will knock at the back door and get some fresh bread from 'their' baker – a practice which is unthinkable with any other shopkeeper. Whatever the reason for this behaviour, it is an indicator of the constant pressure under which bakers and (especially) bakers' wives have to live their life.[4]

The second particular aspect of bakers' wives' daily lives is that they work during the day while their husbands work during the night. Paradoxically, the family business here means not more 'family life' but less. The situation is even worse for bakery workers' wives, and this is one of the reasons why so many bakery workers quit the trade on marriage.

The worst situation is that of a young woman who, knowing nothing about bakery, marries a young bakery worker who wants to set up his own business. As we have explained, she will have to play a part in the strategy of the ambitious young man; the central part, actually. But she does not realise it, or rather she does not realise *what it means* until it is too late.

To become self-employed, the bakery worker needs two things: money and a wife. A *good* wife is a courageous and responsible woman who will work to the utmost of her abilities, without getting much reward (either in standard of living, or time for living) during the first years of marriage. Is it a coincidence? We noticed that several bakers we interviewed told us they got married quite quickly (a few weeks after meeting their wife), and set up their own businesses even more quickly – sometimes right after the honeymoon. One of them made an interesting slip of the tongue. To the question 'when did you marry?' he answered 'je me suis installé, je veux dire, *marié*, en 1966' (I became self-employed, I mean, married, in 1966).

Conversely we found cases of bakery workers who had delayed the decision to become self-employed; by the time an opportunity arose they could not persuade their wives to take a shop because by that time they knew enough about what it meant (in terms of hard work and low rewards) and refused to do it. Their refusal meant that their husbands would never be able to fulfil their lifelong ambition of setting up their own business.[5]

In order that this presentation should not be one-sided, we must add that in a number of cases, the young bride accepted the life project of her husband and contributed gladly to it, getting thoroughly involved in the logic of small business. Such is the case of young women from rural backgrounds, who had worked in factories, or as servants or waitresses. These young women knew what it was like to make a living, when nobody in the world would help them. Self-employment had a very strong appeal for them, for it meant that nobody else would appropriate for himself a sizeable part of their hard work. Besides, these young women, having lived on their own, knew how to plan expenses, to manage a low budget; they were thus ready to adapt to the role of the baker's wife as financial manager of both business and family, and to give priority to the business over the family.

The women who suffer most in the first years as bakers' wives are those who as daughters of farmers or of shopkeepers were living with their parents up to their marriage, or those who as former high school students had already taken up an office job. Not only do they suffer (one of them, a former social worker, told us she had been crying all day long for weeks; she has now adapted well to life as 'headmistress' of a large bakery), but quite often they simply cannot adjust to the new role and quickly the whole project of becoming rich bakers ends in bankruptcy. In this case, husband and wife take up separate salaried jobs and often live quite happily in this way. They stress the fact that 'when the work is over, it's over' and you have long hours to spend together or with the children; while, as long as you are on your own, the necessities of the job impinge on private life to such an extent that they leave no time for anything else. The sociological truth about bakers' marriages seems to be that the relation between husband and wife becomes at once a relation between an artisan and a shopkeeper who got together as business partners.[6]

VII

What is the future of the artisanal bakery? We are neither functionalists, nor prophets; we believe the future cannot be predicted, either by sheer extrapolation or by the intuitions of some genius. History is a process of many struggles and the struggle of many processes. The survival of the artisanal bakery is in itself the daily outcome of a protracted struggle which mobilises not only the artisans, but their wives as well, and the young bakery workers and apprentices. They don't call it struggle, but 'hard work'. However, it is this fantastic amount of hard work which makes for the strength of the artisanal form and which has prevented industry from taking over the bread market. How long will they fight, or rather how long will they continue to accept working so hard for relatively poor results? This is the basic question.

The strength of industry lies in its enormous financial power, and in the supportive complicities it can mobilise at the top of the state apparatus. The strength of the artisanal form is of a different nature; it lies in its people.

It is at the level of the recruitment of its agents that the greatest threat for the artisanal bakery lies. Fewer and fewer apprentices are recruited by bakers. The proportion of apprentices from rural backgrounds is dropping fast, and according to our interviews, it is mainly those from rural backgrounds who are ready to go through the ordeal of setting up their own business. If *this* particular recruitment (of young men from rural backgrounds) becomes exhausted, then it will be the end of all the processes through which the artisanal form reproduces itself; it will be the end of artisanal bakery, or at least so we think.

This drying up of the flow of apprentices is in itself an interesting phenomenon. The professional organisation of bakers is highly conscious of it and has been trying to reverse the trend, without success so far. It is a mass phenomenon – it can be observed in most artisanal trades, and even in industrial crafts. As a result, while there is huge unemployment among youths, employers and artisans look in vain for skilled workers in some crafts; and ageing bakers begin to worry much earlier about finding a young couple to whom the goodwill could be sold.

Of course, bakers and other artisans explain this phenomenon by the fact that 'youths don't want to work any more'. A very interesting statement which opens a whole field for sociological thinking! We will limit our comment to one point: it seems quite true that attitudes towards work have drastically changed in the last twenty years. Urban youths seem to have moved towards a new attitude to life; they get less involved with work as such, and they invest more (psychologically speaking) in consumption, and more generally, in the private enjoyment of life. From a sociological point of view, it is easy to interpret this huge shift in ideology as a result of the shift from an industrial capitalism producing mainly machines and means of transportation, towards a capitalism producing goods for mass consumption; a shift which has been very well described by Baran and Sweezy in their *Monopoly Capital*. (Nowadays the massive unemployment of youths, hence their *poverty*, coupled with this orientation towards consumption issues, produces great sufferings and loss of identity among youths – but this is another story.) It is only among rural youths that one finds, somewhat paradoxically, 'industrial' values, that is some psychic involvement in work as a meaningful activity; a paradox, it seems, but one which is well known to employers who prefer to hire immigrant labour, not only because it is cheaper but mainly because Algerians and (especially) Portuguese have a more 'serious' attitude towards work.

Artisans also have some responsibility in the whole process. The number of those among them who are still willing to take up apprentices and teach them the trade is steadily diminishing. Constrained by the market to work more and more as small capitalists, and to consider like them that time is money, they think of appointing a new apprentice as a loss of time. Mechanisation has suppressed most of the small, unskilled tasks which were entrusted to apprentices (many old bakery workers recall how, during their first year of apprenticeship back in the twenties, they only learned to cut wood, sweep the floor, and deliver bread to restaurants, cafés and private houses). With the suppression of the opportunity to over-exploit the (practically free) labour of young apprentices, the teaching vocation of the bakers is also disappearing.

As a result, it is only in the rural areas that the 'production' of future bakers goes on. It is a paradox, for the artisanal bakery, contrary to what its 'traditional' image would have us believe, has always been mostly an *urban* trade. In French cities it has existed for at least ten centuries, while in the countryside, the peasants cooked their bread themselves (the women did it actually); and it is only at the end of the nineteenth century that the first rural bakers appeared (except in rural-industrial areas where they grew up with the factories).

Although we have not found statistics which would prove it, we believe that the number of rural bakeries grew very fast during the first thirty years or so of this century, thus covering the territory with a dense network of small shops making bread for 500 to 1500 people. It is this network which, as a last resort, saved the artisanal form from extinction by providing it with its main resource: human beings.

Evidence in favour of this hypothesis is given by a comparison between the western industrial countries; for it is precisely in these countries where a large peasantry remains (France, Italy, Spain) that bread is made by artisans; while in the countries where the peasantry has all but disappeared (Great Britain, the United States, Canada), bread is factory-made. This hypothesis may be only partly true, we have not done fieldwork in countries other than France, and there are certainly some processes which we are not exploring at all. Why is it, for instance, that artisanal bakeries have disappeared altogether with the peasantry in Quebec but that some remained in Britain, in Germany or in Belgium? We can only ask the question.

What is interesting, however, in this hypothesis is the chain of mediations that it assumes between the existence of peasantry and the survival of the artisanal form. The relation is by no means simple. The artisanal bakery has always been a preponderantly *urban* phenomenon. Towards the end of the nineteenth century it started diffusing from the local towns into the countryside. Also, rural millers, foreseeing the threat of industrial mills using new sources of energy, cylinder grinding and sophisticated techniques of sifting, moved into baking bread and distributing it to the surrounding farms and hamlets. This extension of artisanal bakery into the rural areas of the country tapped new sources of human labour. A new type of bakery worker began to appear, not the city-born hand of the past centuries, but the country-born worker carrying with him peasant values. Peasant values means, in France, first and foremost, the desire to be on his own; coupled with this fierce individualism, it means also an orientation towards work, well done work whose products bear the mark of their producer.

According to our hypothesis, it is this type of man who was able to 'save' the artisanal bakery when it was confronted with the hard competition of industrial bakery. For, under the mask of continuity, the French artisanal bakery underwent a deep transformation. As the trade progressively lost its economic rewards, the bakers' sons left. In other countries it is this move which probably meant the end of the artisanal bakery. In France, however, relief was to hand: bakery workers with peasant values were eager to take the place of bakers' sons. It cost them very hard work – so hard that it took peasant, not urban, values, to start on the steep path of *installation*. And this is how the rural bakery, after having been created by the urban bakery, saved it from extinction – by pumping new blood into its emptying structures. This human flow made possible the adaptation of the artisanal bakery to the new situation, characterised by the permanent threat of a takeover of the market by industry, and the much lower economic status of the artisanal bakery. The core of the 'reproduction' process of the artisanal form shifted from family inheritance to *installation* of bakery workers with the help of those who are also their exploiters: the master bakers.

The emphasis we put on 'the human factor' may be too strong. In the contemporary context, however, which witnesses the hegemony of economics as the religion of modern times (the core of their ideology), we believe this emphasis is useful. Sheer economic processes may have played a role we have not studied and stressed sufficiently (for example, the price of wheat, which was definitely lower in Britain and the New World than in France, due to the latter country's protectionist tariffs dating back to the 1880s). One should, however, be careful to avoid economic reductionism.

For instance, we have shown that the competition between artisan and industry for control of the bread market takes the form of a competition between two types of products: artisan and industry do not prepare the same type of bread. This, however, is not a pre-condition but a result of the competition itself. The strength of industrial baking lies, amongst other things, in the stability through time of industrial bread. What is a crucial necessity for capitalist production itself, that is the ability to transport through space *and* through time the goods it produces, has been redefined as a virtue of the products themselves: buy them once a week and get rid of the dreariness of daily shopping. But the artisanal bakery could also produce long-lasting bread: throughout the centuries this was the case. Peasant women would bake once a week and big loaves kept their taste for more than one week; in the cities too, a loaf lasted several days. How is it then, that the typical artisanal bread today, the *baguette*, is an essentially 'fresh', hence perishable product? Is this simply because 'the taste of the public has changed'? Or rather, cannot we interpret it as a slow, unconscious move of the artisans themselves towards the enhancement of freshness, the very feature of bread that the industry could not incorporate into its product? This interpretation we quote only as an example of how economic competition on the market (one of the seemingly purest economic phenomena, as it seems devoid of any political component) includes non-economic aspects. The competition is not between prices as such, but between products, which are characterised (briefly said) by a quality/price ratio; and it is through the 'quality' component that the social world slips in again. The 'quality' of bread (or, its use value) means not only its taste as a physical characteristic, but its symbolic meaning, and the social meanings it carries with it: there is some use value in buying fresh bread every day at the same place, from a baker you have 'chosen' from several. Whatever the words used to qualify this use value (sociability could be such a word), buying is not only an economic act but also *a social practice*; and socially speaking, it does not mean the same thing to buy food products, be it the *same* food products, from 'your' local shopkeeper or from a supermarket which could hardly be conceived as 'yours'.[7]

VIII

Lest, however, the preceding paragraphs should be understood as a request to complement the purely economic analysis with symbolic *supplement d'âme* (economic analysis 'with soul added', so to speak), we must briefly develop our conception of the so-called human factor. As we see it, the relations of production do not produce only products; they also produce the men and women who are taken into their web. It is this second aspect of production that we have called *la production anthroponomique*.[8]

When we stressed the importance of peasant values for the new generations of bakery workers, we used the metaphor of people 'carrying' values; we could also have used the expression of 'bearers of (a given) culture'. But these metaphors are somehow misleading. Values are not something that human beings carry on their backs as a load, and that they could suddenly drop. Values are inside them, at the very heart of their psychic structure. Values are social relations made human (social relations, not 'society' as a monolithic whole, as Parsons would have it). We use this expression, not in an idealistic sense, but, on the contrary, as an attempt to build up a conception of man and woman rooted in concrete life and, if you will permit the term, in a materialist philosophy. But materialism is not a philosophy of matter! There is no materialist conception of man (and woman) we know of; but if there was one, it would consider that what characterises a man or a woman is not his body, not even his or her labour power, but his or her psychic structure, which is far more rigid, far more stable through time, than the body.

The body is superficial, almost irrelevant, except as the carrier of *human energy* (a central concept in anthroponomic theory). But human energy itself has two aspects: the physical one, the only one that vulgar Marxism considers when it speaks of 'labour power' (which is the way capitalism, not Marx, defines human energy); and the psychic one. One day is enough for physical energy to be exhausted, it has to be reproduced daily. But it takes years to build up a psychic structure, and once it is shaped, it remains highly stable throughout the whole life. 'The mind is a bone', said a great philosopher (Hegel), which is exactly what we mean. The mind, or rather its psychic structure, is not only a bone, it is *the* main bone of the body. But the psychic structures of a given human being do not come 'from the sky of ideas' (the surrounding ideology); they come from social relations themselves. Social relations penetrate the body, structure its psychic 'central fire'; psychic structure is social structure alive in the heart of the body.[9]

IX

This very brief sketch may look highly abstract (like any first encounters with a new theory); and true enough, these theoretical ideas have been developed mostly through reflection, without any direct reference to concrete observations. But it is all the more interesting that they shed some light on what happens to artisanal bakers.

It all starts with apprenticeship, which is the process through which a young innocent boy of fourteen is transformed into a *boulanger*. In the profession, this word is used for both artisans and bakery workers – most of these referring to themselves not as *ouvriers boulangers* but simply as *boulangers*. And indeed, that signifies something; both bakers and bakery workers have been through the same process of transformation – apprenticeship. It is a long and hard process. When it begins the boy is still like soft dough, he is going to school, without any success, and is waiting for his fourteenth birthday. When this day comes be it in December or in March, he quits school. His parents have talked with a local baker and agreed orally on the conditions. So, the boy packs a few things, says goodbye to his family and leaves. For three years he will be working and living with another family.

The work as we said, starts at two o'clock at the latest. Now, the law forbids putting an apprentice to work before six, but, as the bakers say, if he wants to learn the trade, he has to get up with me. So at two, the baker climbs the stairs and wakes up his apprentice, sometimes with cold water (sleep is deep at this age). A quick coffee and the work starts. Taking the dough, dividing it into small pieces, weighing these pieces one by one, the apprentice, still half asleep, learns to do all these simple acts quicker – he is never quick enough; under the shouting (and sometimes kicking) of the baker, the 'soft dough' of the apprentice starts taking shape. Making two hundred *croissants*, putting them in the oven, not letting them burn, cleaning the trays, getting used to jumping from one move to the next, to following two or three operations at the same time (preparing the next batch while one is being cooked); learning to organise one's work, to struggle against sleep, to avoid letting a finger or a hand be caught in one of the machines; following the rhythms of the bread, keeping going until noon. This is what you have to learn; and as, at the end of a long night, the shapeless dough is transformed into bread, at the end of the three years of apprenticeship, the boy has been transformed into a baker. When the night ends, the bread is baked, so is the apprentice.

Night after night, six nights a week (the seventh is used to catch up on sleep), the trade penetrates the body. It is rather easy to learn how to make bread; an intellectual can do it. But in order to make it *fast* and nightly, you have to transform your body completely. Its natural rhythm has to be reversed, the body must learn to sleep during the day and be awake in the dark hours of the night. The speed of movements has to be augmented. Bakers are known to work very fast without tiring (they get hired easily in industrial factories because of this reputation), it is their body which has been transformed into a quick tool. To learn the trade does not mean to learn how to make bread, but to acquire the rhythm necessary to make it in the artisanal relations of production of today. It also means being able to work fast for ten hours, eat, sleep a little, and go back to work for a few more hours in the afternoon, day after day. The apprentice is the companion of the baker, and if he works fifteen hours a day (which is the average) then the apprentice will have to follow. It means a trained body, which lives on its nerves; and the training, the restructuring of the body is what apprenticeship is all about. So it may be said that while bakers make the bread, the bread also makes the bakers; if the population needs bread to live, the artisanal form needs the bakers' bodies in order to survive. The relations of production produce the people who will reproduce them.

It is only by understanding what happens to their body at an early age that one may understand how the young bakery workers who become self-employed can work so fast for so many hours without collapsing. Some of them, in fact, do collapse (usually through heart attacks), but most of them go on, forcefully imposing on themselves, on their wives, on their workers and apprentices a frightening rhythm of work and life. But, through competition between bakers, this rhythm becomes the rhythm of the *whole* trade, and if one considers not only one bakery but fifty thousand with their long opening hours and the hard work which takes place around the ovens, all this for relatively low economic rewards; if one considers the amount of work invested, then one understands better why it is so difficult for industry to take over the market for bread.

Appendix

Our interest in the artisanal bakery started several years ago. We had no family connection or personal relations with it in any way. The initial idea was to study a particular branch of industry in order to get at the *relations of production*. Daniel's project was to observe the concrete functioning of class relations in French society; he thought social classes could only be understood by studying *class relations* and that, of the many forms class relations take, production relations are the ones which determine all the other forms. He also wanted to choose a branch of production which would produce a very familiar product; bread, wine or shoes, so that his study of class relations would be connected somehow to everybody's daily life.

Bread (that is the bakery) was chosen by happenstance and it was only much later that its political meaning was realised. One of the bakers interviewed described how when the Germans left Paris in August 1944, they took with them all the fuel they could find so that there was no more fuel to bake the bread; and he added, when Paris lacks bread, it means riots and perhaps revolution. He was very proud to recall how he organised teams to go cut trees in the parks and to bake bread with this green wood. *Et Paris n'a pas manqué de pain!*

For several years, this research remained in embryo. Academic authorities in sociology considered the topic irrelevant ('artisanal bakers are disappearing anyway') and the approach inefficient. Daniel stubbornly insisted on collecting life stories, and he should have known that 'nothing can be done with this type of material'. Why not do a nice survey with a representative sample, a good questionaire, and apply his mathematical skills to a sophisticated analysis of quantitative data?

If academics saw no interest in this research project, others did. Some students helped to collect life stories of bakery workers, especially Jacqueline Dufrêne; later on, Renée Colin interviewed bakers' wives. Despite academic scepticism, small funds were allocated by the CORDES (depending on the Commissariat au Plan) to explore the life history method. Then in 1974 we proposed to the CORDES to make a study of the reasons why there were still artisanal bakers in France and not in the other industrial countries. The project was accepted.

We tried to make a survey, but it proved impossible because the non-response rate would have been very high. We were not too sorry about this (the proposal to make a survey was a concession). So we went back to the life history approach, which means that we collected life stories of about one hundred people in three regions of France: Paris and its suburbs, a *département* of the Pyrenees, and an industrial town in northern France.

We mentioned earlier some of the difficulties of fieldwork (with bakers especially). Once, however, we had succeeded in interviewing one baker, it usually became easy to interview others he knew; the same with bakery workers.

Interviews were quite open. To be sure, we knew what we wanted. We wanted to get at the 'material side' of the life trajectory of the interviewed: in which type of family he or she was born, what kind of social constraints had made him a baker, how many hours he worked when he was an apprentice, a young bakery worker and so on. What was the concrete content of the work. We also wanted to know which were the various jobs the man had occupied since apprenticeship; for every job, we tried to get the schedule of an average week. We asked the same questions (concerning work) about the present situation. This focus on work came from Daniel's interest in relations of production.

But bakers and bakery workers, through their life stories, soon taught us that they had other areas of interest: health, money, outdoors activities, and so on. We never asked questions about political ideas, having understood that no matter how the bakers vote (and we have little interest in that), it is by making bread daily, and by keeping the artisanal form alive, that they make politics without knowing it.

Our list of questions (drawn from the questionnaire we wrote for the survey which was not done) always remained implicit. We soon learned that some of the best interviews, or parts of interviews, were the results of a takeover, by the interviewed person, of the control of the interview. Sometimes this takeover would end up with the person unravelling his personal ideology, in which case we tried to interrupt by coming back to specific questions about the facts of his past life (this does not mean that we were uninterested in the core of personal ideologies, that is personal values, but we believed these values expressed themselves in the acts of life, in important choices rather than in discourse, where many external interferences and among them the relation to the interviewer, would jam the authentic expression of inner commitments). But quite often, when a man or a woman started to tell a particular story which obviously was important to him or her, it appeared afterwards that it was important for us too – that is, it was relevant for an understanding of the level of social relations. It seems that in these fortunate moments, people shifted from the status of 'interviewed' to the one of social observer, talking on equal terms with another social observer (the sociologist), to whom they wanted to transmit something they had understood, something of sociological substance.

Step by step we began to accumulate knowledge on the structure and history of social relations in the artisanal bakery (Isabelle did most of the historical study). Life stories, or rather life-story interviews (we seldom held more than one interview – but we remained friends with a number of persons and visit them from time to time to discuss our findings and just chat) gave us acts, *practices*; and from the patterns of practices put together, an image of the structure of social relations slowly began to arise. We were trying to develop a method or rather an approach, which would break with the empiricist approach.[10]

The main difference between what we have done and empiricism is not primarily the use of a 'qualitative' technique, the life story interview. It is quite possible to gather 'qualitative' (or rather, non-quantifiable) data in an empiricist way; actually this is what happens with most 'qualitative' work.

If we succeeded in breaking with empiricism, it is to the extent that during fieldwork we kept our attention focused not on the technique of observation itself (the interview-guide) but beyond, on this level of social relations that we were trying to perceive and elucidate. And this meant actually that we never separated the moment of data collection from the moment of data analysis, as is done in most textbooks of methodology. Questions and hypotheses were discussed from the very beginning of the research, between two interviews, while studying the history of the bakery, and so on, and the interview-guide was constantly modified to include questions on processes which past interviews had started to reveal.

If 'analysis' (thinking?) was there from the beginning, data collection continued until the end of the research. Because we have no quantitative data, we cannot use figures to kind of close and lock our reflection. For instance, we are unable to state how many bakers to-day are former 'authentic' bakery workers (not bakers' sons). If a representative sample had been drawn and enough questionnaires had been gathered, we could state that, say 71.5 per cent of the bakers are former 'authentic' bakery workers who have become self-employed. Because this has not been done, we do not know if this figure is 40 per cent or 80 per cent. We think, however, that sociological research is meant to get at the level of social relations. With our approach, we cannot give accurate measures of social phenomena, but we are able to propose an hypothesis about the social processes which produce them. Had we done this survey, we could have given accurate figures, but most probably we would not have discovered the importance of the social mechanism by which retiring bakers risk all the value of their goodwill to allow young bakery workers to take it over. What is sociologically relevant, a figure, or a process?

One question remains: how can we be sure that our hypotheses represent correctly what is really happening?

This question may be asked at several levels. At the empirical level, it means that, having no representative sample, we have supposedly 'no proof of the validity of our data'. Our answer to this is that we conducted interviews with, for instance, bakery workers until we felt new interviews were not bringing us any new knowledge about the level of social relations. By the way, the fact that there is such a process of *saturation* means that this level of social relations exists indeed! The same saturation was observed with bakers' interviews, and apprentices; less so with bakers' wives, because they are recruited through the somewhat random process of 'love'; but all interviews gave the same results as for the work schedules, hard work, and psychological constraints of the job. This process of saturation of knowledge means that we get a certain representativeness indeed, not at the level of phenomena, but at the level of the social relations which produce them everywhere – be it in Paris, Marseilles, in a local town or in a suburb. We think we are able now, just by looking at a bakery in any part of France, to guess many features of its internal life; and to us this means more than accurate figures.

Still, this does not mean we are sure of our hypotheses. Because our ambition is to describe in depth the social relations as they are (and as they change) we have been led to propose a number of *interpretations* of observed facts and processes. We believe it is our job as social researchers to bring forward hypotheses – to enhance the sociological imagination. But we are not sure it should be our task to *prove* them. We would rather think it is up to the people in the bakery trade to examine whether our interpretations make sense or not.

This is the last challenge and the toughest: to write sociology in such a way that a large public, and first of all the people who are concerned with a particular study, may understand what is said.[11] But the greatest difficulty might be not in finding a readable style of writing, but in accepting in advance being judged by non-sociologists. It is a wonder, come to think of it, how sociologists have succeeded so far in escaping from a public appreciation of their writings. When S. M. Lipset wrote about 'the authoritarianism of the working class', he was confident that no workers could form an opinion about the ideas he proposed, much less express it publicly. When a sociologist writes about some specific attitudes of a whole population, nobody is in a position to answer him (except another sociologist), because everybody appears as some particular individual facing the universality of the sociologist's discourse. These are two examples of how sociologists are protected from direct criticism by the people they are talking about.

By studying a branch of production, it seems we have taken a risk: we know bakers and bakery workers are waiting for our conclusions. Even worse, by refusing to protect ourselves behind percentages, we have aggravated our situation. And by trying to write in a simple way (we are referring here to the book we plan to write – it is obvious that this paper gives but a hint of the complexity of artisanal bakery and its agents' lives), we are lowering the last defence of sociology against public criticism.

The whole enterprise is risky; but risks are irrelevant when compared to the stake, which is to make sociology more relevant to society, or rather to the human beings who make it what it is.

NOTES

1. Life stories confirm the testimony of Bernard Clavel, a young apprentice who later became a novelist. He wrote a book called *La Maison des autres* where he describes the life in a pastry shop at the beginning of the thirties.
2. Actually there are three excellent social mobility surveys bearing on the whole population of France; they have been done by the INSEE in 1964, 1970 and 1976. The 1970 survey has a representative sample of N = 60,000. The sociologist Nonna Mayer, studying the men of this sample who had set up their own business between 1965 and 1970, found out that they belong mostly to two trades, construction and bakery. She also observed that most bakers are not bakers' sons. This conclusion is drawn upon the 23 bakers included in the sample of 60,000 – a small number, but in the very carefully done surveys of the INSEE, even small numbers have a meaning. See Nonna Mayer (1977).
3. The methodology of this research and its overall philosophy are briefly described in the Appendix.
4. Another indicator of this constant pressure is, of course, the fact that the bakery is under discrete supervision by the *Renseignements Généraux*, that is that part of the police which is in charge of intelligence work on the French population itself. Bread seems a harmless thing, but the lack of bread is an extremely powerful social explosive, or rather, a social detonator, which is responsible for many historical uprisings, among them the 1789 Revolution. It has been a constant concern of the highest authorities that the population of the big cities, and especially Paris, gets its daily bread, and at a reasonable price. Actually the price of bread has been decided by the State itself, not by the bakers, for the last 180 years. It is only since August 1978 that the price of bread has been freed from direct State decision. This drastic change in State policy was interpreted by many bakers as a subtle move in favour of the industrial bread-makers. As a result, they were very careful to limit the rise in bread prices to about 10 per cent..
5. The male reader might ask: Why don't they divorce and find another more 'operational' wife? thus forgetting that the obvious instrumentality of marriage for ambitious bakery workers is efficient only because it works in a larger, non-instrumental context, that is traditional marriage as 'love' marriage. If separation was that easy, then we know a number of baker

couples who would not have survived the first year of business because of the wife's reaction to the way of life imposed on her.

6. The 'sociological truth' in this expression means a fair description of the level of social relations. It is *not* 'the whole truth' of the matter. Situations which are the same 'objectively', that is in terms of socio-structural relations, may be lived wholly differently by different people, that is by people differentiated by social origin, family history, life trajectory, and so on – and hence having different systems of values and goals in life.

7. Also the family dinner (*diner en famille*) is still very important in France. It is a kind of daily ceremony for the celebration of the Family; hence the emphasis on food quality and also on the social origin (traditional v. industrial) of this food.

8. We have tried elsewhere to sketch what could be a theory of anthroponomy; it includes, of course, a theory of 'the family', or rather of the various (class) types of families as the main units of production of human beings. It includes also a theory of the *distribution* of human beings into social positions (elsewhere called, somewhat misleadingly, 'social mobility') with emphasis on capital inheritance. Needless to say, this theoretical effort has little to do with the prevailing theory of 'human capital'. See Daniel Bertaux (1977).

9. On this, see Lucien Sève (1974) in which the author tries (and in our opinion, only half succeeds) in laying the groundwork for a materialist theory of 'personality'. Also Bertaux (1973).

10. On the life-history approach, see Daniel Bertaux (1980).

11. As a first attempt to outline the problems involved, see Daniel Bertaux (1978).

REFERENCES

P. A. Baran and P. M. Sweezy, *Monopoly Capital* (Monthly Review Press, 1966).

Daniel Bertaux, 'Two and a half Models of Social Structure', in W. Müller and K. U. Mayer (eds.), *Social Stratification and Career Mobility* (Mouton, 1973).

Daniel Bertaux, *Destins personnels et structure de classe* (Presses Universitaire de France, 1977).

Daniel Bertaux, 'Ecrire le sociologie', *Social Science Information* (February, 1979).

Daniel Bertaux (ed.), *Biography and Society* (provisional title) (SAGE, 1980 forthcoming).

Bernard Clavel, *La Maison des Autres* (Robert Laffont, 1962).

N. Mayer, 'Une filière de mobilité ouvrière: l'accès à la petite entreprise artisanale et commerciale', *Revue Française de Sociologie*, xviii (1977) 25–45.

Claude Servolin, 'L'absorption de l'agriculture dans le mode de production capitaliste', in Yves Tavernier, Michel Gervais and Claude Servolin, *L'univers politique des paysans dans la France contemporaine* (Armand Colin, 1972).

Lucien Sève, *Marxisme et théorie de la personnalité* (Editions Sociales, 2nd edn., 1974).

8 Petty Property: the Survival of a Moral Economy

FRANK BECHHOFER AND BRIAN ELLIOTT

> I do not see class as a 'structure' nor even as a 'category' but as something which in fact happens . . . in human relation-ships. . . . And class happens when some men, as a result of common experiences (inherited or shared), feel and articulate the identity of their interests as between themselves, and as against other men whose interests are different from (and usually opposed to) theirs. (Thompson, 1968, p. 9)

As sociologists it would be easy to find points of disagreement with the notion of class expressed in the preface of E. P. Thompson's celebrated study of the making of the English working class, but whatever its shortcomings, his approach has the considerable merit of forcing us to think seriously and precisely about actual social relationships. In this chapter we want to look at the character of those social relations in which men and women of the petite bourgeoisie are set, at the class experience of those who, in so much of the literature, are ignored or crudely caricatured. As in so many discussions of class, we encounter awkward problems of definition flowing from different traditions of writing, different theoretical stances and different substantive interests. In the previous essays we have brought together accounts which relate to small farmers in a developing colonial territory, small farmers set in and working for a modern capitalist economy, artisanal bakers in France, small businessmen in a socialist country and craftsmen and petty capitalists in developing countries. In what sense can such a diverse occupational set be said to have anything in common? On one thing we can surely agree: these are neither bourgeois nor proletarians. At the same time it is clear that they are unlike the routine white-collar workers in industry, commerce or public administration and they are different too from the bureaucratised professionals or salaried intelligentsia. The one thing they all have – the crucial thing – is petty productive property, and it is property with which they work themselves. It is their labour and very frequently that of their families and kin, that they mix with this property and though a good many also become the employers of hired labour, the scale of that exploitation is typically very small and is an extension of, rather than a substitute for, their own labour.[1]

These are the most fundamental features of what we shall call the petite bourgeoisie and from them flow the stream of experiences which affect the material and social lives and the political sentiments of that stratum that sits uneasily between the major classes of capitalist societies. Some Marxists, like Poulantzas and E. O. Wright, are quite happy to identify a petit-bourgeois *class*, Wright restricting this strictly to the traditional small capitalist elements, Poulantzas attempting to ascribe the term to a much wider range of the population. Weberians too would often accept that such is the distinctiveness of the economic interests, such the commonality of market and work situations that we would be entirely justified in using that term. Others though would hesitate. Gerry and Birkbeck in their essay in this volume put the idea of a petit-bourgeois class aside and following what seems in many ways a sensible lead from Wright, try to explore, in a Third World context, a variety of 'contradictory class locations'. In our own writing and thinking, we too have been chary of the idea of a separate 'class' of petits-bourgeois largely because, like Newby and his colleagues, we have always been impressed by the powerful structural affinities between even petty capitalist and the bigger bourgeois. Talking of a petit-bourgeois *stratum* retains for us what seems an important indication of that linkage. However, our task here is not to legislate in these matters but merely to draw attention to a problem which at the level of serious theoretical discussion has received really very little attention. Our main purpose is to explore the position of the petite bourgeoisie within diverse economies and social orders and to understand how structural location affects their experience of class and status relationships.

The hallmarks of this experience seem to be uncertainty and contingency. The self-employed and small entrepreneurs lack the consistent pattern of subordination which informs all spheres of a manual worker's life in western society yet at the same time it can hardly be claimed that they enjoy the routine, taken-for-granted superiority of the big bourgeois. Running their own enterprises, be they small workshops, or retail stores or service operations, they are forced into some awareness of their vulnerability to change, to the booms and recessions in the economy, to the fiscal and other measures of the state. Small farmers contend with the uncertainties of the weather as well as the vagaries of the political climate. French bakers can be threatened by changes in public taste as well as the looming presence of the manufacturers of 'industrial' bread. The sense of precariousness, of contingency, leads to the awareness of life as 'struggle' and to ambiguity in their relationship to others in the major classes. Small capital is menaced from above and below. Viewed historically, these uncertainties and ambiguities are reflected in the shifting political alliances of the petit-bourgeois. Sometimes, as in the early phase of Britain's industrial development, they are to be found supporting or even sponsoring forms of working class radicalism, at others (and it must be said, more commonly) giving conditional, grudging support to the political forces of the large capitalists. From time to time there have been attempts to express their own special interests through new parties and forms of direct action, at which points we can see very clearly the contradictory elements in their class location, but usually these have been brief outbursts followed quickly enough by a renewed incorporation into the routines of conventional class politics.

Studies of the petite bourgeoisie are in their infancy. For too long it was accepted that this stratum would disappear or that it was politically impotent and economically trivial and outmoded, but recent studies are beginning to cast doubt on all these assumptions. A more thorough and a more humane understanding is beginning to emerge, and it becomes apparent that in studying these minor property holders we can gain considerable insight into the workings of contemporary societies. We can learn a good deal about the pervasiveness and durability of ideas central to the workings of capitalist economies, about ideological and material adaptation to new economic systems, about modes of recruitment to seemingly unpromising occupational positions. We can acquire too a much more thorough understanding of the processes of status group and class formation in societies with widely differing political and economic bases. Above all, the new interest in the self-employed, the small businessmen, the petty capitalists, points up the capacity for survival demonstrated by this 'traditional' sector in modern economies and some of the mechanisms whereby a stratum which is obviously manipulable – both politically and economically – is kept alive, continuously reproduced in slightly different forms over long periods of time.

Persistence: Economic Factors

To say that the petite bourgeoisie persists is not to deny that its character, its composition, the economic functions and interests of its constituents have changed considerably with the evolution of capitalism and the recent creation of socialist economies. But it is to say that in widely varying conditions, and frequently against formidable economic and political odds, men and women using minimal amounts of property have found ways to survive. Sometimes they have accomplished this by defending their old trades, often they have accurately identified and exploited deficiencies in the operations of large companies or of state enterprises. Survival has rested upon continuous adaptation – not always at the level of the individual petit bourgeois, for many have been inflexible and have gone to the wall – but at the level of the stratum as a whole. Adaptation has often been born of dire necessity as migrants flock to towns only to find there is no regular work to be had, or as workers are thrown on to the dole queues in times of recession. As with all small fry, the persistence of the collectivity masks the fact of high mortality, and of depredations by governments and larger enterprises which pose continuous threats to the aggregate's survival. But so far it has survived and it is hard to accept that there are any ineluctable forces which will destroy it.

From generation to generation, the petits-bourgeois reproduce themselves, sometimes simply handing on land, real estate, diverse businesses or entrepreneurial skills from parents to children, at others, recruiting 'outsiders' on the basis of ideological as well as material factors. Daniel and Isabelle Bertaux have provided a vivid account of the process whereby French bakers pass on their businesses not to their offspring but mainly to their bakery workers, to their former apprentices. Our own study of shopkeepers also indicated that most newcomers were not sons and daughters of the retailer but were former shop workers or indeed those with very little prior connection with shopkeeping.[2] Among urban landlords or small farmers, on the other hand, the transmission of the property is much more a family affair. Much urban property was passed on as a source of income and security to female dependents in a family. It could be deliberately 'worked', taken seriously as a business enterprise or treated passively – simply as a source of rent and periodically of capital gain.[3] For farmers, even small ones, the escalating price of land has meant that the chances of being able to buy a farm are remote for all but the wealthy.[4] For both groups, family transmission is also a reflection of the symbolic importance of property. It represents continuity and stability; it is the tangible evidence of survival, even of success.

But the petite bourgeoisie also sustains itself by infusions of 'new blood' from all ranks of society. Sons and daughters of the peasantry raised in a milieu of unremitting toil and defensive independence often adapt more readily to the kind of labour and supposed 'autonomy' of the small enterprises, to petty trading, hawking and manufacture than to the regimentation of factory life. From the urban working class too novices appear, attracted by the relative wealth and the prospect of escape from the most obvious forms of subordination, and even from the elite groups, there are those who supplement their wealth or perhaps check their social decline by joining the ranks of the little businessmen. These are the immediate processes of recruitment in which we can see the maintenance of the stratum as the product of individual actions and sentiments, but of course there is a broader sense in which we can talk of 'society' recreating the stratum from generation to generation through the flux of the economic system. Depressions, recessions, sudden technological advances, the incursions of multi-national corporations with capital intensive enterprises, mergers and take-overs and government sponsored 'rationalisations' – all these alter the texture of the economic and occupational structures, destroying some opportunities, creating others. Some of the dispossessed sink their savings and sweat in some form of small enterprise, some engage perhaps in an expanding technology, quit their jobs to try their hands as entrepreneurs.

Thus, what we call the petite bourgeoisie displays great diversity, containing within it old, even 'archaic' forms of economic activity – craft or artisanal production for instance. It encompasses a wide variety of traders, retailers and dealers and it includes those who run businesses whose role is 'service'. As the character of economics change, so the size and composition of the petite bourgeoisie alters. In the western economies over the last three or four decades, the size of the small business sector has generally declined – nowhere more markedly than in Britain. Within the small business realm small retailers and manufacturers have had a hard time, but as the economy as a whole takes on the character of a 'service economy' so those who attend to and repair our cars, houses and domestic machinery, find expanding opportunities, as do those who cater to our needs for leisure and diversion and personal adornment. Moreover, as large enterprises, public and private, encounter diseconomies of scale, so the idea of subcontracting some of their work becomes more and more attractive. There are some commentators who see here the prospect of a substantial *increase* in the size of the small business stratum, not its continuing decline.

In the Third World millions are drawn into the cities, attracted by the prospects of work and wealth in the newly arrived high-technology industries or in the ranks of the highly centralised administrative and political apparatus that characterises many such societies, especially in Latin America. Few of the migrants actually find work in the so-called modern sector. Some retain a foothold in the rural economy of the urban fringe,[5] but most are accommodated in the 'traditional' or 'informal' sector or in the so-called 'bazaar' rather than the 'firm' economy.[6] They become part of that world of small traders, small producers, dealers, touts and own-account workers. At first glance, many of them seem to live only partly in a market economy, the webs of kinship, ethnic and linguistic solidarities, the ties of neighbourhood and the layers of patronage obscuring their relationship to the dominant economic structure.[7] But as Gerry and Birkbeck show, many of the most menial forms of self employment are in fact tied in with the demands of world-wide capitalist production. Monopoly capitalism in the third world did not emerge out of the gradual concentration of indigenous capitalist enterprise but rather was superimposed on the social and economic structures thrown up by the earlier colonial scramble for raw materials and foodstuffs. The petite bourgeoisie which developed in the centres of colonial administration, providing for the needs of mine owners, the plantation bosses and the colonial elite, has now been joined by the numerous and diversified types of self employment that form an economic penumbra around the multi-national corporations in these countries.

Even in the socialist economies of Eastern Europe, a stratum of small businessmen survives, running small shops that often deal in the goods produced outside the state-run enterprises, providing services, even engaging in minor forms of production. They seem in many ways anachronistic, part of an economic order that has been destroyed. The sense of their being a 'residual' stratum, the sense of their being out of step with the major, modern elements of the economy, their ambiguous location in the system of economic relationships, is even more marked here than in contemporary western economies.

The petite bourgeoisie is like a chameleon, taking its colour from its environment. Thus, the precise nature of relationships with manual workers, with peasants, with factory owners, capitalist farmers, with migrant labour or foreign employers varies widely. But in all circumstances it is a dependent stratum; dependent first and foremost on the dominant economic groups and institutions. It is their decisions, their interests that do most to affect the size and circumstances of the stratum. When it suits large enterprises to buy out the competition from the 'little guys' they can generally do so. Conversely when they want to encourage the emergence of more small concerns, they can provide loan capital, or the kind of technical knowledge that might form the base of new enterprise. They sponsor research into the market situations of small business – as for instance Shell does – and ultimately they can try to persuade governments to assist their efforts on behalf of petty capital.

Persistence: political factors

This last point reminds us that in accounting for the persistence of the petite bourgeoisie, we cannot ignore political inducements and restrictions. Perhaps the importance of political decisions is most evident in socialist states where political management of the economy has entailed the working out of some accommodation with those small businesses which help overcome problems of supply or distribution. Eastern European intellectuals from time to time remind us that there is 'a pluralist' strand in the writings of Marx and Lenin and Kautsky which allows for the co-existence of small producers and retailers alongside the socialised enterprises.[8] But in practice the relationship between the economic planners and the small businessmen has not been an easy one. As Bronek Misztal shows, there have been significant changes in both policy and the overall attitude towards the private entrepreneurs. Indeed, in a country like Poland, the political dependency of small traders is symbolised in the spatial arangements in the cities, where the state-run shops occupy the main streets while private concerns are allowed to do business tucked away in courtyards and back streets, in small, apparently temporary premises.

In other societies too there is political manipulation of small business. Suzanne Berger makes plain the extent to which the survival of the 'traditional sector' in Italy hangs upon political decisions. Politicians trying to cope with the volatility of the economy have recognised the value of a sector which at one time can be encouraged to shed labour needed by the 'modern' enterprises, at another expanded to absorb 'surplus' labour, shaken out by these same firms at points of recession. In Canada, the Trudeau government established a Minister for small business and at federal and provincial level, incentives have been offered to increase the number of small concerns. Government-sponsored studies have revealed the considerable importance of small business in the Canadian economy, whether that is judged by the number of enterprises, the numbers employed or the contribution to Gross National Product.[9] Political support for small business has arisen partly as a result of the lobbying and agitation of business groups but mainly because it is consistent with wider political and economic objectives. Thus, the support is designed to combat unemployment, to help redress gross regional inbalances between the 'have' and 'have not' provinces and to alleviate in some modest way the overwhelming economic influence of the United States. And if this was not enough, government research suggests that in several areas of economy, small businesses were at least as efficient, and sometimes much more efficient, than the big companies.

Governments elsewhere have come to share the scepticism about the economic benefits of bigness. The social costs of processes of 'consolidation' or 'rationalisation' when they involve plants with many thousands of employees, the capital intensive nature of many big businesses, the failure to employ local labour in outlying and depressed regions – all contribute to the doubts. And so too do big business scandals, involving the bribing of foreign officials or the misappropriation of funds or the wilful evasion of environmental standards. Compared with the situation in the 1960s, political opinion seems clearly to have become much less enthusiastic about large concerns and more sympathetic to small business. Even in Britain the political tide appears to have turned and is now running in favour of smaller enterprises. And it is not just the Tory party in which we find this reorientation. Labour and Liberal MPs also cast themselves as champions of the 'oppressed' small businessman. For many years small business as a political constituency was ignored, even by the Conservatives.[10] It was partly because they had become estranged from the party which traditionally offered them at least rhetorical support, that so many turned to the new voluntary associations and lobby groups that sprang up in the middle and late 1970s. Much of the newfound enthusiasm for small business among Tories is a matter of political expediency, designed to win back a bloc of votes, but beyond that there is the so-called 'libertarian' philosophy of the new right in which the small businessman epitomises those virtues of independence and parsimony which it commends. In much of the current talk of 'regenerating' the British economy, the petite bourgeoisie are held by many politicians to have an important, even central, place. Decisions taken by the politicians will moderate the economic forces that affect the survival and character of the petit-bourgeois. Here, as in the economic sphere, their capacity for self-determination is very limited: lacking the consolidated economic weight of big business, lacking the long-established mass organisations of labour, they found themselves without strong party support and without the institutionalised access to government and civil service.

The moral economy of the petit-bourgeois

Dependent strata need sponsors and in recent years the small business sector has acquired some. It has acquired economic sponsors in the form of those big businesses whose owners and controllers have become apologists for small enterprise. In Britain, several large companies have been involved in, or encouraged the formation of, a small business lobby. They do so out of very mixed motives: from a general wish to see a market economy with lots of small competing units; from a wish to see risk-taking and innovation in the hands of little enterprises rather than their own; from a desire to reduce the power of trade unions and from the knowledge that strike rates and union activity are generally much lower in small concerns. Stability, profitability and social control may all be served by the promotion of the small fry. So, big business gives the appearance of accepting some of the current critiques of the major corporations and joins the boosting of small business. In doing this it distances itself from the strictures about the 'unacceptable face of capitalism' and enjoys instead proximity to a defensible, apparently even popular, form of economic organisation.

Small business has also acquired political sponsors. A Tory party trying to win power and acknowledging its neglect of what Gamble called the 'politics of support' set out under Margaret Thatcher deliberately to recapture the allegiance of little capitalists. It formed back-bench committees and even a special Small Business Bureau to that end. But the small business associations and individual small businessmen have been anxious not to tie themselves too closely to a single party. They wanted a broader political base, a wider sympathy, and they sought this through public meetings, protest marches and lobbying. They have succeded in drawing attention to their position, to their struggles, but more than that, they have carried these struggles into the political arena. In order to do that they have had to overcome two formidable difficulties: the disparateness of the various elements of the stratum and the intense individualism that pervades it. Surmounting them has required the formulation and expression of a broad criticism of the functioning of our present economy together with programmes of action intended to persuade government to lift specific impositions. It has been the 'ideological work' which has done most to promote an unusual degree of coordination, if not of unity, among petit bourgeois elements. And identifying and articulating the grievances, the sense of what is wrong in the economy and society, has gone hand in hand with the effort to adumbrate a preferable and morally defensible order.

In many western countries the last few years have seen the mobilisation of many sections of the so-called middle class.[11] Petit-bourgeois discontent has been a most important – arguably *the* most important element in this. The small-business elements have been eager to publicise their hurt. Time and again they attack the same targets: the extent of state intervention in the market with its levying of new taxes, its growing powers to license occupations, to inspect business premises and business records and its attempts to regulate the relationships between employers and employees. Alongside these there are the attacks on the spread of the big corporations. From the perspective of the little man, it looks as though the general drift towards bigness, and toward State intervention, are related. Governments encourage the growth of these concerns, bribing the multi-nationals to set up shop and offering them subsidies and loans when they encounter difficulties. To the petits-bourgeois, it seems that they are being turned into unpaid tax collectors for the state, harried and cajoled by officials from the Customs and Excise and the Inland Revenue, only to find that the money collected (so they claim) is handed not to their kind but to the large 'lame ducks' among the big enterprises. The complaints though are not just about the economic effects of all this, but about what they portray as the collapse of a moral order. Increasingly, in the current spate of unrest, one can hear the defence of a moral economy[12] whose practices and institutions are being daily violated. What underlies the present stirrings is 'an outrage to the moral assumptions quite as much as actual deprivation' (Thompson, 1971, p. 79). Few are really being forced out of business, none are starving but many are aware of widespread changes, social and political, as well as economic, which threaten them. C. Wright Mills' observation that:

> Their economic anxieties have led many small entrepreneurs to a somewhat indignant search for some political means of security and there have been many spokesmen to take up the search for them. (Mills, 1951, p. 33)

seems particularly apt at this time. Some of the news-sheets put out by the new associations in Britain are indeed 'indignant'. 'Tax is theft', 'Mind your own business is the only moral law' are the kinds of slogans that appear in the most strident of them.[13] And there are a great many new associations and new spokesmen. What they are doing though is more than simply identifying economic grievances and pressing for changes; they are involved in the construction of an idealised economic and moral order. Out of the economic and social relations of the small businessmen they establish a moral platform from which the recent actions of governments and corporations can be assessed. Big businesses can be charged with failing to honour their obligations. They deliberately refuse to settle their accounts on time; they cut off orders or supplies to small enterprises without warning; they act to suppress small business innovation and competition when it suits them. Governments too overstep moral boundaries when they pour millions of pounds into foreign-owned companies like Chrysler, when they write off the debts of a co-operative like Meriden, when they give employees 'excessive' security through the Employment Protection Act or empower VAT Inspectors to invade the domestic privacy of small businessmen.

Both the critical analysis and the prescription that we return to an economic order in which smaller enterprises can flourish occur time and again in the recent history of western societies. John Conway provides a nice illustration of this in his treatment of the Canadian agrarian petits-bourgeois. What we are observing is simply the latest manifestation. In the last five years hosts of new voluntary bodies have been formed, 'leagues' and parties established, international conferences held to defend and promote small business and self-employment. And there is much in the attack on big business and on government bureaucracy which earns popular sympathy. It is partly for this reason that governments have responded by setting up Ministers for small business, giving tax concessions, establishing new credit facilities, providing technical advice, bringing speculative capital, technical experts and entrepreneurs together. But there is another reason for the new enthusiasm for small business among the politicians. Capitalist societies face a crisis of confidence. Fuel resources are running out, raw materials are more difficult and costly to obtain, the commitment to growth has begun to wobble and everywhere the gross inequalities inside the industrial nations and between them and the Third World are visible and persistent. Many politicians, especially on the right, are looking for a way of 'remoralising capitalism' and what the petit-bourgeois organis-ations are beginning to offer is a vision of capitalism as a moral system which they can use. In Britain, we are watching the business organis-ations and the right wing of the Tory party and to some extent the media, constructing one of those periodic 'retrospects' in which the joys of a simpler, freer, more competitive economy are sung; in which the multi-nationals supposedly are tamed or wished away; in which the invisible hand steers individual competition along paths of efficiency, prosperity and freedom.

Raymond Williams, writing about the images of 'the country' which appear in English literature over the centuries, comments that ' . . . what seems an old order, a "traditional" society, keeps appearing, reappearing at bewilderingly various dates . . . as an idea to some extent based on experience, against which contemporary change can be measured' (Williams, 1973, p. 35). The petite bourgeoisie in the west have from time to time helped create 'retrospects' not of pastoral societies but of 'traditional' capitalist societies in which free and independent men and women competed in the market place, where monopolies were held at bay, where the state acted as an umpire ensuring that the game was played by the rules. Such a 'retrospect' was an integral part of the turn of the century *Mittelstand* agitations in Germany;[14] similar motifs could be found in the protests about 'co-operative' trading (as unfair as competition from big business) in Britain in the 1930s.[15] It has occurred since the last war – in the debates over the Abolition of Resale Price Maintenance and in the rhetoric of the Freedom Group in the 1960s.[16] What makes its present manifestation remarkable is that the images it conveys, the policies it wants pursued have been taken up not by some fringe group in right wing politics, but by the current leadership of a Tory party whose electoral victory seemed to owe a good deal to their manipulation of this 'retrospect'.

The 'new right' in British politics claims that it is offering a new approach, that compared to the politics of the middle ground previously peddled by both major parties, it provides a 'radical' programme.

> . . . in every kind of radicalism the moment comes when any critique of the present must chose its bearings between past and future. And if the past is chosen, as now so often and so deeply, we must push the argument through to the roots that are being defended: push attention . . . back to the . . . moral economy from which critical values are drawn. (Williams, 1973, p. 36)

The moral economy from which many contemporary right wing values are drawn appears to be an eighteenth- or early nineteenth-century market economy – or rather some highly abstracted and idealised version of this. Hence the urge to 'roll back the state', to allow market forces not government intervention to shape economic activity; hence the opposition to organised labour depicted by the less sophisticated as preventing the establishment of free contracts between employers and employees, by those with a broader understanding as 'necessary', even 'valuable', but now in need of some reform; hence too the distaste for big business and its capacity to squeeze subsidies and concessions from governments. In all this the small businessman becomes a symbol, representing, it is claimed, the virtues of an old order to which we must return if our economic fortunes are to mend and our society and polity be restored to health.

Retrospects occur or are resuscitated at points of important social change. They are called out by fear of change. Their purpose is not to explain, to render intelligible the shifting patterns of social relations, rather it is to give comfort and hope to those who long for a return to the imagined joys of an earlier era . . . 'When Britain was Great . . . when it was the workshop of the world . . . when hard work and wit produced just rewards . . . when the workers knew their place . . .'. Such re-trospects obscure, they do not illuminate, the important historical processes of change which shape our everyday lives. Currently they obscure the changing relations between the west and the Third World suppliers of energy and foodstuffs and raw materials who have acquired collective power and pressed into the open the exploitation which under colonialism and then under monopoly capitalism bound them to the 'metropolitan' societies of Europe and North America. Yet how can we understand the current economic problems of the west without such recognition? The 'retrospect' of a traditional market society also offers no understanding of the changing social relations *within* capitalist systems: the modest but undeniable advances in material standards of the mass of the working class population; the partial erosion of old conventions of deference; the emergence of new strata; and the realignments of status groupings. The 'retrospect' sketches the shape of a prior order but offers no historical comprehension of the real framework of structural relations which supported it.

In surviving, the petite bourgeoisie demonstrates the viability of small-scale capitalism and in its periodic mobilisations it calls for the defence of a previous and apparently desirable social order. In this way it plays a significant role in the ideological servicing of contem-porary capitalism, in the successive efforts to recapture the sense of capitalism as an historically progressive force. This wins it friends and defenders.

Property and social relations

If that 'retrospect' which owes so much to the petite bourgeoisie
conceals contemporary social relations or produces a truncated analysis
of them, our task must be to lay them out for inspection as clearly as we
can. At the centre of the social world of the petit-bourgeois lies petty
property. Property is not a thing but a relationship, something historically
conditioned, constantly changing. Owning some small property has
meant that the petit-bourgeois could derive economic benefit from the
sale, rent or mobilisation of the productive powers of that property.
Traditionally he has had some control (by no means total) over the flow
of work processes and over the use made of the capital invested. He has
had rights over the sale of any product or the income from the provision
of services; he could hire, fire and set the levels of pay for his workforce.

Today, as always, small businesses depend primarily upon family
labour, on the sweat of wives and children. Without such inputs of
labour, large numbers of the smallest enterprises would go to the wall.
Daniel and Isabelle Bertaux have shown how crucial it is for the French
baker to have a wife who will keep shop for him. Marriage 'binds' her to
this work, the business, as much as to her husband. In our own study of
shopkeepers, we found a similar pattern. A good many in our sample
were 'Mom and Pop' stores as Mills called them. And it is not only retail
stores or bakeries that have this character, but small firms of the most
diverse kind – farms, hotels, restaurants, minor workshops and service
enterprises – often are staffed by a family with a minimal amount of
additional labour. This familial basis to the activity sets many at odds
with the dominant form of social organisation in which work and family
life are sharply segregated. It means that husbands, wives and children
are often bound together in the most basic task of earning a living. It also
means that many small bourgeois employ only a few hands, so, unlike
the owners of large modern enterprises, they cannot be viewed as
extractors of large 'surpluses' from luckless workers. Relying so heavily
on family effort they are engaged very frequently in a kind of self-
exploitation rather than exploitation of proletarians.

Having very few contracted workers means that the relationships in
the bakery, grocery store, the small garage or whatever are often highly
personalised. The 'boss' works alongside his 'labour force'. Often the
'labour' is recruited from the networks of kinship, friendship and
neighbourhood and thus there are 'non-contractual' elements in the
relationship from the start. In a society where large impersonal
institutions mould much day-to-day living this personalising of work
relationships may be welcomed by both sides. To the boss it often gives
an additional measure of personal and immediate control to buttress
that which comes from working side by side with his labour force. He
knows his workers and does not negotiate with them through any

'union' channels. This can lead to rates of pay well below those set for workers in the large enterprises and the consequent use of the classically vulnerable sources of labour – women, youngsters, immigrants. But it looks too as though some employees choose to work in small enterprises and have little more sympathy for the unions than do their employers. Most small businessmen, in Britain at least, dislike trades unions, not just because the latter fight for higher wages, but because their whole approach and style represent that highly organised, large-scale world which independent entrepreneurs generally try to keep at arm's length. And those who work in small concerns often value the modest 'scale' of the work unit and the face to face social relations within it. Whether or not they initially 'chose' to work in little businesses the chances are that if they stay in them, many workers come to share many of the predelictions and values of their employers. This after all is how one stream of recruitment is assured. The moral economy then is a cultural mould. Basic beliefs, patterns of social and occupational aspiration, diverse attitudes, tastes[17] and interests are given structure by the everyday experiences of the encapsulating routines of petit bourgeois life.

Running your own business not only binds you into a small set of relations in the workplace, but also, through the demands it places on your time, it limits the opportunities for other social contacts. Franz Pappi's study of patterns of interaction gives some indication of the boundedness of the social world in which many small businessmen move. In the little time there is for leisure and recreation there is a marked tendency for like to meet with like. Work constrains the social networks of the petit-bourgeois more rigorously than those of some other 'middle-class groups', producing highly selective associational patterns. This relative isolation encourages a rather narrow and individualistic interpretation of their world which compounds the structural restrictions on forms of collective action. Most small businessmen are 'loners', not 'joiners' and large, politically effective associations among them are rare. Resisting 'organisation' becomes normative. It takes some profound changes in economic and political relations to transform social consciousness, and overcome their resistance to collective action, which makes the present spate of coordinated agitation all the more significant. Historically these factors have limited the political force of the stratum in Europe and North America, and in the Third World it looks as though similar structural and cultural elements will prevent the 'lumpen-bourgeoisie' from fulfilling any revolutionary role there.

Long hours, exiguous rewards and poor conditions, three salient features of much minor enterprise, are often borne by owners and workers alike because of what it is hoped they will ultimately bring. For the petty businessmen themselves there is the hope of a 'comfortable' –

not a lavish – standard of living and the chance perhaps to 'promote' their children into less arduous careers.[18] For the hired hands – for some of them – the hope is that one day at least all the hard work will be for themselves. They will be able to set up on their own. Workers and bosses alike are tied to their work and to each other, in part by the threads of aspiration. Men and women in diverse cultures are drawn to small business because it appears to offer some chances of self-direction, some prospects of self-development. Small seems beautiful, if in contrast to the apparently rigid structures of the society at large, it allows a freedom to take immediate and obvious responsibility for your own fate. This is one of the reasons why self-employment in some form often seems attractive and defensible to intellectuals who absorb and transmit long-standing ideas about the desirability of the individual realising his or her own potential, developing his or her persona in the fullest way. And this establishes a point of confluence in the streams of 'radicalism' of both left and right. Here, in this sector of the economy, it seems there may be fewer constraints on that process than will be found elsewhere. There is little doubt that this idea of a kind of freedom continues to attract new recruits and the weaving of myths about such limited sovereignty turns it into a cultural strand that can be laced into the programmes of various bourgeois political 'leagues'. It is this strand that leads some among the small business world in Britain to join and commend organisations like the National Association for Freedom, organisations which point to the erosion of certain liberties, privileges and perquisites enjoyed by middle-class groups in Britain, and urge collective defence of these. They have looked to the associations of petit-bourgeois for support. Not that their interests are simply or even seriously congruent with those of the small businessmen: they are not. But they can play on the fears of this group, point to the threats it faces and demand that it 'keeps faith' with old and hallowed precepts of a moral economy that is being challenged. There is sleight of hand involved here. NAFF really represents the interests of established elites, but their call has been heeded by some among the small business community.[19]

That some old ways, old relationships *are* threatened seems very plain to many who make their living in the small business world. Their awareness may be restricted to the 'proximate' changes; they may have only very dim apprehensions of the broader structural changes but they do recognise that the pivot of their working lives, their property, is itself being changed. The rights which it has conferred have gradually been made less absolute, more conditional. Take for instance property in the form of domestic buildings. The private landlord, particularly in Britain, has been hedged about with major restrictions on rents since World War I, and today with tenants given greater rights of tenure, the economics of landlordism are such that most owners simply want the opportunity to sell out. The landlord no longer has the kind of authority over his tenants that he once had; he can be forced to improve his property or face compulsory purchase; his right to levy the maximum rent is no longer absolute. Old landlords in particular resent these changes. For them they symbolise the loss of economic power and the loss of status of local petty property-owning bourgeois. Their decline corresponds with the rise of public housing, which is to say with the political influence of organised labour. Such people are sharply aware of a world they have lost.[20]

Other small businessmen in Britain protest about the job security given to workers in recent pieces of legislation. Again they complain about the curtailment of their rights as property holders. They no longer possess, by virtue of ownership, the unconditional right to sack a workman.[21] At the same time, their right to the surplus generated in their businesses is subject to close control since they must collect major consumer taxes which have to be passed on to the State. Traditional norms of 'privacy' accorded private property can be violated by tax inspectors and this occasions yet another sense of change in the moral economy of small property. One could add to this their resentment over the physical planning restrictions which affect business as well as domestic property or the outrage at decisions by government to control by 'licence' many who want to run little enterprises, but all make substantially the same point: that what is at issue is not just, not principally, an economic hurt – it is a moral hurt of which they complain.

It is this, we believe, more than any other single factor which occasions those ripples of middle-class discontent that have washed over most advanced western societies in the last few years. The petite bourgeoisie, and those who sympathise or try to make common cause with them, are responding to the rapid changes in social and occupational structures which have accompanied the growth of monopoly capitalism and the supportive and interventionist policies of western industrial states. They are responding to the growth in the political and economic strength of organised labour which in most of these societies has at least won some form of welfare provision to cushion the worst aspects of exploitation.

With the economies of the west in some disarray, with the fear of deep and lasting economic recessions, the orchestrated protest of small business has helped carry into power a number of right wing governments which will try (in more or less good faith) to protect and even to restore the moral economy of the petite bourgeoisie.

NOTES

1. In an earlier article (Bechhofer and Elliott, 1976), we used technology as one of the variables in our definition of the petite bourgeoisie, arguing that we should exclude concerns set up to exploit high technology (we were thinking of the 'Route 128' phenomenon). It seemed to us that the basis of their market power was the extremely specialised and sophisticated knowledge of their founders. It was knowledge rather than capital they were trading on. Further reflection perhaps suggests we should exclude them because so often they appear to involve little investment by their owners but a good deal by public agencies, banks and other institutional sources of finance capital. The traditional petit bourgeois works mainly with his own or his family's capital and invests a good deal of hard work but generally rather little esoteric knowledge. The problems of definition are considerable and rest in part on our great ignorance of contemporary entrepreneurship and the roles of capital and knowledge within most small enterprises.
2. For some discussion of this see the papers with our colleagues Monica Rushforth and Richard Bland; Bechhofer, Elliott, Rushforth and Bland (1974) and Bland, Elliott and Bechhofer (1978).
3. See Elliott and McCrone (1975) and McCrone and Elliott (1979).
4. Newby and his colleagues have produced an excellent book in which the economics of farming in Britain are well treated. See Newby, Bell, Rose and Saunders (1978).
5. See for instance Alison MacEwan's discussion of patterns of work in an Argentinian shanty town (MacEwan, 1974).
6. Two good recent volumes in which the 'political economy' of Latin American and other third world cities is described and analysed are Lloyd (1979) and Roberts (1978).
7. See L. Lommitz' account of social networks and patterns of economic assistance (Lommitz, 1978).
8. In his paper 'Marxism and Pluralism' delivered to the International Political Science Association Study Group on Social and Political Problems of Pluralism, April 1978, Professor Stanislaw Ehrlich included the following from Kautsky (no precise reference given):

   > Small enterprises may assume various forms of property ownership. They may complement large state or community establishments, receive from them raw materials and implements and provide them their own products – or they may produce for private customers or for the public market.

   and elsewhere:

   > The most varied kinds of ownership of means of production: state, local community, company (consumers' associations, producers' unions) or private may exist side by side in a socialist state.

9. For some indication of the government view see *Small Business in Canada: Perspectives* (1977).
10. Gamble (1974) documents the Tory neglect of what he calls the 'politics of support' especially during the Heath administration 1970–4.

11. For instance, in France elements of Poujadism still flourish. Apart from Nicoud and his party, there is the 'Union of Frenchmen of Common Sense', the 'Upper Council for the Middle Classes' as well as a number of organisations to link the interests of professionals to those of the artisans and self employed. In Denmark we have seen the formation of the Progress (anti-tax) Party, in California there was the revolt of the ratepayers expressed through Proposition 13. In Britain we have seen the formation of vigilante groups like Civil Assistance and GB 75, Ratepayer Action Groups, associations aiming at broad value changes, like the National Association for Freedom and a host of organisations representing the self employed and small business elements. The most important of these is the National Federation of the Self Employed.
12. The idea of a 'moral economy' we take from Thompson (1971).
13. See *Counterattack*, the journal of the Association of Self-Employed People.
14. The best account is that by Gellately (1974).
15. See Killingback (1978).
16. A brief description of the Freedom Group can be found in Thayer (1965).
17. Franz Pappi's paper suggests that even aesthetic standards are shaped in this way so that there are discernible differences in the preferred styles of petit bourgeois, grand bourgeois, professional and the like. We know of no systematic evidence on this matter in Britain but the experience of interviewing a good many 'middle class' respondents over the last decade leads us to think he is right. As part of wider systems of belief, aesthetic judgments and predilictions deserve much closer scrutiny. Living in societies where consumption patterns have assumed great social and ideological as well as economic significance, it is high time more research effort was directed to this issue.
18. See again Bland, Elliott and Bechhofer (1978).
19. Inspection of the 'house journal' of associations like the National Association for Freedom (now called simply the Freedom Association) and the National Federation of the Self-Employed, reveals the tensions as well as the affinities between these bodies. Interviews with leaders of these and many other recently formed 'middle-class protest' organisations provide evidence of the efforts made by value-oriented movements like NAFF to 'capture' the petit-bourgeois constituency.
20. This theme is discussed in Elliott and McCrone (forthcoming).
21. It is interesting to note that within the first few weeks of office, the new Tory government in Britain initiated modification of the Employment Protection Act to restore powers of dismissal to small employers.

REFERENCES

F. Bechhofer, B. Elliott, M. Rushforth and R. Bland, 'The Petits Bourgeois in the Class Structure: the Case of the Small Shopkeepers', in F. Parkin (ed.), *Social Analysis of Class Structure* (London: Tavistock, 1974).
F. Bechhofer and B. Elliott, 'Persistence and Change: the Petite Bourgeoisie in the Industrial Society', *European Journal of Sociology*, XVII (1976) 74–99.

R. Bland, B. Elliott and F. Bechhofer, 'Social Mobility and the Petite Bourgeoisie', *Acta Sociologica*, **21** (1978) 229–48.

B. Elliott and D. McCrone, 'Landlords in Edinburgh: Some Preliminary Findings', *Sociological Review*, **23** (1975) 539–62.

B. Elliott and D. McCrone, *Property and Power in a City* (London: Macmillan, forthcoming).

A. Gamble, *The Conservative Nation* (London: Routledge & Kegan Paul, 1974).

R. Gellately, *The Politics of Economic Despair* (London: SAGE Publications, 1974).

N. Killingback, 'Retail Traders and Co-operative Societies', in J. Garrard *et al.* (eds.), *The Middle Class in Politics* (London: Teakfield, 1978).

P. Lloyd, *Slums of Hope?* (Harmondsworth: Penguin, 1979).

L. Lommitz, The Survival of the Unfittest', in R. Schaedel, J. Hardoy and N. Kinzer, *Urbanisation in the Americas from its Beginnings to the Present* (The Hague: Mouton, 1978).

A. MacEwan, 'Differentiation Among the Urban Poor', in E. de Kadt and G. Williams (eds.), *Sociology and Development* (London: Harper & Row, 1974).

D. McCrone and B. Elliott, 'What else does someone with capital do?', *New Society* (31 May 1979) pp. 512–13.

C. W. Mills, *White Collar* (New York: Oxford University Press, 1951).

Minister of State, Small Business, *Small Business in Canada: Perspectives* (Ottawa: 1977).

H. Newby, C. Bell, D. Rose and P. Saunders, *Property, Paternalism and Power* (London: Hutchinson, 1978).

B. Roberts, *Cities of Peasants* (London: Edward Arnold, 1978).

G. Thayer, *The British Political Fringe* (London: Anthony Blond, 1965).

E. P. Thompson, *The Making of the English Working Class* (Harmondsworth: Pelican Books, 1968).

E. P. Thompson 'The Moral Economy of the English Crowd in the Eighteenth Century', *Past and Present*, 50 (1971) 76–136.

R. Williams, *The Country and the City* (London: Chatto & Windus, 1973).

Author Index

Subject Index

Africa, South, 128
agriculture
  co-operation in, 9–10, 19–20, 28,
    56, 69
  development of, 5, 31, 39
  in free market, 4, 42
  returns to, 44
  as source of wealth, 11
  in Third World, 122, 129, 131, 134
  See also farmers
America, 13, 51, 155, 159, 171, 188
America, Latin, 186
America, North, 13, 128, 158, 193, 195
artisans, 74, 91–2, 106–7, 131–3,
    135–6, 140, 155–81 *passim*,
    182
Australia, 128

bakers, 155–81 *passim*, 185
  future of, 169–73
  making of, 174–6
  patterns of work, 161–3
  recruitment of, 164–9
  statistics on, 156–8
  wives of, 163–4
Belgium, 171
Britain, viii, 38–9, 41–2, 67, 107–9,
    158, 171–2, 188–9, 191–3,
    195–7
business
  small
    as family business, 47–51, 163–4
    as reservoir of labour, 83–6
    economic advantages of, 77–83
    role in Poland, 103–4
  big
    attitude of farmers to, 65

Canada, 1–37 *passim*, 155, 171, 188,
    191

capital, 2, 21, 48, 53, 133
  in agriculture, 42, 52–3
capital-intensive enterprise, 62, 66,
    77–8, 84–6, 122
capitalism, 1, 6, 10, 32, 74, 93, 122,
    129–30, 136
  belief in, 147–50
  development of, 4–6, 10, 16, 20, 32
  farming under, 40–44
  mode of production in, 122–4, 134
  Populist critique of, 6–7
  relation of production in, 121–2,
    136, 146, 155
capitalist(s), 2, 3, 12–13, 59, 91, 108,
    124
class(es), 4, 29, 96, 103
  agrarian petite bourgeoisie as, 9, 28
  analysis, 123–125
  contradictory relations of, 124–7,
    139, 141–3, 150–1, 183
  formation, 111, 114, 121–2, 141–2,
    142–8 *passim*, 152, 184
  lower middle, 90, 100–3
  middle, 49, 66, 82, 104, 105–20
    passim, 190
  perception of, 65–6
  relation between, 1, 4, 15, 106, 108,
    111
  social, 73–4, 95
  structuration, 106, 110–15
  structure, 67, 112, 115, 123, 182
    rural, 38–70 *passim*
  upper, 58, 66
  working, 8, 12–13, 17, 24, 47, 64,
    113–14, 116, 122
Colombia, 122, 127, 136–9, 140, 145,
    149
commodity production, petty, 5, 6,
    121–154 *passim*
  defined, 128

204